NEW HAVEN PUBLIC LIBRARY

3 5000 09460 9

D0078599

OFFICIALLY WITHDRAWN
NEW HAVEN FREE PUBLIC LIBRARY

## DATE DUE

| | | | |
|---|---|---|---|
| DEC 0 8 2008 | | | |
| MAR 2 1 2009 | | | |
| | | | |
| | | | |
| | | | |
| | | | |
| | | | |
| | | | |
| | | | |
| | | | |
| | | | |

GAYLORD                                                         PRINTED IN U.S.A.

# PATRONIZING
# THE ARTS

*Painting by Mark Tansey (American, born 1949),* The Innocent Eye Test, *1981, oil on canvas, 78 × 102 inches. The Metropolitan Museum of Art, Partial and Promised Gift of Jan Cowles and Charles Cowles, in honor of William S. Lieberman, 1988 (1988.183).*

# PATRONIZING
# THE ARTS

## Marjorie Garber

PRINCETON UNIVERSITY PRESS • PRINCETON AND OXFORD

Copyright © 2008 by Princeton University Press

Published by Princeton University Press, 41 William Street, Princeton, New Jersey 08540

In the United Kingdom: Princeton University Press, 6 Oxford Street, Woodstock, Oxfordshire OX20 1TW

All Rights Reserved

Library of Congress Cataloging-in-Publication Data

Garber, Marjorie B.
   Patronizing the arts / Marjorie Garber.
     p. cm.
   Includes bibliographical references and index.
   ISBN 978-0-691-12480-3 (hardcover : alk. paper)   1. Art patronage—
United States.  2. Arts—Economic aspects—United States.  I. Title.
   NX705.5.U6G37     2008
   707′.973–dc22

                  2008017726

British Library Cataloging-in-Publication Data is available

This book has been composed in ITC New Baskerville with Trajan Pro display

Printed on acid-free paper. ∞
press.princeton.edu
Printed in the United States of America

10  9  8  7  6  5  4  3  2  1

707.973 GARBER
Patronizing the arts /
35000094609491
MAIN

*To my colleagues and students in*
*Visual and Environmental Studies, and*
*to the friends and patrons of the*
*Carpenter Center for the Visual Arts*

Integri sint curators,
Eruditi professores
Largiantur donators
Bene partas copias.

—James Bradstreet Greenough,
*Harvard Hymn*

# CONTENTS

# ACKNOWLEDGMENTS

I would like to express my gratitude to Sara Bartel, Sol Kim Bentley, Eliza Hornig, Giulio Pertile, Matthew Sussman, and Moira Gallagher Weigel for their invaluable assistance with this project. My warm thanks also to the colleagues, students, and friends to whom this book is dedicated.

# PREFACE

THE ARTS are doubly patronized in America today. On the one hand, they are supported, financially and institutionally, by foundations, corporations, universities, and private donors. On the other hand, they are condescended to, looked down upon, considered as recreational rather than serious work. None of this is new, and little of it has changed very much over the last several years.

In what follows, I will argue that the two kinds of patronizing are not only related, but also interimplicated: that the system of arts patronage has led to both a devaluation of art-making and performance and, with equally damaging results, to their *over*valuation, aligning the "creative arts" with aesthetic transcendence rather than with work that can be assessed within the traditional canons of scholarship.

This dynamic, of over- and undervaluing the arts, is in my view both inevitable and dialectical. It is not a *problem*, per se, in that it needs to be—or can be—resolved. Rather, it is a condition of art-in-the-world, a consequence of the fact that works of art (whether they are paintings, poems, plays, or architectural designs) have come to be aligned with possessions, objects, taste, and desire, rather than with progress, reason, logic, or social welfare. But whether or not art "makes the world better," or "makes us better people," in some mystical-secular-cultural-ethical way, artworks, and artists, are part of a market economy, as well as of a libidinal economy. Indeed, the relation between those two economic spheres is close to the heart of the question of patronage, and of patronizing in its double sense.

By undervaluation, then, I mean the idea that art is an add-on, a recreational activity, something that supplements the real hard work of, say, economics or politics or medicine or physics or business. Thus when school budgets are tight, the first things to be cut are classes in art or music. No one would think of cutting science or history. In these examples, art suffers from being considered somewhat worthless for the work of the "real world." Overvaluation, on the other hand, results in a different sort of difficulty in the placing of values upon art and its products. Some people feel that it is beyond the realm of regular experience, therefore the *work* of art (art as object and as process) is also beyond, or even above, a normal discussion of valuation and evaluation—it is "priceless," as they say.

This overvaluation of art seems closely akin to what Freud described as the overestimation of the object, which he considered to be the normative condition of being in love. "In connection with this question of being in love," he wrote, "we have always been struck by the phenomenon of sexual overvaluation—the fact that the loved object enjoys a certain amount of freedom from criticism, and that all its characteristics are valued more highly than those of people who are not loved."[1] Freud's "object" here is a "loved object," not a "material possession," but the trajectory of feeling is, I believe, the same. We might compare the bromide, attributed to humorist Gelett Burgess, "I don't know anything about art, but I know what I like"—a saying tellingly similar to Justice Potter Stewart's statement about hard-core pornography, "I know it when I see it."[2]

As we will see, when we take up the analogies between art and science and their implications for the value of the arts in modern culture, the idea that art is related to love, and thus, in an etymological as well as a pragmatic sense, to the *amateur*, has had some negative effects upon the idea of art-making as a *profession*. One persistent notion, inherited from and cultivated—in some quarters—since the Romantic period, has been that to be an artist is to suffer, and that suffering, including economic privation, is a testing ground for the true artist and his or her calling. This conviction has led, upon occasion, to the claim that somehow if *artists* don't suffer and compete to succeed, their *art* will suffer, so that funding them will actually lower the standards of art. Despite the fact that our culture values museums, art collections, and professional theater and ballet companies, there is a certain resistance to the idea of art-making as a *job*, and also as a *major* in a college or university setting.

A survey by the Urban Institute cited statistics to illustrate what is called "an American paradox"—that while 96 percent of Americans said they were "greatly inspired" by art and "highly value" it in their lives, only 27 percent "believe that artists contribute 'a lot' to the good of society." It is worth taking note of a certain double bind here that underwrites this "American paradox." If contemporary art is not considered "work" or art-making a "job," nonetheless (or, perhaps, *therefore*) art— once certified as art, by patrons, collectors, curators, reviewers— becomes an object of desire, of worth. Critics have developed a vocabulary of transcendence to describe such things in the world, a vocabulary that includes words like "great" and "universal" and "timeless." The opposites of these terms, assuming that they had opposites, would ground the work in its time, place, and conditions of production and consumption—the *materiality* of the work of art. The idea of art as transcendent implies that it is not tied to experiment, practice, rehearsal, rewriting, error, correction, reconstruction, and so on—that is, to the processes of scholarship, science, business, and so on. By experiencing art as "other worldly," the quite worldly aspects of its production are often misplaced.

Yet the training and support of artists is a serious, time-consuming and, indeed, often a costly business, since it involves issues of space, materials, equipment, and personnel—what are often lumped together under the forbidding word "resources." Any serious commitment to the arts today, though, will have to begin with an understanding of their interrelationship (studio art, film, video, photography, installation, music, dance, performance, theater) and of the essential necessity to provide, precisely, the vital resources of space and materials—a studio, a dance floor, a display or installation space, for each artist and every group.

Even today, when corporations, venture capitalists, instruments of government, and art aficionados vie for the role of patron, and when publicity, flattery, and celebrity are part of the habitual currency of the art market, there is no guarantee of escaping the mutual misprision of patron and patronized, and their tendency both to overestimate and underestimate each other. But this misprision, I hope to show, is both inevitable and, ultimately, salutary. It's a starting point, a place of debate and fruitful contestation, an opportunity to discover what is at stake in various kinds of analysis, observation, and cultural performance (whether the performance in question is an interview, an installation, an exhibition, or a scholarly article).

The advent of what I will be calling the "visual intellectual," and of cognate artists in performance, music, and other residual and emergent art forms, provides a timely showcase for the seriousness and pervasiveness of art-making in venues that cross over from academia to public life. Arts venues, universities, curators, and interested donors in the public and private sectors should see this as a moment of challenge and opportunity. When high interest—in the general culture, among students, in the worlds of commerce and celebrity—come together with the belated recognition of the centrality of the arts and art-making for humane life in a complex world, there is a strong incentive to work collaboratively to take advantage of this conjunction. Committed and knowledgeable participants can bring these elements together in projects and programs that no one entity can sustain alone.

If the goal is to envisage and bring about a mode of patronage without patronization, at all levels of artistic performance, it is essential for artists to have a chance to speak, and advocate, in conjunction with their patrons—whether those patrons are financial supporters, trustees, gallerists, impresarios, art collectors, audiences, employers, peers, or fans. For what we need is an understanding of the way in which patron and artist, production and consumption, art and science, transcendence and application, theory and practice, are part of a cultural dialogue, in which each complements, interrupts, and challenges the other.

# PATRONIZING
# THE ARTS

# 1

## THE PARADOX OF PATRONAGE

> TIMON: *What have you there, my friend?*
> PAINTER: *A piece of painting, which I do beseech*
> *Your lordship to accept. . . .*
> TIMON: *I like your work,*
> *And you shall find I like it.*
>
> —TIMON OF ATHENS

ARTISTS HAVE ALWAYS had patrons. From the time of Maecenas, a wealthy Etruscan noble who supported Virgil and Horace and was duly celebrated in their verse, to the Medicis and later the popes, and then to Isabella Stewart Gardner and the Guggenheim and MacArthur Foundations, rich sponsors have often supported painters, sculptors, and poets. And inevitably, these relationships have been loaded—fraught with over-, and underestimation, with pettiness as well as generosity, with disdain as well as desire.

The artist had the talent, and the patron the money. In some cases, though by no means all, the dynamic of the relationship involved forgetting this key and defining fact. Artists, who often have very little money, could occasionally live as if they were rich, or at least live *among* the rich, receive invitations to their parties, and be received at their city and country homes. And patrons, who have often, though by no means always, possessed considerable artistic vision and taste, could experience pleasure in a creative society of people and be made to feel that their place in the world might transcend the means by which they came to financial and social prominence. By mobilizing the fantasies that artists have about patrons, and vice versa, productive instances of patronage can be forged and precipitated.

For example, when he wanted to raise funds to rebuild Shakespeare's Globe Theatre, the American actor Sam Wanamaker put together a highly effective coalition of philanthropic socialites, actors, and British and American academics. Each was possessed of a quality or attribute lacking in, and admired by, the others—wealth, fame, charisma, gravitas.

A complicated and contradictory mixture of deep gratitude and powerful resentment is thus built into the dynamic of patronage. Which of these two will predominate in any given encounter between patron and protégé is never entirely predictable, although the volatility of their bond has been the stuff of many historical biographies and romanticizing films, such the 1984 hit *Amadeus* and the 1988 French period piece *Camille Claudel* (featuring Gérard Depardieu as Auguste Rodin and Isabelle Adjani as his eponymous admirer/*amante*). Indeed, as we have already noted, the relationship between patron and artist often follows the psychic structure of a love affair, with attendant fantasies, appropriations, misunderstandings, and disappointments. The more disinterested this relationship appears, the greater is its capacity to surprise and disconcert one party or the other—or both.

The histories of words are often suggestive, and the history of "patron" is no exception. The word stems originally from the Latin *pater*, "father," and the connections with, or analogies to, a system of patriarchy are not incidental but central. Many of the ambivalences of that familial power relation reemerge in the context of patronage. The Latin *patronus* means "protector of clients" (whether those clients were individuals, cities, or provinces); the "former master of a freedman or freedwoman"; and an "advocate or defender." The English word "patron" quickly acquired the meaning of "one who takes under his favor and protection, or lends his influential support to advance the interests of, some person, cause, institution, art, or undertaking."

A patron was once also a "donor," who commissioned works of art, like altarpieces, for churches and other institutions. In recognition of this generosity, using the medieval and early modern versions of Photoshop, the artist carefully inserted an image of the donor into the work of art: a donor kneeling in prayer at the foot of the cross, a donor in close proximity to a saint. Nicholas Rolin was the chancellor of the Duke of Burgundy, Philip the Good (from 1422 to 1457). He was fortunate enough to have lived in the time of Jan van Eyck and Rogier van de Weyden, court painters to Philip the Good, and so he is prominently on display in van Eyck's *Rolin Madonna* (where he kneels opposite the Virgin, wearing a gold brocade jacket trimmed with mink) and in van der Weyden's *Beaune Last Judgment.*

Medieval and Renaissance paintings and stained-glass windows regularly display such donors, dressed in the height of modern fashion, posing unselfconsciously (and without a hint of anachronism or blasphemy) in the same panels as naked saints and the crucifixion. In 1493 a guild of wealthy citizens and craftsmen from Haarlem in the Netherlands commissioned a sumptuous illuminated manuscript as a welcoming gift to a monastery, the Hermits of St. Augustine, who had undertaken to pray for the guild's members. The manuscript is a virtual "Who's Who of Haarlem," with donors depicted at the bottom of almost every page, kneeling in prayer next to saints or other religious figures.[1]

In centuries past, patrons were mentors, sponsors, and agents for the artists they took under their protection. The painter lived with the patron and tried to obtain commissions from the patron's friends. Artists were members of the household retinue, rather than godlike creative beings; sometimes they even wore livery, in order to indicate their dependent status. The baroque artist Andrea Sacchi entered the household of Cardinal Antonio Barberini in 1637 and was placed in a category with three slaves, a gardener, a dwarf, and an old nurse. In 1640 he was promoted, joining other pensioners like writers, poets, and secretaries. Jan van Eyck was *peintre de monseigneur* (court painter) in the household of Philip the Good, paid—according to the terms of his contract—not for his work itself but for his availability to do it. Anthony van Dyck was the court painter of Charles I. These were patronage relationships of a kind that seldom exists now. There were, of course, variations on this pattern. Some artists worked exclusively for single, powerful patrons, while others, like their twenty- and twenty-first-century counterparts, might paint, and then exhibit, without knowing who would purchase their work. Transactions could be mediated by dealers or dilettantes, domestic or foreign—"but," as Francis Haskell noted, "artists [in Baroque Italy] usually disliked the freedom of working for unknown admirers, and with a few notable exceptions exhibitions were assumed to be the last resort of the unemployed."[2]

In the realm of literature, the patron emerged as an especially important figure with the rise of print culture. Indeed, it has been suggested that it would make more sense to list and catalogue early modern works by the names of their patrons than by the names of their authors, since patronage was a much more powerful system than authorship in that period, and the imprint of the patron's interests on the collectivity of the work he or she sponsored might be more telling than any assessment of the author's supposed subjectivity. Only with the development of the system of copyright, in the eighteenth century, did authorship really become the major factor in determining who "owned" a written work. This paradigm shift had far-reaching implications for literary patronage. The seventeenth-century poet and playwright Ben Jonson, famously sensitive on the question of his social place, expressed satisfaction at the way he was treated at Penshurst, the home of the Sidney family,

> Where the same beer and bread, and self-same wine
> That is his lordship's, shall be also mine.
> And I not fain to sit (as some this day
> At great men's tables) and yet dine away.
> Here no man tells my cups; nor standing by
> A waiter, doth my gluttony envy; . . .
> Nor, when I take my lodging, need I pray
> For fire, or lights, or livery; all is there; . . . .
>                     (Jonson, "To Penshurst" [1616])

In this case the rather touchy poet felt, or wished to feel, like a guest rather than a servant in the house of his patron. But patronage was often less comfortable and more intrusive than the Penshurst ideal. Classic quotations on the topic are telling. We might compare the observation of the Painter in Shakespeare's *Timon of Athens*—"When we for recompense have prais'd the vile, / It stains the glory in that happy verse / Which aptly sings the good"—with Francis Bacon's testy remark that "books (such as are worthy the name of books) ought to have no patrons but truth and reason." But in fact books in this period often *did* have patrons and dedicatees, and in many cases the favor of the patron was crucial to the economic survival of the writer.

Perhaps the most famous contretemps between patron and "patronized" in English letters was the public quarrel between Dr. Samuel Johnson and his supposed patron, Lord Chesterfield. Johnson had sought Chesterfield's assistance, without success, at a time when he was in deep financial need, and was hard at work on his pathbreaking *Dictionary of the English Language*. Chesterfield was completely unresponsive until, many years later, the dictionary at last appeared in print, at which point it was belatedly accompanied by Chesterfield's endorsement. Johnson's celebrated letter of rebuke, dated 1755, is a model of its kind:

> My Lord:
> I have been lately informed by the proprietor of the World that two Papers in which my Dictionary is recommended to the Public were written by your Lordship. To be so distinguished is an honour which, being very little accustomed to favours from the Great, I know not well how to receive, or in what terms to acknowledge. . . .
> Seven years, My lord have now past since I waited in your outward Rooms or was repulsed from your Door, during which time I have been pushing on my work through difficulties of which it is useless to complain, and have brought it at last to the verge of Publication without one

Act of assistance, one word of encouragement, or one smile of favour. Such treatment I did not expect, for I never had a Patron before.

[. . .] Is not a Patron, My Lord, one who looks with uncon-cern on a Man struggling for Life in the water and when he has reached ground encumbers him with help. The no-tice which you have been pleased to take of my Labours, had it been early, had been kind; but it has been delayed till I am indifferent and cannot enjoy it, till I am solitary and cannot impart it, till I am known, and do not want it.

In Johnson's *Dictionary* itself the first definition under "patron" was equally to the point: "One who countenances, supports or protects. Commonly a wretch who supports with indolence, and is paid with flattery." It was after Johnson's experience with Chesterfield that he famously altered a couplet in his poem "The Vanity of Human Wishes." In the 1749 version of the poem, adapted from a satire of Juvenal, Johnson had catalogued a litany of woes, all concerned with the harshness of poverty:

There mark what ills the scholar's life assail,
Toil, envy, want, the garret and the jail.

The penurious scholar worked, starved, competed with others for his livelihood, slept in an attic, might wind up in debtor's prison. But in 1755, after the spat regarding the *Dictionary*'s patronage, he replaced the humble but anodyne "garret" with the far more pointed and personal "patron." Henceforth the list of grievances would read, uncompromisingly,

Toil, envy, want, the *patron* and the jail.

The fact that a patron could so readily be summed up as part of the problem, rather than presented as the solution to it, tells the whole story in brief—for Johnson's London, and for the ages.

Many recent writers, following Jürgen Habermas, have de-scribed the eighteenth century as a time of expansion of the public sphere, with attendant pleasures and dangers. Nowhere was this clearer than in the changing market for art and literature. Thus, for example, in a study forthrightly titled *Painting for Money: The Visual Arts and the Public Sphere in Eighteenth-Century England*, art historian David Solkin discusses "artists and writers about art who embraced the realities of a burgeoning market economy." In this period, he notes, "for the first time in English history, paintings became an object of widespread capital investment; and alongside other cultural producers who contributed to an increasingly active trade in luxury goods, artists soon learned that many rules they had long accepted as absolute imperatives would have to give way to the higher laws of supply and demand."[3] During the first half of the eighteenth century, painters continued to work for individual patrons on commission, as they had in previous centuries. However, a new mode of display, the exhibition, created an increasingly important space for commercial competition among painters and sculptors. Ironically, the same century that produced Immanuel Kant's famous definition of beauty as "disinterested" (*interessenlos*) also propelled art into the fray of commerce and the challenge of public taste—that is, into modernity.

Portrait painting, long a favorite of patrons and a mainstay of artists' incomes, came under particular criticism as a species of "self-love." Portrait painters, one observer said acidly, are "chiefly obliged" to the

> *Vanity* and *Self-love* of their Employers, Passions which must ever be gratified, and the Owners of them are ever ready (though Remiss upon other Occasion) to open their Purses to the irresistible Flattery of Portrait Painting. . . . For be the Taste and Fashion of the Times what they may, or let them vary ever so much, or be they ever so preposterous— it is impossible for the Craft of Man to invent a Method to prevent the Sale of Portraits and Looking Glasses.[4]

(Recall the painter poking fun at the "glass-fac'd" flatterer in *Timon of Athens*.)

Was a patron a vain narcissist or a generous underwriter and collector? The tension produced by these two ostensibly incompatible models of patronage emerges in the debates between two major eighteenth-century institutions: the Society of Artists of Great Britain and the Royal Academy. The Society fostered annual exhibitions for the sale of artwork. However, the Academy remained resistant to the notion of a general public that might consume art in a free marketplace. Sir Joshua Reynolds concisely presents the position of the Academy in his third *Discourse on Art*:

> Be as select in those you endeavour to please, as in those whom you endeavor to imitate. Without love of fame you cannot do anything excellent, but by an excessive and undistinguishing thirst after it, you will come to have vulgar views; you will degrade your style; and your taste will be entirely corrupted. It is certain that the lowest style will be the most popular, as it falls within the compass of ignorance itself; and the Vulgar will always be pleased with what is natural, in the confined and misunderstood sense of the word. . . . I MENTION this, because our Exhibitions, while they produce such admirable effects, by nourishing emulation and calling our genius, have also a mischievous tendency, by seducing the Painter to an ambition to please indiscriminately the mixed multitude of people who resort to them.[5]

Patrons continued to receive bad press at the hands of some of the most eloquent and nimble satirists of English literature and English art. William Blake, himself no fan of art schools, academies, or Sir Joshua Reynolds, wrote a series of torrid epigrams on the bad taste of the age, and particularly on the folly of aspiring English collectors. "You must agree that Rubens was a Fool / And yet you make him master of your School," begins a short poem addressed "To English Connoisseurs," and another chants "Rafael Sublime Majestic Graceful Wise . . . Rubens Low

Vulgar Stupid Ignorant," and so on. Yet another of these barbed verses is entitled, with a fine diminuendo,

> On the Great Encouragement
> Given by English Nobility to Correggio Rubens
> Rembrandt Reynolds Gainsborough Catalani
> DuCrowe & Dilbury Doodle

But perhaps most striking among the frank and vivid epigrams that have been collected under the heading "On Art and Artists" is a little dialogue between the poet (who was also, of course, a painter and engraver) and a powerful allegorical woman whom he addresses as "Mother Outline":[6]

> "O dear Mother Outline! Of wisdom most sage,
> What's the first part of painting?" She said: "Patronage."
> "And what is the second, to please and engage?"
> She frowned like a fury, and said, "Patronage."
> "And what is the third?" She put off old age,
> And smil'd like a siren, and said, "Patronage."[7]

In this delectable piece of Blakean fantasy, woman is divided into a familiar set of three parts (old wise woman, fury, siren), and the elusive and allusive word "Patronage" is given a full operatic performance in all of its contradictory dimensions: first oracular, then hissing, and finally, enduringly, seductive. Blake's "patronage" hovers in the air, a ghostly afterimage, the smile of the siren lingering after the rest of the scene has faded. (A biographical aside: Blake's own experiences with patrons were largely unhappy. When he died in August 1827, he was destitute.)

As we have seen, the change of economic structures in the industrial age produced a shift in the patronizing class. No longer did nobility, royalty, and gentry have a monopoly on becoming donors; nor were persons of humbler station the exclusive recipients of their largesse. Victorian patrons were often members of the rising middle class, while some of the artists they patronized were gentry, or, at the least, moved in sophisticated social circles. One result of this social reversal was that the new patrons, less confident about their knowledge of art history, began to pour money into the purchase of new art.[8] Here is the classic formulation of Lady Elizabeth Eastlake, an author and critic who was also the wife of the president of the Royal Academy, and director of the National Gallery.

> The patronage which had been almost exclusively the privilege of the nobility and higher gentry, was now shared (to be subsequently almost engrossed) by a wealthy and intelligent class, chiefly enriched by commerce and trade; the notebook of the painter, while it exhibited lowlier names, showing henceforth higher prices. To this gradual transfer of patronage another advantage very important to the painter was owing: namely, that collections, entirely of modern and sometimes only of living artists, began to be formed. For one sign of the good sense of the *nouveau-riche* consisted in a consciousness of his ignorance upon matters of connoisseurship. This led him to seek an article fresh from the painter's loom, in preference to any hazardous attempts at the discrimination of older fabrics.[9]

Thus the upwardly mobile Victorians began to collect "contemporary art." Art contemporary to *themselves*, of course—the works of painters like Frith and Landseer. They may not have known much about art, but they knew what they liked, and bought it.

Artists either complied with their new class of patrons, or grumbled—in public and private. Dante Gabriel Rossetti, who had made himself vulnerable to a particular patron's wishes because he wanted to avoid the judgment of a public exhibition, complained in a letter to Ford Madox Brown about Frederick Leyland, a wealthy Liverpool shipowner, who had been his generous supporter: "I have often said that to be an artist is just the same thing as to be a whore, as far as dependence on the whims and fancies of individuals is concerned."[10]

J. M. Whistler had a similar relationship, and a similar break, with Leyland, when Whistler's extravagant and beautiful design for the Peacock Room in Leyland's house proved too costly for the patron's taste. Leyland paid only half the requested two hundred guineas, and the two parted company acrimoniously. When Whistler subsequently went bankrupt, he was not reticent about blaming the situation on his former patron.

### *Patronizing Modernity*

Throughout Europe, the pattern and personalities of patronage shifted over time, as economic circumstances changed and artists began to negotiate on their own, acknowledging the need to sell or place their work. This shift, indeed, laid the groundwork for the modern system that integrates artists in a network of social and fiscal relations. The French Academy—like its British counterpart—had actively discouraged its members from combining the sale of art with artistic production, forbidding artists "to do anything to permit the confounding of two such different things as a mercenary profession and the status of Academicians."

But a new group of dealers representing painters and sculptors began to develop in France—and elsewhere—in the nineteenth century. Renoir, for one, declared, "there's only one indicator for telling the value of paintings, and that is the sale room."[11] Gauguin had been a stockbroker. Both Theo van Gogh and his better-known brother worked as dealers for many years, and, indeed, Vincent regarded his brother as both an aesthetic collaborator and a representative.[12] Picasso was represented by Daniel-Henry Kahnweiler and then by the entrepreneurial Paul Rosenberg, who set up for his client gallery exhibitions from Paris across Europe and then in the United States. By the 1930s—the decade in which the Museum of Modern Art's powerful director, Alfred Barr, mounted a retrospective of Picasso's work—the relationships among galleries, dealers, curators, and museum exhibitions had been fashioned into a highly beneficial and workable patronage system. This system functioned well into the later twentieth century, and it is still preeminent today.[13]

Twentieth-century writers, too, continued to have their patrons. Once again, this relationship often remained highly ambivalent: talent and money were equally eroticized, and some species of creative ingratitude was perhaps inevitable. The patronage relationships of modern authors were often further complicated by social and personal issues such as class, sex, and race, all of which exacerbated both the difference between patron and patronized and their mutual imbrication. One striking example may perhaps stand for many others.

A wealthy white widow, Charlotte van de Veer Quick Mason, became the patron of several key figures in the Harlem Renaissance, including Alain Locke, Zora Neale Hurston, Aaron Douglas, and Langston Hughes. Mason, who liked to be called "Godmother," gave funding to support black artists, but required a certain degree of reciprocity. She shared the view of many at the time that Negro art and culture were suffused with spirituality and primitive energy, and vocally differed with Frederick Douglass, the "father of African art," when he disagreed with this romantic ideal. Her story provides an all-too-vivid example of the doubled valence, and danger, of "patronizing the arts." Mason gave funds to underwrite the play *Mule Bone*, coauthored by Hurston and Hughes (later, when she withdrew her support from Hughes, a rift developed between the two writers, and Hurston claimed the play as her own). The dapper Hughes was asked to cut back on his social life, and received gifts of clothing and opera tickets. Mason also asked him to accompany her to balls and other public functions. She advised him on the content and tone of his first novel, *Not Without Laughter* (1930), and he was ultimately dissatisfied with some of the changes she suggested.

In his autobiography, Langston Hughes wrote about the difficulties of this patronage relation: ". . . having just been through a tense and disheartening winter after a series of misunderstandings with the kind lady who had been my patron.

She wanted me to be more African than Harlem—primitive in the simple, intuitive, and noble sense of the word. I couldn't be, having grown up in Kansas City, Chicago and Cleveland."[14] Langston Hughes split from Mason in 1930, although he wrote her letters seeking to reinstate the connection. And he lost touch, as a result of the schism, with Locke and Hurston, who remained loyal and indebted to their "Godmother" for patronage and support.

With certain exceptions—like the $100 million-plus donation that the heiress Ruth Lilly made to *Poetry Magazine* in 2002[15]— literary patrons are less visible today than in previous decades and centuries. Perhaps this is because the profession of "writer" has now attached itself to a brave new world of publishing and contracts, agents and editors, bookstores, magazines, and journals, not to mention the worlds of self-publishing (pioneered in the nineteenth century by Emily Dickinson and Walt Whitman) and the world of the weblog. Writers often teach writing, either in colleges and universities or in evening programs, summer institutes, or institutions for "life-long learning." The creative writing lectureship or professorship and the book contract— tantalizingly described in *six* or very occasionally *seven figures*— are the patronage units of the present day.

### Postmodern (Post-)Patrons

The twenty-first century continues to see analogous transformations in the business of the visual arts: contemporary patronage networks increasingly include not only collectors but also gallerists, who perform a number of the financially sustaining and personally inspiriting roles that were fulfilled in earlier years by the individual patron. Dealers like Leo Castelli and Illeana Sonnabend (both based in New York) have given monthly stipends to the artists affiliated with their galleries, sometimes supporting them through years of meager sales. Some dealers assist with production costs, which can be significant in certain cases. Take Jeff Koons, for instance, whose forty-three-foot-high topiary sculpture *Puppy* required not only a steel frame but the laborious installation of hundreds of living flowers and plants. Although the standard activities connected with representing artists remain—placing the work in private collections or in museums, photographing and archiving new work, and so on—the modern dealer is also a friend, confidant, personal manager, and publicist.[16] And in the world of the "art star," the world of present-day art, gallerists are also competing with one another for high-profile artists, and artists are switching galleries and representation in a series of economic moves that resemble the "free agency" in professional sports.

In practice, dealers have long been part of the process of taste-making at the heart of this new structure of art-world patronage. However, this social and economic fact has sometimes struck observers as contravening a cherished notion of art. The fact that the critic Roberta Smith, writing in the *New York Times* in celebration of the booming Chelsea art scene, has to defend it against accusations that it is "dealer driven" in contrast with the purer "artist-driven" Soho, draws attention to the persistent romanticism of this idea of pure art. "The dealers," wrote Smith,

> are exactly what's best about Chelsea. As small, basically family-run businesses, commercial galleries are the closest link between new art and the everyday public. Unlike increasingly corporate, supposedly non-profit museums, they are run by one or two people who decide what will go on view, without having to get permission from a director, board of trustees or corporate sponsor—and admission is free. The dealer may even look longer and think harder than his or her museum counterparts, because the dealer's own money is on the line. And the link between the art and the public is especially direct in Chelsea; the glass-fronted spaces currently in favor allow pedestrians to see a great deal of art without ever leaving the sidewalk.[17]

That galleries should have come to rival museums in the ambitiousness of their exhibitions—another point Smith makes—says something suggestive about the current state of arts patronage. And the "backlash" against the Chelsea scene, which condemns it as overly commercial and homogeneous, "a consensus of mediocrity and frivolousness" according to one gallery dealer, is likewise indicative of the unease produced by the specter of artistic success and its indebtedness to dealers, to museum donors, and to the public.

Many of today's artists still work on contract or on commission. While this practice is most visible among architects, it is also common to some other studio artists. They may occasionally find wealthy patrons who are also deeply knowledgeable about contemporary art—patrons like Eli Broad, a collector and sponsor, who built two Fortune 500 companies over five decades, before turning to a full-time life of what is now called venture philanthropy; or Agnes Gund, president emerita of the Museum of Modern Art, a lifelong collector of modern and contemporary art, and an early patron of major artists like Robert Rauschenberg, Mark Rothko, and Jasper Johns. But despite all the language one hears about "modern Medicis," by and large most artists are independent workers, not contracted to patrons in the old Renaissance fashion, which is to say that they are in fact *dependent* on grants from foundations and the government, and on teaching, to support their studio work and exhibitions.

Here is where government, academia, commerce, and the arts come together in a potentially fruitful but also contestatory relation.

### Culture Vultures

Like "hodgepodge," "higgledy-piggledy," "legal eagle" (or "legal beagle"), and "fag hag," all current entries in the *Oxford English Dictionary*, the phrase "culture vulture" has a built-in pseudo-logic based upon its rhyme. Also, newspapers love it. It is a term that catches the eye in a headline. (Here are some recent sightings: "The Candidates as Culture Vultures." "Why the Queen

Is No Culture Vulture." "Material Girl Turns Culture Vulture." "Hungry French Culture Vultures Feed on Eng Lit.")[18]

But it is also, of course, a phrase with a history.

By the time the term "culture vultures" appears in Dylan Thomas's *Quite Early One Morning* (1954), it has already acquired a negative connotation. The context, alas, is "A Visit to America," a description of the voracious and indiscriminate appetite for visiting artists, novelists, and lecturers making their way, and their income, from Europe to America. The date of this devastating little account is 1953, but—allowing for globalization and for some slight shift in gender politics away from the automatic derogation of women's clubs—the narrative is not unfamiliar. Let me treat you to Thomas's unbeatable prose:

> See the garrulous others . . . . gabbing and garlanded from one nest of culture-vultures to another: people selling the English way of life and condemning the American way as they swig and guzzle through it; people resurrecting the theories of surrealism for the benefit of remote parochial female audiences who did not know it was dead, not having ever known it was alive; people talking about Etruscan pots and pans to a bunch of dead pans and wealthy pots in Boston.[19]

While today it is obligatory for performers to speak highly, even fawningly, of their audiences—every baseball and football player thanks the fans—in those earlier, more robust, and less politically correct times visiting lecturers, from Sigmund Freud to Oscar Wilde, were happy to be lionized while privately, and not so privately, deploring the comical limitations of their audiences. Thomas takes the measure of both sides. As you can see, the garrulous—and bibulous—lecturers come in for as much genial irony as the culture vultures. But—as you can also see—the term has a powerful persuasiveness. Call it the flip side of "patronizing"—in this case the protégé patronizes his public, if only for a New York (or Boston) minute. But Dylan Thomas was, happily, atypical, and even he took more pleasure in the access to his admiring public than he was here willing to acknowledge.

## *Patrons of Culture*

The relation between an individual patron and his or her pro-tégés was always, of course, only one model of "patronizing the arts." Participatory patronage meant that many people could be "patrons" in a sense that came closer to cultural consumption than to cultural production. As early as the time of Charles Dickens the notion of the "patron" had come to mean sponsor in a slightly different sense, a sense that continues in arts organizations (and fund-raising) today. In Dickens's brilliant novel *Our Mutual Friend*, the kindly common man, Mr. Boffin, who has unexpectedly inherited the estate of his rich employer, voices his impatience with patronage as a mode of social climbing for the middle class:

> "Patrons and Patronesses, and Vice-Patrons and Vice-Patronesses, and Deceased Patrons and Deceased Patron-esses, and Ex-Vice Patrons and Ex-Vice Patronesses, what does it all mean . . . ?
>
> "I can't go anywhere without being Patronized. I don't want to be Patronized. If I buy a ticket for a Flower Show, or a Music Show, or any sort of Show, and pay pretty heavy for it, why am I to be Patroned and Patronessed as if the Patrons and Patronesses treated me? If there's a good thing to be done, can't it be done on its own merits? If there's a bad thing to be done, can it ever be Patroned and Patronessed right? Yet when a new Institution's going to be built, it seems to me that the bricks and mortar ain't made of half so much consequence as the Patrons and Patronesses; no, nor yet the objects. I wish somebody would tell me whether other countries get Patronized to anything like the extent of this one! And as to the Patrons and Patronesses themselves, I wonder they're not ashamed of themselves. They ain't Pills, or Hair-Washes, or Invigo-rating Nervous Essences, to be puffed in that way!"[20]

Allowing for Mr. Boffin's uncommon frankness—this is the Emperor's New Clothes moment for modern patronage—his description of contemporary Patrons and Patronesses, "puffed" on the playbills and plaques of cultural institutions, has a disquietingly familiar (and modern) ring. "The art patrons of the Renaissance," S. N. Behrman observed shrewdly, "had themselves painted into the pictures they commissioned; because their American counterparts lived too late to have this service performed for them, they had to gain their immortality by buying collections and putting them in public museums."[21] The Frick Collection. The Guggenheim Museum. The Getty Institute. The Morgan Library. The Kimbell Museum. The Broad Center for the Arts. Today "patron" and "donor" are carefully calibrated levels of fund-raising at cultural institutions like museums and theater companies. And instead of the image of the donor, we have the donor's name, whether corporate or personal, inscribed on the entablature or the letterhead.

If Dickens's litany of "ex-vice patronesses" and so forth seems excessive, consider the patronage options open to a twenty-first-century donor. At the American Repertory Theatre in Cambridge, Massachusetts, contributions are gratefully recorded and acknowledged from generous supporters who run the fiscal gamut from guardian angel to archangel to angel, and then, shifting from the celestial to the merely terrestrial sphere of giving, to (in order of generosity) benefactor, producer, partner, patron, and finally sponsor. What can be gleaned from this Great Chain of Funding is, among other things, that the principles of grade inflation function at all levels of cultural taxonomy. The once exalted patron is now near the bottom of the heap, while even the angel, long a term of endearment in the annals of theatrical management, is trumped—and out-trumpeted—by the guardian angel.

Arts venues have long been naming opportunities indebted to the generosity of individual patrons or corporate sponsors. The Art Institute of Chicago offers Ford Free Tuesdays, courtesy of the car-maker, not the foundation. New York's storied

Broadway theaters now include the American Airlines Theatre (formerly the Selwyn), the Ford Center for the Performing Arts (aka the Lyric and Apollo Theaters), and the Cadillac Winter Garden (founded as the Winter Garden in 1911, adopted by the Cadillac motor company in 2002). Boston's Citi Performing Arts Center, once called the Metropolitan Theatre (1925) and later the Music Hall (1962), was renamed CitiWang Center for the Performing Arts in 1983 after a generous gift from philanthropist An Wang, founder of Wang Laboratories.

This onomastic explosion in the arts corresponds, it is perhaps needless to say, to the general tendency to put a corporate or commercial brand on other entertainment venues, notably sports stadiums. Among major-league baseball teams, the Texas Rangers play at Ameriquest Field, the Detroit Tigers in Comerica Park, the Chicago White Sox at U.S. Cellular Field, the San Diego Padres at PETCO Park, the Philadelphia Phillies at Citizens Bank Park, the Tampa Bay Devil Rays at Tropicana Field. These are the names as of this writing, but there is no guarantee that they will remain so. The naming rights function like high-end billboards; Chase Field, the home of the Arizona Diamondbacks, was previously Bank One Ballpark. The former Enron Field, home of the Houston Astros, is now Minute Maid Park, although Houston is not renowned for its orange groves. And I have not even mentioned the Allstate Sugar Bowl (formerly the Nokia Sugar Bowl) or the Tostitos Fiesta Bowl.

Perhaps the winner in this name-change sweepstakes, though, is the golf tournament known from 2004 to 2006 as the Cialis Western Open, the second oldest professional golf tournament in the United States. Beginning life as the Western Open, it became in the palmy eighties the Beatrice Western Open (named after Beatrice Foods, not Dante's ideal love), and then in rapid succession the Centel Western Open, the Sprint Western Open, the Motorola Western Open, the Advil Western Open, and then the Cialis Western Open. In 2006 the event was scheduled for a complete makeover, and was renamed the BMW Championship. From Cialis to BMW—talk about the Ultimate Driving Machine.

It may be hard to top these commercial and cultural transitions, but the arts are doing the best they can to keep up. Like other kinds of institutions, the visual and performing arts have long offered naming opportunities for bricks and mortar, as well as for endowments: a gift from Laurence A. and Preston Robert Tisch made possible, in 1982, the purchase and renovation of space for what would become the Tisch School of the Arts at NYU, and philanthropists Edythe L. and Eli Broad made a major contribution to enable the construction of the Broad Art Center at UCLA. Buildings, galleries, theaters, and museums are traditional beneficiaries of sponsor generosity.

But a new aspect of arts patronage has now entered the fray, with the decision of ballet companies to auction off, not their theaters or seats, but their top dancers. As Erika Kinetz reported in the *New York Times*, "American ballet companies have recently begun allowing donors to sponsor individual dancers, for amounts that range from $2,500 to $100,000 a year. Some ballet companies even compile and distribute rosters, which look eerily like shopping lists, specifying their dancers' ranks and prices." In nineteenth-century Europe and America, liaisons between rich men and female dancers were sometimes fostered by management. But the *Times* article focused—perhaps as a sign of the times (and the *Times*)—not on men sponsoring women, but instead on women sponsoring men.[22]

Two large color photographs of smiling women and the male dancers they had paid top dollar to sponsor adorned the top half of the Dance page. And the text emphasized that this sponsorship was "practical" and "friendly," not "intimate" or erotic. The sponsor of an American Ballet Theatre principal dancer gave cooking tips to his girlfriend (another principal dancer with the company). The sponsor of a male dancer with the Atlanta Ballet planned to invite him home for dinner with her four sons. For his part, the dancer acknowledged his sense of obligation to his patron—"to be quite frank, they are paying your salary"—and said he planned not only to accept the dinner invitation ("I would definitely rotate my schedule to accommodate anything") but also to cook her dinner and send her birthday gifts.[23]

The sponsor is not always a single individual; several of the ABT sponsors were couples or family groups. In other cases, as with the Houston Ballet, the company asks donors to "endow a dancer position, in the manner of an endowed chair at a symphony or university, rather than to sponsor an individual artist."[24] This practice both protects the funding—if a dancer leaves the company, the funding stays—and also guards against overpersonalization. But the American Ballet Theatre posts the patron's name on its Web site: "Mr. ——'s performances at American Ballet Theatre are sponsored by ——."

A full-color spread in the *New York Times Magazine* heralded the rise of a long-suppressed type, the "patron sweetheart."[25] Full-color, full-page photographs in the style of a *Vogue* or *Vanity Fair* magazine cover featured five New York women, most in their thirties, one a youthful twenty-six, each surrounded by works of art they collect or sponsor. The information in the captions reflects this curious combination of art patronage and personal shopping. Thus the description of Allison Sarofim, the daughter of two wealthy Texas art collectors, ends, "Sarofim's own collection includes the Rothko over the fireplace. Zac Posen dress, $1,600." Another patron was identified not only by "the three paintings by de Kooning that surround her but also by her Chloe dress, $2,560. *www.neimanmarcus.com.* Christina Addison earrings, Manolo Blahnik sandals." The price of the dress and the Neiman Marcus Web site from which you could buy it were given in the text.

This feature appeared in the *Times* Style pages, not the Art section, and a certain amount of having-it-both-ways journalistic schadenfreude seemed to accompany the description of its subjects, described in the article as "not Bergdorf blondes looking for a cause between collagen injections and lunch at Le Cirque" but rather "the behind-the-scenes movers and shakers, planning the parties, picking the art." What is probably most telling, and most symptomatic, is the evocation, in the first line of the brief (one-paragraph) article that accompanies the glam photographs, of the telltale M-word. *M*, for Medici. Here is the opening sentence: "The fall, for Manhattan's young Medici types, can be grueling—with galas and openings and armory-size antiques-fests clogging up the social calendar well into winter."

Let's leave aside for a moment the fact that the armories of the Medicis were quite possibly clogged with weaponry rather than with antiques. The idea of these "patron sweethearts" as young Medici types is, nonetheless, both alluring and suggestive.

We are, in fact, in the midst of a full-scale Medici revival in popular culture—the second time as farce. A four-part series on PBS in 2004 was called *The Medici, Godfathers of the Renaissance*, and the Mafia analogy was insistent and deliberate. CBS's *60 Minutes* went to Italy to observe the exhumation of the Medici family tombs by some historians of medicine, in a program entitled *Tales from the Crypt* (broadcast October 3, 2004). But why was this headline stuff for *60 Minutes*? The double valence of the Medicis (lurid family history, patrons of high culture) made them both irresistible and contemporary. The Medicis-R-Us. Or so we would like to think.

Indeed this idea—that there is a new class of American Medicis, movers and shakers who are patrons of the arts—has been a tempting one for more than half a century. For Senator John F. Kennedy, even as he campaigned for the presidency in 1960, this was a role to be fulfilled by an enlightened government. As he wrote in a letter to the editor of the periodical *Musical America* (which describes itself today as "the business source for the performing arts"), "There is a connection, hard to explain logically but easy to feel, between achievement in public life and progress in the arts. The age of Pericles was also the age of Phidias. The age of Lorenzo de Medici was also the age of Leonardo da Vinci. The age of Elizabeth was also the age of Shakespeare. And the New Frontier for which I campaign in public life can also be a new frontier for the American arts."[26] In this case the Medici function was to be fulfilled not by the individual patron but by the government. And as we are about to see, this mode of sponsorship, too, has its pitfalls.

## A Late Frost

At John F. Kennedy's inauguration in 1961, he sought to emphasize the difference between his White House and Dwight Eisenhower's by incorporating a celebrated American poet into the proceedings. The poet he chose was Robert Frost, then in his eighties, a former poetry consultant to the Library of Congress. After Kennedy's own stirring remarks—"Ask not what your country can do for you—ask what you can do for your country"—he turned the podium over to Frost, who had written a new poem, entitled "Dedication," for the inaugural occasion. (The poem was later published as "For John F. Kennedy, His Inauguration.") But—as anyone who saw these events on television will vividly recall—Washington, D.C. had just emerged from a winter storm, and the glare of the sun on the snow blinded Frost from seeing his text. (In those long-ago days, his poem was on a piece of paper, blowing in the wind, not mounted invisibly upon a teleprompter.) Although Kennedy and Vice-president-elect Lyndon Johnson tried to shield the aging poet's eyes from the sun, he could not read. So Frost abandoned his occasional poem and recited, instead, one he knew by heart, the familiar and powerful poem called "The Gift Outright":

> The land was ours before we were the land's.
> She was our land more than a hundred years
> Before we were her people. She was ours
> In Massachusetts, in Virginia.
> But we were England's, still colonials,
> Possessing what we still were unpossessed by,
> Possessed by what we now no more possessed. . . .
> Such as we were we gave ourselves outright
> (The deed of gift was many deeds of war)
> To the land vaguely realizing westward,

But still unstoried, artless, unenhanced,
Such as she was, such as she will become.[27]

The poem today sounds, in a way, astonishingly politically incorrect, full of paeans to mastery, ownership, and expansion, ignoring the preexistence in "our" land of many native peoples, many prior stories, arts, and enhancements, not to mention the practice of slavery that made the rhetoric of possession seem double-edged at best. Ishmael Reed would observe many years later, "Frost's poem is the last gasp of the settler sensibility. It says the country was created so it could be occupied by Europeans."[28] This is the danger of trying to patronize poets who are still alive: they might write something the patrons—or a later cultural sensibility—find embarrassing. But it is not the business of poetry to be politically correct.

"The Gift Outright" was, and is, a powerful poem, stirring in its rhythms, patriotic in its themes, the perfect complement to Kennedy's own clarion call to the nation. Originally written in 1942, in the midst of World War II, it was a hot war poem for a cold war time. Whether they admired it or deplored it, those who were there remembered it. Poet Derek Walcott, who noted all the flaws in the poem, had this to say about the occasion: "By then as much an emblem of the republic as any rubicund senator, with his flying white hair, an endangered species like a rare owl, there was the old poet who, between managing the fluttering white hair and the fluttering white paper, had to recite what seemed more like an elegy than a benediction."[29] And another poet, Galway Kinnell, recalled the moment, memorably, in his poem called "For Robert Frost."

> I saw you once on the TV,
> Unsteady at the lectern,
> The flimsy white leaf
> Of hair standing straight up
> In the wind, among top hats,
> Old farmer and son

Of worse winters than this,
Stopped in the first dazzle

Of the District of Columbia,
Suddenly having to pay
For the cheap onionskin,
The worn-out ribbon, the eyes
Wrecked from writing poems
For us—stopped,
Lonely before millions,
The paper jumping in your grip,

And as the Presidents
Also on the platform
Began flashing nervously
Their Presidential smiles
For the harmless old guy,
And poets watching on the TV
Started thinking, Well that's
The end of *that* tradition,

And the managers of the event
Said, Boys this is it,
This sonofabitch poet
Is gonna croak,
Putting the paper aside
You drew forth
From your great faithful heart
The poem.[30]

This image, genuine twenty-four-carat American pathos with a timely touch of *King Lear*, depends for its effectiveness—and it is very effective—upon the contrast between the frail, aged man and the robust, powerful poem. (And also, we might note in passing, upon the contrast between the oral and the written, the former, in this case, a kind of guarantor of authenticity.

"Putting the *paper* aside . . . You drew forth / From your . . . *heart* / The poem.")

What would have happened if Frost had read, instead, the poem he had composed for the occasion? Here is how "Dedication" begins:

> Summoning artists to participate
> In the august occasions of the state
> Seems something artists ought to celebrate.
> Today is for my cause a day of days.
> And his be poetry's old-fashioned praise
> Who was the first to think of such a thing.
> This verse that in acknowledgement I bring
> Goes back to the beginning of the end
> Of what had been for centuries the trend;
> A turning point in modern history.[31]

The poem ends—and would have ended, that cold and sunny January day—with a trumpet blast and a bathetic thump:

> It makes the prophet in us all presage
> The glory of a next Augustan age
> Of a power leading from its strength and pride,
> Of a young ambition eager to be tried,
> Firm in our free beliefs without dismay,
> In any game the nations want to play.
> A golden age of poetry and power
> Of which this noonday's the beginning hour.

All things considered, I think we may be thankful for that gust of wind and that blinding glare that replaced an "occasional" poem of far lesser merit, written under the pressure of patronage, with a better poem written without it. The event, watched by millions on television, gave new (if brief) prestige to poetry in America, and—as the *New York Times* noted years later, "earned [Frost] unofficial recognition as the poet laureate of the United States."[32] And yet there were many who did take exception to the "American exceptionalism" expressed in his poem.

The next president to invite a poet to speak at his inaugural was Bill Clinton, thirty-two years later. The poet was Maya Angelou, and the poem, "On the Pulse of Morning," was the first actually written and performed for the inauguration of a president. It is never possible to guess at a poet's motivation or inspiration for writing a particular poem, but some aspects of Angelou's verse seemed to suggest that she had read Frost's "The Gift Outright" (the poem he *performed*, not the poem he *wrote* for the Kennedy inaugural) and that she was speaking back to it. She cited, for example, all those who might have been thought to have been excluded from Frost's colonial "gift":

> the Asian, the Hispanic, the Jew,
> The African, the Native American, the Sioux,
> The Catholic, the Muslim, the French, the Greek
> The Irish, the Rabbi, the Priest, the Sheik,
> The Gay, the Straight, the Preacher,
> The privileged, the homeless, the Teacher.

Predictably, the poem itself got mixed reviews, though many people praised the poet's energy and delivery. "I felt that woman could have read the side of a cereal box," said novelist Louise Erdrich. "Her presence was so powerful and momentous." A "prominent poet" who declined to have his name used told a reporter for the *Washington Post*, "I was hoping that it would be short, and it was long," adding that "Maya Angelou is to Robert Frost as Bill Clinton is to John Kennedy." "The Gift Outright" had been sixteen lines long; "On the Pulse of Morning" was thirteen stanzas long and took five and a half minutes to read. Rita Dove, who had won a Pulitzer Prize for her own poetry, sought to reposition Angelou's poem as part of a different genre of verse: "I wouldn't compare it to a poem I'll read over and over again in silence. That's not the kind of poem it was meant to be. It's a song, really."[33]

On the other hand, the poem certainly served a political purpose. Bill Clinton said he loved it and would hang a copy in the White House. "Having a black woman poet was a wonderful symbol," said Louise Erdrich, and it was Angelou's presence as symbol, personality, and inspiration that lingered after the event. The poem itself promptly became a best seller, underscoring Maya Angelou's reputation as a poet of the people, rather than a poet's poet. The fact that she had written the poem became as important as the poem she had written.

At Clinton's second inaugural, Arkansas poet Miller Williams read a poem called "Of History and Hope" (it will not be forgotten that Bill Clinton was a native of Hope, Arkansas; Maya Angelou had also ended her poem, perhaps subliminally, "with hope").

But since that time this presidential precedent has fallen into abeyance. As the Associated Press reported in January 2001, "President-elect Bush has decided not to include a poet at his inauguration. A spokeswoman for the Presidential Inaugural Committee, Natalie Rule, cited no reason for his decision."[34] The AP writer, succumbing to temptation, began this brief item, "It'll be an inaugural with no doggerel."

### Once More, O Ye Laurels

Robert Frost was an unofficial "poet laureate," working—and writing—on behalf of the head of state, but the title "laureate" was not awarded to poets in the United States until more than twenty years after his death. The history of this curious office, in effect that of government poet, will suggest some of the complications that come about when the patron is the king, president, governor, or (most complicated of all) "we the people." The result, as you will see, is not always sanguine or salubrious.

The term "laureate" literally means "crowned with laurel leaves," or "bays." (As Andrew Marvell puts it, in a poem about the resistance to worldly fame, "How vainly men themselves amaze / To win the palm, the oak, or bays."[35]) According to Greek mythology, the god Apollo, patron of poetry and music, chased the nymph Daphne, who fled to a riverbank, where with the help of a river god she was transformed into the laurel tree;

Apollo thenceforth wore a laurel wreath as a sign of his love for her. Ancient and medieval poets were often literally crowned with laurel wreaths. The most famous paintings of Dante show him thus bedecked. Petrarch's beloved Laura was both a lady named "Laura" and a laurel tree (*il lauro*). The poet makes love to the idea of poetic fame. When she dies, he writes poems. The death of Laura becomes the birth of the laureate.

In England, Ben Jonson had been an "unofficial" laureate for James I, a literary king, but the office itself was created in the time of Charles II, and the first real "poet laureate" of Britain was John Dryden, appointed in 1670. A record of that time lists the new court officer among others of "His Majesties Servants in Ordinary," including "One Geographer, One Historiographer, One Hydrographer, One Library Keeper, one Poet Laureat, one Publick Notary." The original fee for the Laureate was £100, plus a "butt of sack." (When a later laureate tried to get the payment in wine converted to a payment in cash, the wine was mysteriously *included* in the £100 fee by the thrifty monarch—a case of wine turning into water, rather than the other way around.)[36]

Initially the official laureate was a combination of panegyrist and propagandist—a role that is no longer held in government by a poet, but is nonetheless recognizable as a function of several of our paid officials. The two occasions for which "occasional poems" were required were New Year's Day and the king's birthday, on each of which the laureate was to produce an ode that would be set to music and performed in the presence of royalty. Early laureates labored mightily under these thankless tasks—the Hanoverian Georges were particularly tin-eared when it came to English poetry.

Dryden himself was already a celebrated poet and dramatist when he was appointed to first official laureate. (It is worth noting that most of the next several laureates were dramatists, not—as today—lyric poets.) Documents of the period describing the new laureate call him "the most ingenious and learned John Dryden."[37] But a roll call of his successors will indicate the degree to which fame can be fleeting: Thomas Shadwell, Nahum Tate, Nicholas Rowe, Laurence Eusden, Colley Ciber, William Whitehead, Henry Pye, and Alfred Austin are no longer household words, if they ever were, although—to be fair— it is also the case that Wordsworth, Tennyson, Robert Bridges, and John Masefield have held this (increasingly symbolic) post. Some who were asked declined the honor, not wishing to spend their time writing birthday odes to kings.

In the nineteenth century the office became overtly ceremonial, no longer requiring "any onerous or disagreeable duties." Queen Victoria's prime minister Robert Peel wrote to Wordsworth, who had initially turned down the post, "Do not be deterred by the fear of any obligations which the appointment may be supposed to imply. I will undertake that you shall have nothing required of you." The laureateship was an honor, offered simply because of Wordsworth's "eminence as a poet."[38] Wordsworth accepted it in the same spirit, as an honor that expressed "a sense of the national importance of Poetic Literature."[39] We should notice that this tribute came at the end of his career, not when Wordsworth was a young radical but when he was an old and established figure. Aged seventy-three, and long resident in the Lake District far from London, Wordsworth borrowed a suit of court clothes from the literary socialite Samuel Rogers in order to attend a levee at the behest of the sovereign, then returned immediately to the mountains and the lakes. In the seven years that ensued between his appointment as poet laureate and his death, he never wrote a poem, or indeed so much as a line of poetry, in connection with the office.

This lack was made up, and more, by the laureate who followed, Alfred Tennyson, who held the rank for forty years, and wrote much distinguished and moving occasional verse. It is worth noting, though, that even Tennyson disliked the implications of the title. "Writing to order is what I hate," he said. "They think a poet can write poems to order as a bootmaker makes boots."[40] Despite this reluctance—born, it should be noted, from the bad reputation the word "laureate" had acquired since its first official use in England—it was Tennyson, more than any other poet, who gave prestige and meaning to the modern role of poet laureate. He fulfilled the promise implicit in Wordsworth's wistful phrase about the "national importance of Poetic Literature." Tennyson became, in effect, England's poet, the poet of the English language, of Englishness, and of English patriotism, at a time of high colonial and world expansiveness. "The Poet of the People," he began to be called. The American poet James Russell Lowell would hail Tennyson as "The Laureate of the Tongue as well as the Nation."

Tennyson's poetry was frankly patriotic, and through it he advised and admonished, using poetry as a mode of public policy. Cardinal Manning thought his poem about the need for a stronger fleet "ought to be set to music and sung perpetually as a National Song in every town of the Empire."[41]

After Tennyson's death, Stéphane Mallarmé, writing from the vantage point of France, felt called upon to comment on the laureateship and its discontents, suggesting that England had misunderstood its "superb deceased" poet: "One nation has the right to remain unfamiliar with the poets of another; it so badly neglects its own! That misunderstood title of poet laureate, in addition, sounds like a license to engage in boosterism, seems almost to designate some sort of versifying comrade, inferior to the gossip columnist."[42]

Tennyson's successors, down to the most recent laureates, Ted Hughes and Andew Motion, have increasingly served public roles, although they have been roles connected with education and public outreach, not with policy. Motion, indeed, has penned a poem on Princess Diana and two poems on the queen mother—one on her hundredth birthday, one on her funeral—all published in a volume called, not without irony, *Public Property*.

So the English model of the poet laureate went from one kind of patronage to another. How has the United States, so often emulous of England in matters of high culture, envisaged the role of national poet?

## *American Idol*

In 1985, in the wake of a long campaign by Senator Spark Matsunaga of Hawaii, himself a writer of poetry as well as a virtuoso
of the harmonica, Congress changed the title of the consultant
in poetry to the librarian of Congress, a little known and little
noticed official. Henceforth the poetry consultant would be
known as the poet laureate. Notice how comparatively recent
this is. From Joseph Auslander in 1937 to Gwendolyn Brooks in
1985–86 the title of poetry consultant had stood alone, adorning the resumes and the reputations of such luminaries as
Allen Tate, Robert Lowell, Elizabeth Bishop, Robert Frost, and
Maxine Kumin. But Matsunaga felt the title gave insufficient
visibility to poets and poetry. Indeed his first idea was that the
laureate would be selected and appointed by the president of
the United States (in 1985 that would have been Ronald Reagan). But the legislation was changed to keep the appointment
in the hands of the librarian of Congress.

The poet laureate gets a stipend of $35,000 (importantly,
this is not government money, but the income from a private
gift). Robert Penn Warren, who had been poetry consultant
forty-five years earlier, was the first to hold the new title—a title
a more recent laureate, Robert Pinsky, has viewed with some
ambivalence. "'Laureate' is more royal sounding and Americans are suckers for that," he said. "'Laureate' has cachet, but
it also sounds like you're serving an elite group." For Pinsky
the combination of a small stipend, a very small travel budget,
and a nonexistent staff made the implied task of "trying to
constantly create culture" a virtual impossibility, and one that
made the laureate, whoever he or she might be, a "huckster for
poetry."[43] (Compare Mallarmé's "license to aid boosterism.")

Robert Penn Warren made it clear when he accepted the
appointment that he would not serve if he were "required to
compose an ode on the death of someone's kitten." He would
not, he said, be a "hired applauder."[44] More specifically, he
would distinguish his role from that of his British counterpart.

"Of course, it's not the same thing as the English version. There they write stuff celebrating the throne. I don't expect you'll hear me writing any poems to the greater glory of Ronald and Nancy Reagan. Why should I?"[45]

Again as a small footnote to history we might note that Senator Matsunaga, who had wanted to "upgrade" the position of poetry consultant so as to "provide young American poets with role models," and who was not himself involved in the search process, had rather expected the first American laureate to be Gwendolyn Brooks, who was then the incumbent poetry consultant. ("I thought they might have just promoted Brooks right away," he said, "but I guess they're waiting till next year to start it up," he told David Remnick at the *Washington Post.*) The designation of Robert Penn Warren as the first first poet placed in the office a very distinguished writer who had already been poetry consultant (and who was a white man, not a black woman).

The first female laureate was Mona van Duyn (1992–93); the first black woman to hold the office, Rita Dove, was appointed the following year. The laureate for 2004–06, Ted Kooser, was a retired Nebraska insurance executive who has written ten volumes of poetry about the Midwest. The description of Kooser offered by the librarian of Congress, James Billington at the time of his appointment, says a good deal about just how representative the American laureate was now expected to be: "Ted Kooser is a major poetic voice for rural and small town America and the first poet laureate chosen from the Great Plains. His verse reaches beyond his native region to touch on universal themes in accessible ways." Regional, universal, accessible. These are the key words of modern laureation. (Kooser's reply was in kind. "We poets out here don't get a lot of attention, and now I will and I have some trepidation over that.")[46]

By contrast, Kooser's successor, Donald Hall of New Hampshire, was heralded as "a poet in the distinctive American tradition of Robert Frost." He lives in a white clapboard farmhouse in New Hampshire on land settled by his maternal great-grandfather, and encountered Frost at the Bread Loaf Writer's

Conference when he was only sixteen, before going on to Harvard, Oxford, and Stanford. But Hall was also seen as a potential advocate for artists, unafraid of political controversy or plain speaking. It was noted that when he served on the advisory council of the National Endowment for the Arts during the first Bush administration he called those who interfered in the awarding of arts grants "bullies and art bashers." (Billington, asked about this history, said he wasn't aware of it, but that in any case the poets laureate "are chosen for their poetry, not chosen to make a statement about anything else.")[47]

But Hall's bluntness seems to have extended as well to debunking grumpy ideas about the death of poetry ("Death to the Death of Poetry" was one of his essays in 1989) and to what he calls the "McPoem": "The McPoem is the product of the workshops of Hamburger University," he once wrote, in an essay called "Poetry and Ambition," and "every year Ronald McDonald takes the Pulitzer." Poems, he contended, "must not express mere personal feeling or opinion—as the moment's McPoem does. It must by its language make art's new object." Eastern newspapers—the *New York Times*, the *Boston Globe*—rejoiced in the return of the laureateship to the neighborhood, each offering an editorial urging Hall to speak out freely and bluntly; as Verlyn Klinkenborg noted, "There's always the temptation for the laureate to find some anodyne ground to stand on. But these are not anodyne times."[48]

Times change, laureates change. When Hall's term was up, a "fellow New Englander"[49] with a very different history and style was appointed the fifteenth poet laureate. Charles Simic, born in Yugoslavia, is a former MacArthur fellow and a recipient, in 1990, of the Pulitzer Prize for poetry. The *New York Times*, which deployed the "New Englander" tag (Simic teaches at the University of New Hampshire) to mark the transition from one national poet to another, nonetheless stressed the differences. Simic was a "surrealist" with a "dark view," declared the *Times* headline, and Simic himself was quoted as saying that his residence in the United States was a product of history: "Hitler and Stalin were my travel agents." Nonetheless he declined in an interview to address the question of "the role of poetry in culture," preferring to quote a student he had met in an El Paso school in 1972, who had said that the goal or purpose of poetry was "to remind people of their own humanity." (Nineteen seventy-two, the year of the Watergate break-in, the shooting of Governor George Wallace, Jane Fonda's visit to Hanoi, the massacre of eleven Israeli athletes at the summer Olympic Games in Munich, and the reelection, by a landslide, of Richard Nixon as president of the United States, might have been a good year to be reminded of one's humanity, though it is not quite clear what would be involved in such an aide-mémoire.)

Simic was approvingly described as a poet of "disconcerting shifts" and "sinister imagery" (the *Times* here quoting, as its authority, a previous review in—of course—the *New York Times*).[50] The same review had also characterized him as a poet with a "blunt plainspoken delivery punctuated with colloquialisms and deadpan ironies," views echoed by librarian of Congress James H. Billington, who told the *Washington Post* that Simic's work was "surreal and surprising, commonplace yet dreamlike," and "has both shades of darkness and flashes of ironic humor."[51] In 2007, with the Iraq War going badly and President Bush's popularity ratings hovering around 30 percent, irony, darkness, and surrealism were again mentionable qualities in connection with the highest poetic appointment in the land.

If one laureate is a good thing, would more laureates be better? This, too, we could say, is the American way with culture.

Indeed many of the *states*, it turns out, also have poets laureate—at present, close to forty states plus the District of Columbia. (The numbers change from time to time, since some states have subsequently discontinued these—largely unpaid—posts; or, as in the case of Pennsylvania, "have no plans to fill" them.) State laureates vary from the eminent (John Ashbery was poet laureate of New York; Grace Paley, poet laureate of Vermont) to the local and idiosyncratic. Songwriter John Denver was poet laureate of Colorado from 1974 until he died in 1997.

And the tasks of the state laureates have also varied widely. Some travel from schools to bookstores to libraries to Rotary Clubs, bringing poetry and literature to new audiences. The poet laureate of New Hampshire (Marie Harris) was asked to write a commemorative poem celebrating the minting of the New Hampshire quarter. Her poem, "Common Coin," praised the famous profile of the state's Old Man of the Mountain— which (unlike the poem, and the coin) subsequently collapsed three years later. Some laureates serve for life—like John Denver—others for as little as a year, like the poet laureate of the state of Texas, who is appointed together with a state musician and two state artists, one for two-dimensional media and one for three-dimensional. According to the statute, "the individuals designated as the poet laureate, the state musician, and the state artists do not receive any pay or emolument."

It may not be lucrative, but that does not mean the position has been without controversy, or peril. Amiri Baraka (the former LeRoi Jones) was poet laureate of New Jersey until after the September 11 World Trade Center bombings, when his poem, "Somebody Blew Up America," was deemed incendiary because of its anti-Israel—and some say anti-Semitic—sentiments. The position of New Jersey laureate, which was created in 1999 and pays $10,000 for a two-year term, was worded in such a way that Baraka could not be fired, and he refused to resign, so some state legislators tried to abolish the position, and succeeded in July 2003.

The laureateship of California is a position for which poets apply—or, as it turned out, don't apply, since many of the state's best-known writers decline to do so (Adrienne Rich, Gary Snyder, Lawrence Ferlinghetti . . . ). Quincy Troupe, a poet, performer, and editor who did apply, and became California's first official poet laureate, later resigned when it was learned that he had falsified his resume (claiming to have graduated from Grambling State). In the wake of the scandal—it turned out he had never passed *any* courses at Grambling, though in his first admission he said he had studied there though not earned a degree—Troupe also resigned from the writing faculty of UC San Diego and returned to New York.

### (First) Ladies Bountiful

One striking, though not surprising, fact about these U.S. poets laureate and the enterprise of the public support of poetry is that they sometimes seem to be, or to become, the properties of the first lady rather than of the governor or the president. The patronage of poetry, and the arts in general, is still women's work in the United States. California's first lady Sharon Davis announced the appointment of California's first official poet laureate in 2001, although there had been "unofficial" California-state poets, appointed for life, since 1915. And Laura Bush, as first lady of the United States, has been closely associated with the National Endowment for the Arts and its chair, poet Dana Gioia.

As Jacqueline Kennedy had once brought high culture (and decorative arts) to the White House, and Lady Bird Johnson identified herself with the "beautification" of America's highways (clearing them of billboards, planting flowers and trees), so Laura Bush, trained as a librarian, committed herself to cultural education. She and Dana Gioia collaborated to produce two blameless, but toothless, family-focused public projects, *Shakespeare in American Communities* and *American Masterpieces: Three Centuries of Artistic Genius*. The Shakespeare program, as its title suggests, was aimed at outreach and at "introducing" Shakespeare to children and families. Indeed, the official publicity materials stressed this even to the point of faint risibility, noting that the plays to be performed featured "famous families such as the Montagues and the Capulets, and memorable characters including Desdemona and Othello."

As for *American Masterpieces: Three Centuries of Artistic Genius*, the three centuries of the title turned out to be the eighteenth, nineteenth, and twentieth. Representatives of the current century (described by columnist William Safire as "today's edgy artists"[52]) were not in evidence. Instead the program featured "yesteryear's greats" (that's Safire again), from Aaron Copland to Georgia O'Keeffe. The highly touted $18 million budget increase for the arts, after several years of cuts, was the largest proposed increase in National Endowment for the Arts (NEA) funding in twenty years. But all of that money was to go to underpin these new programs, programs in cultural exposure and cultural tourism—programs that would "introduce" Americans to the time-tested artists of the past, and not to the fast-moving, untested art world of their own time. This is a certain kind of arts patronage. But it reveals both the advantages, and the deep-seated problems that arise, when government patronizes the arts.

The programs for *Shakespeare in American Communities* and for *Three Centuries of Artistic Genius* are perfectly pleasant initiatives. Not only will they do no harm, they will surely do much good. But the keywords of the Bush/Gioia initiatives are "introduce" and "family," and neither of these has much to do with the patronage of contemporary art. (As with Dr. Johnson and Lord Chesterfield, the patronage for current work may come too late to be of benefit to the artists whose achievements are most visionary.)

When the poet Robert Bly accepted the National Book Award for Poetry in 1968 he invoked the moral authority of the radical intellectuals of his time, who had spoken up—and acted up—against the Vietnam War:

> We have some things to be proud of. No one needs to be ashamed of the acts of civil disobedience committed in the tradition of Thoreau. What Dr. Coffin did was magnificent; the fact that Yale University did not do it is what is sad. What Mr. Berrigan did was noble; the fact that the Catholic church did not do it is what is sad. What Mitchell Goodman did here last year was needed and in good taste. . . .
>
> In an age of gross and savage crimes by legal governments, the institutions will have to learn responsibility, learn to take their part in preserving the nation, and take their risk by committing acts of disobedience. The book companies can

find ways to act like Thoreau, whom they publish. Where
were the publishing houses when Dr. Spock and Mr. Good-
man and Mr. Raskin—all three writers—were indicted? . . .

You have given me an award for a book that has many
poems in it against the war. I thank you for the award.
As for the $1,000 check, I am turning it over to the draft-
resistance movement, specifically to the organization called
The Resistance.[51] (March 6, 1969)

The most dated part of this speech is the amount of the check.
Today's National Book Award winners each get $10,000 and a
crystal sculpture.

But there is something moving, still, about this spectacle of a
poet trying to change the world with "many poems against the
war"—and a thousand-dollar check. Especially when we contrast it to the cancellation of the proposed White House Conference on "Poetry and the American Voice," convened by First
Lady Laura Bush for Lincoln's birthday, February 12, 2003.


### The Live Poets' Society

Mrs. Bush made cultural headlines when she declared, "There's
nothing political about American literature."[54] The occasion was
a flood of new poems by poets invited to the White House for
Lincoln's birthday, a day set aside for a symposium on the works
of Emily Dickinson, Langston Hughes, and Walt Whitman, but
intersecting, as it happened, with the onset of the war in Iraq.
The White House event, which was to be called "Poetry and the
American Voice," was jettisoned—the word used at the time was
"postponed," but the conference was never rescheduled—after
almost two thousand poets responded to an email suggestion by
Sam Hamill, editor of the Copper Canyon Press, that they send
him poems and statements opposing the war. Hamill planned to
create an anthology of poems to present to the White House.

The singularity of the "American voice" was belied by this
chorus of dissidence, articulated by concerned objectors. The

result was that the voices of contemporary American poets were silenced—at least in terms of official sponsorship. The White House put out the following statement: "While Mrs. Bush understands the right of all Americans to express their political views, this event was designed to celebrate poetry." Katha Pollitt, writing in the *Nation*, observed ironically that it was "just like old times," recalling an occasion "when Robert Lowell refused to attend a poetry symposium at the Johnson White House to protest the Vietnam War."[55]

As many commentators pointed out, Whitman, Hughes, and Dickinson were odd choices if the point was to be somehow above politics. Pollitt remarked that

> Whitman's epic of radical democracy, *Leaves of Grass*, was so scandalous it got him fired from his government job; Hughes, a Communist sympathizer hounded by McCarthy, wrote constantly and indelibly about racism, injustice, power; Dickinson might seem the least political, but in some ways she was the most lastingly so—every line she wrote is an attack on complacency and conformity of manners, mores, religion, language, gender, thought.

She noted that Whitman was gay ("as perhaps were Hughes and Dickinson," she wrote carefully), and that these "quintessentially American writers" were also profoundly "subversive."[56]

Instead of live poets (unpredictable, ungovernable, uncontrollable) performing "Poetry and the American Voice" in real time (on five-second delay to allow for poetry malfunction), with all their flaws, eloquences, impertinencies, and importunacies, the event planned for Lincoln's birthday 2003 was to be a celebration of a particular vision of the past. That Whitman, Hughes, and Dickinson were all "war poets" is in its own way indisputable. That they would have been comfortable houseguests, in person, in any White House, is very much to be doubted.

When war with Iraq did come, the laureates spoke, on both sides of the Atlantic. In response to the U.S. war in Iraq the British poet laureate, Andrew Motion, wrote a thirty-word poem, "Causa Belli," and published it in *The Guardian.*

> They read good books, and quote, but never learn
> a language other than the scream of rocket-burn.
> Our straighter talk is drowned but ironclad;
> elections, money, empire, oil and Dad.

As Poetry International commented at the time, "There are several precedents in British literature of anti-war poems written by poet laureates, the most famous of which is 'The Charge of the Light Brigade' by Alfred Lord Tennyson, written after the Crimean war. However, the practice is far from common." (The Tennyson poem, as readers of Virginia Woolf will recall, contains the haunting line "Someone had blundered.")

The then-U.S. laureate, Billy Collins, not known as a political poet, signed an anti-war petition (together with Nobel laureate Derek Walcott, Richard Wilbur, John Ashbery, Robert Creeley, Charles Simic, James Tate, and others). Collins told the Associated Press,

> If political protest is urgent, I don't think it needs to wait for an appropriate scene and setting and should be as disruptive as it wants to be. I have tried to keep the West Wing and the East Wing of the White House as separate as possible because I support what Mrs. Bush has done for the causes of literacy and reading. But as this country is being pushed into a violent confrontation, I feel it increasingly difficult to maintain that separation.[57]

The East Wing and the West Wing may here stand for "private" and "government" patronage. As we have seen, it is not only modern day laureates who find it difficult, often impossible, to keep them apart. But manifestly there are benefits to government patronage of the arts, in the form of grants, visibility, encouragement, reward, and even celebrity.

# 2

---

## GOVERNING ASSUMPTIONS

BOTTOM: *Get your apparel together, good strings to your beards, new ribbons to your pumps; meet presently at the palace; every man look o'er his part: for the short and the long of it is, our play is preferred.*

—A MIDSUMMER NIGHT'S DREAM

TESTIFYING BEFORE the Subcommittee on Select Education of the House of Representatives Committee on Education and Labor in 1978, author John Updike was characteristically blunt about the question of public patronage of the arts:

> I would rather have as my patron a host of anonymous citizens digging into their own pockets for the price of a book or a magazine than a small body of enlightened and responsible men administering public funds. I would rather chance my personal vision of truth striking home here and there in the chaos of publication that exists than attempt to filter it through a few sets of official, honorably public-spirited scruples.[1]

The Updike of 1978 was, of course, already famous and well established as the author of prize-winning novels and short stories (the unnamed "magazine" here is presumably the *New Yorker,* where Updike had been a regular contributor since 1957). His celebrity is presumably one reason he was invited to appear before the subcommittee. But a novelist and critic, especially a successful one, has relatively low set-up costs: in 1978 these would not even have included a computer. And the cost to the consumer/collector of an example of Updike's work—"the price of a book or a magazine"—is, manifestly, on a different scale from the cost of a painting, sculpture, or mixed-media installation. Few artists can afford to be as independent, or as insouciant, as John Updike was on this occasion. Yet the resistance to submitting a "personal vision" to the "official . . . scruples" of public arbiters, however "enlightened and responsible," remains a key question for the notion of government-supported art. The gentle irony implied in the reference to those "honorably public-spirited scruples" suggests that, even if their hearts are in the right place, these well-meaning bureaucrats can in practice know little that is pertinent about the making or evaluation of art.

What should be the role of lawmakers, government agencies, and interested public officials in the patronage of the arts? Hands-off? Hands-on? Handout? How does such state support cohere with the independence and "personal vision" of the artist?

"Great art is sustained and strengthened by great patronage. Poor patronage discourages and diminishes art,"[2] wrote the former deputy chairman of the U.S. National Endowment for the Arts Michael Straight in a book published just two years after Updike's testimony. He was speaking not only of the goals of the NEA but of the great patronage eras of the past, citing William Butler Yeats's 1912 poem, "To a Wealthy Man Who Promised a Second Subscription to the Dublin Municipal Gallery If It Were Proved That the People Wanted Pictures."

> You gave, but will not give again
> Until enough of Paudeen's pence
> By Biddy's halfpennies have lain
> To be "some sort of evidence"
> Before you'll put your guineas down . . .
> What cared Duke Ercole, that bid
> His mummers to the market-place,
> What the onion-sellers thought or did
> So that his Plautus set the pace

For the Italian comedies?
And Guidobaldo, when he made
That grammar school of courtesies
Where wit and beauty learned their trade
Upon Urbino's windy hill,
Had sent no runners to and fro
That he might learn the shepherd's will. . . .

There could hardly be a less populist message: Yeats's claim is that aristocrats and men of taste should lead, rather than consult or follow the popular will. The "Paudeens" and "Biddies" of modern Ireland should content themselves with "pitch and toss" or other folk amusements, and leave the cultural planning to those with taste and vision. But despite Yeats's evocation of Duke Ercole of Ferrara, Guidobaldo, Duke of Urbino, and Cosimo de Medici as models for the visionary patron, the poem failed as a political intervention. The "wealthy man," Lord Ardilaun, did not give a second gift, and the "pictures" in question, a group of French paintings collected by art dealer Hugh Lane, and now the nucleus of the Hugh Lane Gallery in Dublin, were dispatched by their collector to London for an exilic stay of sixty years.

In this case the appeal to national and municipal patronage, voiced by a poet to a wealthy donor, foundered on the request for "some sort of evidence" that the people wanted art—and were willing to pay for it, to the limit of their own abilities.

But what is "great" patronage, and what is "poor" patronage? For Michael Straight, great patronage provides "discernment," "resources," and "restraint"—the good patron chooses the artist well, gives sufficient space, scope, and funding for good work, and declines to meddle in the process or in the result. (For Straight's model of poor patronage, we can presumably invert these terms: a poor patron lacks taste or judgment, provides insufficient funding, and mucks in where he or she is not wanted, whether at the level of the commission or at the level of execution.) Since as an NEA administrator he is trying to map these notions of individual patronage onto a state agency, the criteria seem, again, pretty clear: the job of any patron (agency, corporation, individual, academic, and so on) is to pick the right candidates and give them what they need to get their work done.

What artists need, and what will most benefit our culture, is the wise restraint that actually manifests itself as disinterested but informed support. Can such informed and confident disinterestedness be found, as Straight had hoped, in a government agency?

In what follows I want to explore the recent history of U.S. government patronage, using the twentieth-century history of arts funding in the United Kingdom as a particularly useful comparison index to developments in the United States. But contemporary art is, manifestly, not a national, but rather a global, enterprise, with festivals from the Venice Biennale and the Basel Art Fair to Documenta, held every five years in Kassel, Germany, and artists exhibiting their work internationally in museums, galleries, and on the Internet. The "art world" is a world phenomenon, and arts policy in other nations has an effect upon artists and on art. A brief survey of the varying strategies by which modern states have attempted to patronize the arts—with particular attention paid to the history of government funding in Great Britain and the United States—reveals not only a diversity of possible approaches, but also a recurring set of questions and difficulties concerning expertise, bureaucracy, stewardship, politics, censorship, and taste. The persistence with which these issues reemerge suggests that they are not incidental, but fundamental, and that by examining them we can illuminate something significant about the nature of state patronage.

### Nation Stakes

Government sponsorship of the arts in the Netherlands, in France, and in Germany, is both more thoroughgoing and less contested than in the United States, and has functioned well to support experimental as well as classic and classical work, in visual arts, performance, museum exhibitions, and the like. Funding for the arts in Japan, and in various nations in Africa, has followed models derived in part from European or U.S. practice, but has developed in ways reflective of local interests, political concerns, and national resources.

In Germany, arts funding is ordinarily administered on the state and municipal levels, with the majority of funding going to the cultural institutions owned and operated by the cities (opera companies, symphonies, museums, theaters, ballet companies, and so on) but with some funding also designated for independent artists, who apply to the arts ministry and have their applications judged by specialists from each genre (music, theater, dance, film, photography). "Most larger cities," writes composer William Osborne, an American who lives and works in Europe, "own a number of ateliers which they make available to visual artists on a permanent basis, and most cities own black box and studio theatres for smaller experimental and guest productions." Thus most German cities have many more full-time jobs for musicians, choirs, and ballet dancers, and many cities of moderate size (by U.S. standards) have more than one orchestra, and/or more than one opera house. As for private sponsorship of the arts, it is "rarely encouraged and is viewed with mistrust," Osborne reports. "They feel this will lead to less funding based on the sporadic whims of patrons who often have superficial tastes. Embarrassingly, it is often referred to as the American model."[3]

The Dutch Ministry of Education, Culture, and Science has a budget that is the largest of any Dutch government agency—by one reckoning it was equivalent, adjusted for population size, to the U.S. military budget. In 2003 the ministry spent about twenty-five dollars a year for every Dutch citizen (compared, for example, to about forty cents per citizen in the U.S. National Endowment for the Arts). Grants are usually overseen by independent foundations with specific expertise in arts fields, and cities spend even more on the arts than does the central government. The famed Stedelijk Museum in Amsterdam, for example, gets 95 percent of its budget from the city. Artists can get support for projects, travel, and studios, and get social security payments without having to produce work. Dancers who can't dance anymore get retraining grants, and money is even available in the form of interest-free loans for those who want to collect Dutch art. In recent years there has been an increased interest in seeking out private funding, but there is no comparable system of private philanthropy in the American model—the long-standing system depends upon state and civic support. "We consider it a proof of civilization," said the director of the Mondrian Foundation, which distributes millions in public money each year to the visual arts. "It will never be banished."[4]

In France, public support of the arts in the twentieth and twenty-first centuries has been highly centralized and relied on the operations of a state bureaucracy of cultural affairs. Private, philanthropic contributions along the lines suggested by the "American Model" have been, by contrast, relatively insignificant. Although tax incentives for philanthropy do, in some measure, exist, the contributions of philanthropists remain relatively negligible, as do earned and commercial income for arts institutions and nonprofit organizations.

In the decades since the end of World War II, France has been a strong "designer state," with cultural policy shaped to a great extent by its president and his ministers. Following the centralized, administrative-state tradition of the Jacobin and Napoleonic periods, the de Gaulle government established the Ministère de la Culture in 1959, with the writer and intellectual André Malraux at its head. The first tasks of the Ministry were to restore major national monuments and to create *maisons de la culture* in the provinces. Although this emphasis shifted a bit under Jack Lang, the Socialist minister of culture in the 1980s and early 1990s, Malraux's twofold approach has left a lasting imprint on French cultural policy.

The French system of state support for the arts and culture has been aptly characterized as "an integral part of national

life, indeed of the national identity."[5] Thus there is considerable ministerial control, with the majority of funding going to
a small number of highly regarded organizations, and an emphasis on the support of artists and the creation of art, rather
than on audience and publics. The government supports the
arts far more extensively in France than it does, for example,
in Britain, and the support of culture comes from regions, departments, and communes, as well as from the top. Subsidies
(and tax breaks) for films as well as museums, theaters, and visual artists underscore France's national identification with culture, while the Cultural Services of the French Embassy treats
French artists, filmmakers, playwrights, and musicians as what
they are—a major diplomatic resource.

Another constant feature of government funding of the
arts in France has been an obsession with *grands travaux*—
with major projects like the Centre Pompidou and the Musée
d'Orsay, both conceived in the 1970s. François Mitterand, who
was president of France from 1981 until 1995, transformed the
face of Paris as has no one since Baron Haussmann in the
reign of Napoleon III, with the pyramid and the new Louvre,
the Bibliothèque nationale, La Defense, the Institut du Monde
Arable, Opera Bastille, and the new Ministry of Finance. The
stated goal of Mitterand's head of the Ministry of Culture, Jack
Lang, was to maintain a cultural budget of *1 percent of the total
national budget.*

There has been some decentralization of cultural policies in
France in recent years. However, arts funding remains an important tool of national policy—as the remarks of Dominique
de Villepin, the controversial French prime minister, about the
necessity of reviving the French visual arts and the French presence in world culture, suggest. De Villepin complained that
France lacks a national and nationalistic organ to promote
French culture that would be as effective as the British Council; he established several prizes and an exhibition to rival the
Tate Britain Triennial at the Grand Palais, as well as an organization called Cultures-France to rival the British Council.

Since World War II, the national cultural policy of Japan has largely resembled that of the United States, on which it has consciously patterned itself in many respects. Following the founding of the NEA in 1965, the Japanese government established a counterpart: the Agency for Cultural Affairs (ACA) within the Ministry of Education, founded in 1968. The ACA, unlike the NEA, initially emphasized the preservation of existing artworks and the maintenance of museums and religious sites over providing financial support to living practitioners. It was not until 1990 that the ACA would announce a more comprehensive strategy for funding current work, with tax incentives based on the American example and designed to encourage private-sector sponsorship. (These have been varyingly successful; one perennial problem that the ACA has faced since 1990 is the failure of the Finance Ministry to grant institutions the "nonprofit" designation that they require to provide tax breaks for private donors.)

In the interim, in 1978, the Japanese Diet also established the Japan Foundation by a special legislative act. This autonomous, nonprofit corporation, the equivalent of a German Goethe Institute or Alliance Française, was charged with fostering a positive image and facilitating cultural exchange abroad. It has served as a complementary force to government initiatives in the time since its founding, devoting a great deal of its resources to bringing foreign artists to Japan and encouraging collaborations between Japanese and non-Japanese practitioners.[6]

Most African countries with national cultural policies loosely follow a continental European model. Senegal's primary agency, the Ministère de la Culture et du Patrimoine, closely resembles the French Ministry and funds a wide range of projects, in fashion (*mode*) and cinema (*cinéma*) as well as in more traditional categories, such as visual art, theater, and dance.[7] South Africa has a system of public support for the arts administered almost exclusively at the national level. The National Arts Council, which was established in 1997—when it assumed the role of the former Foundation of the Creative Arts—is funded entirely by the country's central government. (The annual budget currently stands at approximately US$3.6 million.)[8] The Council, much like the German Kulturstiftung des Bundes, provides grants in the following categories: music and opera; literature; visual arts; craft; theater and musical theater; dance and choreography; and "multidiscipline," with resources explicitly allocated to categories ranging from living expenses, to stipends for materials, to exhibitions and performance, to workshops and conferences and documentation and research. As in France and Germany, "development officers" assigned to each area are responsible for judging entries.

While these various national—and international—initiatives are all of considerable interest, and each brings to the table some practices that might well be imitated or emulated elsewhere, the contexts are different enough to make comparisons either very broad or rather oblique. Let us return, then, to something highly particular within individual national practices—that is, to the question of whether a government has, or should have, any role at all in sponsoring or supporting the arts. Not surprisingly, on this question—as on so many—there have been vehement opinions, often vehemently expressed and vehemently opposed.

### Mingling, Meddling, and Interfering

"God help the Minister that mingles with art!" declared the British prime minister Lord Melbourne in 1830.[9] Melbourne's ejaculation, recorded in Haydon's diaries, has often been misquoted as "God help the minister that meddles with art!"[10] And in at least one case the word "minister" has been transmuted to "government," producing a quite different exclamation: "God help the government that meddles with art."[11]

Minister or government? Meddle or mingle?

What difference does it make?

"Meddle," like "mingle," means to associate or mix with— and both words have at one time or another meant "have sexual intercourse"—but the word "meddle" also carries a strong secondary meaning of interference, and has often been used to imply improper intrusion into affairs that are not one's own business.[12] The permutations of Lord Melbourne's ringing phrase have been taken to mean that governments should stay out of the art business. According to Haydon, Melbourne more specifically envisaged a quarrel with the guardians of the flame about the question of which artists to fund, remarking with some irritation: "I'll get the whole [Royal] Academy on my back!"[13] That is to say, it was not so much the arts themselves as their self-appointed custodians that aroused this politician's concern.

Lord Melbourne's anxiety was certainly prescient, in light of the long history of infighting among twentieth-century governmental organizations and agencies and the art-makers they were designed to "patronize." But the persistent painter would not take no for an answer. On a subsequent visit to Melbourne, Haydon raised the question once again, and reported the incident, with nice novelistic touches, in his diary:

> He looked round with his arch face and said, "What now?" as much as to say, "What the devil are you come about—Art, I suppose!" "Now, my Lord," said I, "Do you admit the necessity of State support?" "I do not," said he. "Why?" said I. "Because," said he, "there is private patronage enough to do all that is requisite." "That I deny—," I replied, at which he said, "Ha! ha!"
>
> He then went to the glass, & began to comb his hair. I went on: "My Lord, that's a false view; private patronage has raised the School in all the departments where it could do it service, but High Art cannot be advanced by private patronage." "But it is not the policy of this Country to interfere," said he. "Why?" "Because it is not necessary." "You say so, but I'll prove the contrary." "Well, let's hear," said Lord Melbourne, "where has it ever flourished?" "In Greece, Ægypt, Italy." "How? By individual patronage?" "No, my Lord, *alone* by the support of the State." "Has it

flourished in any Country without it?" "No. How can your
Lordship expect it in this?" He did not reply.[14]

"High art cannot be advanced by private patronage." "But it is
not the policy of this Country to interfere." Presumably Haydon's plaint about high art has to do with the importunities of
patrons, who want timid or flattering art, or who, at least, having paid the piper, expect to hear some favorite tunes. When
Melbourne demands to know where state patronage has flourished, keeping a wary eye on his visitor in the mirror, Haydon
swiftly delivers a classic litany of greatness past: ancient Greece
and Egypt, Renaissance Italy.

Why would the Britain of the nineteenth century not want to
follow their example, in developing art of a quality consistent
with its high political and imperial ambition? Perhaps because of
the liabilities implied by Melbourne's expression "to interfere,"
resonant with the double-entendre possibilities of "meddle" and
"mingle." Because the ambiguous and volatile relationships that
have historically ensnared benefactors in "patron trouble" seemed
best for a responsible statesman to avoid.

The critic and essayist William Hazlitt, formerly Haydon's
ally, came to oppose his view, although for rather different reasons than those cited by Lord Melbourne. "Professional art is a
contradiction in terms," wrote Hazlitt with determined finality.
"Art is genius, and genius cannot belong to a profession."[15] As
we will see, this preoccupation with the question of "genius"
recurs frequently in discussions of patronage and of its relationship to the professional practice of art. Many modern commentators still agree with Hazlitt: the genius is inimitable, not
a "professional" but an original. By this logic, funding was, in a
sense, doomed by paradox: the training, schooling, and fostering of professional artists could only by this logic support the
wrong artists, the nongeniuses.

Throughout the nineteenth and into the twentieth century,
suspicion of the value of public funding of art and artists in

Britain persisted in multiple arenas, particularly among those who were concerned with more direct modes of support for the urban or the rural poor. Art was a luxury, not a necessity. British journalist, politician, and farmer William Cobbett—a contemporary of Melbourne, Haydon, and Hazlitt—who had written pamphlets as a young man under the name of "Peter Porcupine," was also bristly later in his life about government support for culture. Elected to Parliament in his twilight years, he inveighed against public spending on the arts rather than on the needs of the working people: "Of what use, in the wide world, is the British Museum?" he demanded on the floor of the House of Commons. "Sixteen thousand pounds granted for the support of such a place are sixteen thousand pounds thrown away."[16]

Such testiness was not perhaps entirely typical, but the idea of investing in the arts for the public good remained largely a goal for individual philanthropists rather than for the government throughout this period. With the onset of the World Wars, however, international events conspired to help advocates of state patronage break through the kind of resistance Haydon had encountered from Lord Melbourne. Entertaining both the troops and those on the home front became an expedient priority. In order to organize performances for dispirited soldiers in World War I, a group called the Entertainments National Service Association (ENSA) was created. The same group was revived in the Second World War. And in December 1939, thanks to a £2 million gift that the American railway millionaire Edward Harkness had made a decade earlier in order "to conserve the heritage of Great Britain in all its aspects," the Committee for the Encouragement of Music and the Arts was founded in London.

"CEMA," as the Committee was known, came into being with the explicit objective of bringing arts and culture to a war-weary populace, while also providing financial support to performers who were out of work because of wartime conditions. Behind this practical plan—and, indeed, in plain view in its guiding principles—was the belief that England should not suffer a cultural defeat at the hands of its enemies. Indeed, the explicitly stated goal of CEMA was "the preservation in wartime of the highest standards in the arts of music, drama, and painting."[17] That is, there were pragmatic, political, and indeed nationalistic incentives behind the British government's assent to patronize the arts in the mid-twentieth century. And while the organizations founded in this moment of international crisis survived and even flourished in subsequent decades, the interests that initially motivated the creation of ENSA and CEMA have continued to shape debates regarding state patronage in the United Kingdom until the present day.

One of the most persistent disagreements regarding the proper use of state funds for the arts can be seen in the contrasting leadership styles of the first two chairs of CEMA. The first head, appointed in 1939, was Lord De La Warr, the president of the Board of Education, who supported amateur regional theater in the northeast of England and in the Welsh valleys and Lancashire, and groups like the Music Travellers, which gave concerts in churches, air raid shelters, and internment camps for aliens.[18] However, the emphasis initially placed on regional and indigenous arts for public culture shifted abruptly with the appointment of the Cambridge economist John Maynard Keynes as CEMA's new chairman in 1942.

Keynes—now Lord Keynes—was a Bloomsbury habitué, a lifelong friend of Virginia and Leonard Woolf, husband to the ballerina Lydia Lopokova, and the former lover of painter Duncan Grant. He objected, on both artistic and fiscal grounds, to the priority that his predecessor had placed on popular culture. Keynes "was not the man for wandering minstrels and amateur theatricals," observed Kenneth Clark, the director of the National Gallery and Surveyor of the King's Pictures.[19] "He wanted to know why the Council was wasting so much money on amateur effort," Mary Glasgow, Keynes's longtime assistant, added. "It was standards that mattered, and the preservation of serious professional enterprise, not obscure concerts in village halls."[20] As a result, Keynes professionalized both CEMA and the arts it supported, focusing on performance venues like the Old Vic, Sadler's Wells, and the Royal Opera House at Covent Garden.

Many observers had expected that CEMA would cease its operations after the war. However, when the time came to review the organization and its utility in 1944, Keynes and others waged an impassioned campaign for continued state patronage. Ideally Keynes would have liked a balance of private donors and public support, but increasingly he came to realize that government financial involvement was necessary, at least for the time being.[21] Though wary that state patronage might develop into a "bottomless sink," Keynes nonetheless helped instigate an important shift. Under his leadership, CEMA was transformed from a tool for reminding the British masses of the vitality of their culture during a state of emergency into a permanent fixture of the peacetime government. Renamed the Arts Council of Great Britain, the arts agency began, after the war, to offer grants for writers and other producers of art. It seemed a halcyon moment for public patronage.

The moment, however, was fleeting. Keynes's death from a heart attack in 1946 prevented him from taking up the post as the Arts Council's first chairman, and his insistence on the priority of the "fine arts" was modulated by his successors over time to include, once again, the local, the regional, the emergent, and the young—that is, precisely that range of arts that had been fostered by ENSA and CEMA, at least under the leadership of De La Warr, and that Keynes had gradually phased out. By 1965, with the issuance of a government White Paper (*A Policy for the Arts: The First Steps*) the shift in emphasis was complete, and funding for the arts was returned to the aegis of the Department of Education, where it had been until Keynes's reorganization of the Arts Council. The tension between high and low, fine and popular, elite and populist, local and urban, or however else one wanted to describe it—a tension that in fact underlies almost all discourse about the arts in any time or place—was now officially inscribed in the documentation about government support of the arts in Great Britain. The era of Young British Artists was on the horizon. But so was the renationalism of the various sections of "Britain." In 1994 the Arts Council was divided to form the Arts Council of England, the Scottish Arts Council, and the Arts Council of Wales.

### As the World Turns: The Changing "Heritage of Great Britain"

The tension between what we might roughly designate as the "local" and the "cosmopolitan" has only grown more complicated in recent years, as the globalization of the art world inevitably changes the terms of the De La Warr/Keynes opposition. These days, the sense of cultural identity mobilized to justify the founding of CEMA—and, indeed, the identifiable "heritage of Great Britain" that it was funded to "conserve"—has become increasingly difficult to pin down. At the same time, disagreements concerning what constitutes "art" in any case continue to prompt vociferous public sparring on all sides.

Consider the case of the Turner Prize, awarded annually to a British visual artist under fifty, and named for the painter J.M.W. Turner. The Turner Prize has been controversial since its inception in 1984. Organized by the Tate Museum, and thus highly "canonical" and "British" in at least one sense, the Turner has nonetheless often been awarded to makers of "edgy" art. In 1992 winner Damien Hirst exhibited a cow and calf in formaldehyde, titled *Mother and Child, Divided.* In 1998 Chris Ofili exhibited a painting, *No Woman, No Cry* (acrylic paint, oil paint, polyester resin, paper collage, map pins, elephant dung). The list could go on. The Turner Prize, which reliably inspires a media circus, is funded primarily by corporate sponsors. However, the fact that the prize is given by a government organization (the Arts Council) to an artist whose work is—at least metonymically—designated as "British" implicates it in a tangle of issues that persistently surround state patronage. What say should members of the public themselves have in these matters of high culture?

The winners, and all those considered for the Turner Prize, are by requirement "British artists." But what is a "British" artist in the twenty-first century? Chris Ofili, who won the prize in 1998, is of Nigerian descent. Born and raised in London, he won a scholarship that enabled him to travel to Zimbabwe, where he was influenced by local cave paintings and materials like the infamous dung. Yinka Shonibare, one of the four finalists in 2004, was likewise born in London of Nigerian parents, and moved to Lagos at age three, where he spoke Yoruba at home and English at school. Shonibare works with "African" fabrics that are made in the Netherlands and exported to London. Kutlug Ataman, also a 2004 finalist, was born in Istanbul, where he has lived periodically, and now makes his residence in Buenos Aires; he received his B.A. and M.F.A. in film from the University of California. Tomoko Takahashi, a shortlisted finalist in 2000, was born in Tokyo, while the Turner Prize winner that year, photographer Wolfgang Tillmans, was born in Germany; both artists attended British art schools and exhibited in Britain and worldwide. Beirut-born Mona Hatoum, shortlisted for the prize in 1995, and Anish Kapoor, the 1991 Turner Prize winner, who was born in Bombay, both studied at British art schools. Kapoor's work was chosen to represent Britain in the 1990 Venice Biennale, and Chris Ofili's, in 2003.[22]

In short, even a cursory survey makes clear that the question of a national prize for "British art" or a "British artist" has been opened up by both the global art world and the realities of immigration, international marriages, and schooling. When we look back to the questions that Keynes provoked about the comparative merits of funding "wandering minstrels and amateur theatricals" or "serious professional enterprise," what is clear in any case is that the underlying paradigms of the regional versus the urban, and the local versus the cosmopolitan, have dramatically evolved. National art is now global. And—to evoke another issue raised annually by the Turner Prize and present since the founding of CEMA—the high is low, and the low is high.

Dung and gold mixed together—which is the more precious, and which the more prosaic? That almost-witty coinage, "avant garbage," marks a truism rather than a contradiction. And a number of almost-witty organizations, carrying out their critique of the art establishment, have in fact drawn attention to precisely the difficulties that the state as patron faces in meeting the expectations that its citizens have for "art."

In 1993, at the height of the manufactured outrage surrounding the Turner Prize's annual canonization of "best British artist," the £20,000 prize awarded by the Tate Gallery and beneficent Patrons for New Art was shown up by a new accolade, valued at twice the sum (a cool £40,000). The K Foundation's "Prize for the Worst British Artist," selected from the Turner short list, was in its first iteration given to the *same* artist who won the Turner, the sculptor Rachel Whiteread.[23] Informed that the money would be burned unless she accepted it, Whiteread took the funds and distributed them as grants to ten young artists, with a substantial sum left over to contribute to a homeless shelter.[24] And of course everyone—the Tate, the Turner Prize, the K Foundation, and the artist—got a healthy helping of publicity.

It is hard to guess how John Maynard Keynes—either the young "Maynard" of the Bloomsbury years, who often participated in such pranks, or the mature patrician of the BBC broadcasts, the *Times,* and the *Listener*—would have responded to such a well-heeled stunt at the cultural expense of New Art. Indeed, messages sent by such instances of state patronage and the public spectacles that attend them are mixed. In the Whiteread case one public institution, the Tate Gallery, supported an honorific award for edgy art, while another branch of government, a local city council in the East End of London, remained determined to destroy a prize-winning artwork on schedule, rather than extend the exhibition for several weeks to accommodate crowds of visitors. The intervention of the

K Foundation was itself a performance, of course (the Foundation's other moment of fame came when its two founders publicly burned £1 million in £50 notes). But the existence of a prize for a British artist under fifty, with attendant international publicity and the sponsorship of a group named the Patrons of New Art, raised the visibility of both "new art" and the opportunities for patronage. (I should note as a point of interest that although the Tate Gallery—or the various Tate Galleries: Britain, Modern, Liverpool, and St. Ives—is a quintessentially British institution, there is a separate organization called American Patrons of Tate with an address, and a tax-exempt status, based in New York.)

### The Right to Study Painting: State Patronage à l'Américain

In an often-cited letter to his wife Abigail, John Adams outlined, in 1780, what was, in effect, a genealogy of intellectual and cultural life for himself, his family, and the new American nation: "I must study Politicks and war that my sons may have liberty to study . . . Mathematicks and Philosophy, Geography, natural History, Naval Architecture, navigation, Commerce and Agriculture, in order to give their Children a right to study Painting, Poetry, Musick, Architecture, Statuary, Tapestry and Porcelaine."[25] The statement is as ambiguous as it is programmatic. Did Adams mean by this ordering to imply that the arts were a third-order concern? Or, rather, that they constituted a culminating value for the nation and its citizens? It is worth considering the language he uses, both the sequence of fields of learning (from politics to porcelain) and the sequence of verbs and moods: "I must study . . . that our sons may have liberty to study . . . in order to give their children a right to study." This progression, moving from *must* to *may* and from *liberty* to *right*, is both elegant and determinative. The gift of a *right* in the third generation suggests a strong and important entitlement, especially, perhaps, when the word is used by a writer who would help to engineer, a few years later, the

Massachusetts Compromise, which in turn cleared the way for the Bill of Rights to the U.S. Constitution.

To study, of course, does not mean to practice. These are arts both public and private, and their study is as important for patrons as it is for the artists themselves. The range of fine arts indicated in John Adams's letter to his wife describes not only art forms but the emoluments of gracious living. "Painting, poetry, music, architecture, statuary, tapestry and porcelain" are the furnishings of culture, and their study is the necessary preamble to wise patronage as well as to the practice and making of art.

What has become of John Adams's tricolon in more recent decades? Are we, as citizens of a rich, Western democracy now *entitled* to study painting? Does our government have an obligation to protect this right? And, if so, can the government protect it without getting caught in the thicket of misunderstandings that emerge when the patron-patronized relation is grafted onto such nebulous entities as "tax dollars" and "the American public"?

In the United States, as in Great Britain, state patronage organizations first emerged in response to a national crisis. Over the course of their somewhat briefer history, institutions like the National Endowment for the Arts and the National Endowment for the Humanities have also often found themselves in many of the same quandaries that have troubled CEMA and the Arts Council, from the days of De La Warr and Keynes to those of Hirst and Ofili. The recapitulation of the familiar problems in America with respect to the benefits of regionalism versus those of cosmopolitanism—and the liabilities that arise from funding art that "ordinary" citizens might dismiss as "bad"—reappear here, suggesting that they reflect problems deeply embedded in the structure of state patronage.

The usual story told about the United States as compared to the United Kingdom in terms of arts funding is that Britain has become dependent upon government grants at every level, accepting the importance of public patronage, while in the

United States the tradition of private, individual, and corporate patronage, begun by the barons of industry in the nineteenth century and continued by their descendants, has always held center stage. In comparison to the state grants available in Great Britain and continental Europe, the support that the American government provides to its artists has been both less well funded and less widely endorsed. However, the history of government sponsorship in the United States over the course of the last century is complex, and a closer look at American arts funding before the creation of the National Endowments is revealing.

### Public Works of Art: Federal Funding Schemes to Midcentury

In the early years of the Great Depression, Harry Hopkins—a close adviser to Franklin Delano Roosevelt and a future architect of the New Deal—began administering work-relief for artists in New York State. As early as 1932, Hopkins was employing down-and-out artists to teach classes and to work on decorations for public institutions (post offices, hospitals, courthouses). When Roosevelt became president of the United States, however, he appointed Hopkins to run the Federal Emergency Relief Administration (FERA), inherited from Herbert Hoover and expanded by the Federal Emergency Relief Act. It was the Department of the Treasury, rather than FERA, that was to become "in effect one of the world's greatest art patrons" over the course of the 1930s.

Historically American state patronage had been directed primarily at the decoration and enhancement of monuments, not at the artists who did the work. However, with the inauguration of what came to be called the Public Works of Art Project, a program of work-relief for professional artists was developed under the auspices of the Treasury. In the seven months of its existence, before it was superseded by what became the Treasury's Section on Fine Arts, PWAP employed some 3,750 artists working on over 15,000 works of art, albeit at low wages. This marked, as one commentator observed, "the first time the government had subsidized an art project of national dimension."[26]

By the midthirties, a still more extensive national program was under way. Created in 1935 as a subdivision of the Works Progress Administration (WPA), it included the Federal Writers' Project, the Federal Theatre Project, the Federal Art Project (with separate easel and mural divisions), and the Federal Music Project. Known collectively as Federal Arts Project Number One—or "Federal One," for short—this initiative was intended to benefit both out-of-work artists and the general public. Yet, it encountered a number of points of difficulty and resistance— points that, we begin to see, are deeply embedded in the structure of the state as patron in modern culture.

For all of their progressive energies, each of the "patronizing" initiatives of the Roosevelt administration also tapped into a certain strain of cultural conservatism or populism, especially in backlash against the heady experimental days of the twenties, which had produced Dada, Surrealism, and the expatriate poetry of Pound, Eliot, and Gertrude Stein. In the United States the tension between regional arts and "high" or cosmopolitan art was consolidated by the Great Depression and the proliferation of federal agencies developed during the New Deal.

Perhaps in an attempt to avoid controversy, the Federal Writers Project tended to focus on local and regional themes. Although the Writers Project did provide funding for emergent writers like Ralph Ellison and Richard Wright, by far the largest amount of support went to the crafting of a series of state travel guides—a program developed specifically to mollify those who thought all the money would otherwise flow to the big cities. Most of those who worked on these projects did not gain further reputations as writers, although a few well-known figures did participate and survive to tell the tale. John Cheever contributed to the New York guide; Saul Bellow, wishing to avoid the tedium of work on the travel guides, found himself instead performing an equally mechanical task: compiling lists of magazines held in the Newberry Library. Writers employed by the Project were expected to work a regular day, 8:00 A.M. to 5:00 P.M., and in general, both bureaucracy and censorship impeded their efforts. Even the Project's textbook industry, which incorporated local histories, oral culture, interviews with former slaves, and aspects of ethnography and folklore, became the object of suspicion, since over time (and especially after World War II), these books came to be regarded as leftist tracts, or FDR boosterism.[27]

Regionalism and localism did not, in this case, provide an escape from political critique. Even the travel guides, anodyne as they might be thought to have been, did not please all audiences: the Massachusetts guide was said to have too much in it that was prolabor and antiestablishment, not to mention its views on Sacco and Vanzetti. Several mayors banned the book in their home towns, and the state governor ordered a purge of objectionable passages and the dismissal of the author.[28] There continued to be controversy regarding government patronage of the arts.

Regionalism also played an important role in the government funding of theater. In comparison with the work of solitary writers, theater groups under the New Deal flourished. Public performances had an immediate effect, in small towns and cities as well as in urban areas. And collaborative activities sometimes produced material innovations—for example, the new electronic lighting boards and backstage projections, both funded under the Federal Theatre Project. The Theatre Project was directed by Hallie Flanagan, a playwright (and the first woman ever awarded a Guggenheim Fellowship),[29] and strongly supported by First Lady Eleanor Roosevelt. But it was inspired, as well, by one of America's most successful playwrights.

Elmer Rice, the author of plays like *The Adding Machine* and *Street Scene*, agreed with Hallie Flanagan, and with FDR's adviser Harry Hopkins, that "men and women of high professional standing had been reduced to the status of vagrants"[30] by the Depression and its aftermath. Rice proposed an ambitious plan for the government purchase of regional theaters in a hundred cities around the country, and the recruitment to them of actors who had migrated to the large cities, and could be encouraged to return home. Thus regionalism—and permanent local companies—would solve the problem of urban unemployment, even as a few certified stars (Helen Hayes, John Barrymore) would be contracted to make appearances in these theaters across the country.

Flanagan's plan for the Federal Theatre Project, designed along similar lines, said explicitly—in terms that would later be a red flag for some members of Congress—that the goal was not only "caring for the unemployed but recreating a national theatre and building a national culture."[31] But ultimately the project of returning actors to their original home communities was dropped, and the idea of building theater audiences in small towns across the country became a secondary concern. The plan, it seemed, was impracticable: neither actors, nor big-city companies in New York and elsewhere, were willing to tour or travel in this way, and there were no funds to allow them to do so. The relief system did not provide for moving the population from one district to another.

The Federal Theatre Project launched the careers of artists and writers like Arthur Miller, Orson Welles, Marc Blitzstein, John Houseman, Canada Lee, and Will Geer. But the very fact that theater tended to be collaborative rather than solitary seemed—in the 1930s as in the English Renaissance—to provoke suspicion. Brilliant innovations like the *Living Newspaper*, which dramatized current social issues like housing, race, the agricultural depression, labor unions, and public utilities, interweaving documentary facts with fiction, were regarded as inflammatory. (It would be many years before Anna Deavere Smith's *Fires in the Mirror: Crown Heights, Brooklyn, and Other Identities* was hailed as a breakthrough on Broadway). Certainly the left press—the *Daily Worker, New Masses, New Theatre*, and other journals—supported the FTP, which engaged social issues and political controversies. Flanagan was called to testify before the House Un-American Activities Committee (HUAC), where her answers were frank but impolitic, and Congress dissolved the Federal Theatre

Project in 1939. Martin Dies, the chairman of HUAC, was particularly virulent in his criticism, and Republican J. Parnell Thomas asserted that "Practically every play presented under the auspices of the Project is sheer propaganda for Communism or the New Deal."[32]

### Handwriting on the Wall

One of the models for publicly produced art, and a politically ambivalent one, was the successful Mexican mural movement of the 1920s. The American painter, sculptor, and muralist George Biddle wrote to President Roosevelt in 1933 to urge that the administration support a similar project:

> The Mexican artists have produced the greatest national school of mural painting since the Italian Renaissance. Diego Rivera tells me that it was only possible because Obregon allowed Mexican artists to work at plumbers' wages in order to express on the walls of the government buildings the social ideals of the Mexican revolution. The younger artists of America are conscious as they never have been of the social revolution that our country and civilization are going through; and they would be very eager to express these ideals in a permanent art form if they were given the government's cooperation.[33]

Biddle himself was a scion of an old and moneyed family, a classmate of Roosevelt's at Groton and at Harvard (which is doubtless why his letter was not only written to FDR but also read and answered). His commitment to socially conscious art, and to government funding for the arts led to works like *The Tenement*, a federally commissioned mural for the Department of Justice Building in 1935.

As for Roosevelt, his response was, apparently, a typical mix of interest and caution. He reportedly told Biddle that he didn't want a bunch of young zealots painting Lenin's head on the Justice Building—as Diego Rivera had done in a mural at

Rockefeller Center commissioned by Abby Aldrich Rockefeller. Rivera had offered to balance the Lenin portrait with one of Abraham Lincoln; instead he was paid off and dismissed from the job, and the offending image was covered with a drape. Near midnight on February 10, 1934, workmen carrying axes destroyed the mural, and the furious Rivera never consented to work in the United States again. The *New York Times* reported that his supporters compared the treatment accorded Rivera with the way Michelangelo had been treated by the popes.[34] Yet despite these reminders of lofty patronage gone wrong, Biddle's earnest correspondence with FDR led directly to the founding of the Federal Arts Project of the Works Progress Administration. Whether this fact should be regarded as a triumph of social conscience or an old-boy handshake is, perhaps, of less importance than the palpable result: artists were paid by the government to make art.

But what kind of art? And who would decide? The Rockefeller-Rivera fiasco was sufficiently in peoples' minds that the government yielded to local pressure from time to time, altering designs and details to suit its audience. The famous Forty-Eight State Competition of 1939–40, a nationwide contest to design murals for post offices across the country, produced a set of winning designs that were organized in a traveling exhibition. But at least one design, Fletcher Martin's prize-winning "Mine Rescue" for a post office in Kellogg, Idaho, was rejected by the local inhabitants because of its graphic depiction of danger in the mines. Martin was compelled, in the words of one commentator, to "create a less dramatic reference to local reality."[35] A mural by Ben Shahn for the Bronx post office was to include an inscription from Walt Whitman—until a Jesuit from nearby Fordham University lodged a protest. Biddle's *Tenement* was conceived as part of an ambitious mural program on Society Freed through Justice—but some observers objected that its depiction of poverty was inartistic. *America the Mighty*, a powerful twelve- by fifty-foot mural on the subject of war commissioned and executed for the War Department by Kindred McLeary in 1941, became an awkward relict when the building on Twenty-first Street became the Department of State, and the mural was covered from 1954 to 1977 for "diplomatic" reasons.[36]

A different political motive sparked the creation of a mural in the Department of Interior, with the provocative (and appropriate title) *An Incident in Contemporary American Life.* The "incident" was the Lincoln Memorial concert given by singer Marian Anderson on Easter Sunday, April 9, 1939, after the Daughters of the American Revolution denied her the use of Constitution Hall because she was black. In response, Eleanor Roosevelt resigned from the DAR, and Secretary of the Interior Harold Ickes, a strong supporter of civil rights, provided the use of the Lincoln Memorial for the concert, which was attended by some 75,000 people. Money was raised by public subscription for the mural, which was painted by Mitchell Jamieson in 1942.

Mural painting, although much in vogue at the time for the ornamentation of public space, was not the only kind of subsidized visual art under the aegis of the Federal Art Project. Jackson Pollock, for example, was employed by the New York Easel Division of the Federal Art Project for the entire duration of the project, from 1935 to 1943. Artists were free to paint whatever they liked, and to produce as much work as they wished, so long as they submitted one painting every four to eight weeks for allocation to some public venue, for which they were paid, on average, ninety-five dollars a month. Pollock's *Landscape with Train* (1937) and *Landscape with Factory* (1938), both produced for the WPA Federal Art Project, were apparently acquired by a plumber who thought he could use the painted canvasses as pipe insulation, only to discover that oil paint, when heated, gave off a foul smell. The Pollock landscapes, some paintings by Mark Rothko, and other works were rescued by a framer and restorer who purchased them for about five dollars each.[37] Nor were representational paintings and social realism the only favored modes. Ad Reinhardt's geometric abstractions, and a major mural by Arshile Gorky (*Aviation: Evolution of Forms under*

*Aerodynamic Limitations*, Newark Airport Administration Building, 1935–36, later destroyed) were among the works that the Project sponsored and supported.

It is important here to underscore the consistent debate and tension, among government officials, between sponsoring works and sponsoring artists. Holger Cahill, who directed the Federal Art Project from its beginning to its liquidation, conceived of the project's central purpose as work-relief. "The primary objective of the project is the employment of artists who are on the relief rolls," he wrote in 1935. "The Federal Art Project will draw at least ninety per cent [sic] of its personnel from relief. The project is planned in the belief that among these artists will be found the talent and the skill necessary to carry on an art program which will make contributions of permanent value to the community." The goals of the Project—"to secure for the public outstanding examples of contemporary American art; through art teaching and recreational art activities to create a broader national art consciousness and work out constructive ways of using leisure time; through services in applied art to aid various campaigns of social value; and through research projects to clarify the native background in the arts"[38]—were, Cahill believed, completely compatible with the idea of nurturing poor artists and allowing them to develop their own talents.

By contrast, the Section on Painting and Sculpture (later the Section on Fine Arts) at the Treasury Department, led by its chief, Edward Bruce, began with the description of the work ("to secure suitable art of the best quality for the embellishment of public buildings") and then sought out appropriate artists to perform it, using expert advice and juried competitions. In this case the primary objective set out by the Treasury secretary was a "high standard" of quality certified by "people throughout the country interested in the arts and whose judgment in connection with the arts has the respect of the Section."[39]

Opposition to Federal One, which escalated in Congress during 1938 and 1939 (based in part on claims of "Communist subversion in New York City"),[40] led to the abolishment of the program in September 1939, and the complete cutoff of funds for the Federal Theatre Project, presumably deemed the hottest of the hotbeds. The other three projects—music, writing, and art—were now partially foisted onto the states for cost-sharing, and anyone who had been supported by them for as long as eighteen months was dismissed; the "relief" aspect of the WPA was thus effectively undermined. The onset of World War II allowed for the conversion of the arts initiative into the Graphic Section of the War Services Program, and by the middle of 1943, the projects had been shut down completely. HUAC, of course, remained. And armed with old names from the WPA days (Arthur Miller, Pete Seeger), the Committee could look about for new targets, even those not explicitly funded by the U.S. government or the states.

"Regional," "vernacular," "local," "folk," "amateur," "community"; "urban," "urbane," "cosmopolitan," "professional," "experimental," "aesthetic." No matter which terms are used to mark this consistent, and persistent, split, it is one that has divided funders and supporters for as long as there have been patrons of the arts. Is the role of the arts to uplift the many, to provoke the few, to enhance lives, or to challenge them? As we will see shortly, this dichotomy, between subsidizing the art project and subsidizing the artist, would come to color the postwar "culture war" debates in a very significant way. Even in the late thirties and forties, political currents were at work, laying the groundwork of suspicion against artists more homegrown and less overtly "leftist" than Diego Rivera.

The history of government support for the arts in the early and mid-twentieth century both complicates and illuminates the debate about patronage in the United States in more recent years. We are used to thinking of the era of repression and witch-hunting presided over by HUAC as a postwar or cold war phenomenon. It was in September of 1947 that HUAC began to interview "friendly witnesses" who would testify against supposed

Communists and subversives in the Hollywood motion-picture industry, producing the infamous blacklist that prevented many artists and writers from working in the entertainment industry. But it makes sense to see that the congressional "oversight" of such activities was encouraged and prompted by government-sponsored art programs, and that the habits of suspicion and paranoia (or meddling, mingling, and interfering) were already well established before the cold-war HUAC onslaught against artists and their politics. Thus by the time the National Endowment for the Arts was passed by a divided Congress in 1965 the arguments against—as well as for—government arts patronage were already in place. Moreover, the oppositional roles had been cast.

## Lovers' Quarrels

As we have seen, John F. Kennedy set a standard for government attention to arts and culture in the United States, deftly inserting the poet Robert Frost into his inauguration ceremony. In October 1963 Kennedy spoke at the groundbreaking ceremony for the Robert Frost Library at Amherst College. Frost, a former member of the Amherst English faculty, had died, at age eighty-seven, in January of that year.

In the audience on this occasion was another poet, Archibald MacLeish, whom Kennedy had known at Harvard, where MacLeish held the chair of Boylston Professor of Rhetoric and Oratory from 1949 to 1962. Kennedy's words at the Frost Library dedication constitute his most extended remarks on the role of the artist in society, and stand not only as a benchmark of presidential eloquence in the arts of rhetoric and oratory but also as a striking and instructive contrast with the "culture wars" of subsequent decades.

> The artist, [said Kennedy] however faithful to his personal vision of reality, becomes the last champion of the individual mind and sensibility against an intrusive society and

an officious state. The great artist is thus a solitary figure. He has, as Frost said, a lover's quarrel with the world. . . . If sometimes our great artists have been the most critical of our society, it is because their sensitivity and their concern for justice, which must motivate any true artist, makes him aware that our Nation falls short of its highest potential. I see little of more importance to the future of our country and our civilization than full recognition of the place of the artist.

Kennedy went on to defend artistic freedom ("We must never forget that art is not a form of propaganda; it is a form of truth") and also, in the process, to express some worries about the connections between politics and art ("In free society art is not a weapon and it does not belong to the spheres of polemic and ideology"). But his caution, though voiced on the side of the heroic and solitary individual, did not require the silencing or neutering of political opinions. Rather, he sought to distinguish, for postwar America, the role of art in a democratic society. "It is the highest duty of the writer, the composer, the artist to remain true to himself and to let the chips fall where they may." And he concluded with a ringing endorsement that echoed the hopes of John Adams in his letter to his wife:

> I look forward to an America which will reward achievements in the arts as we reward achievement in business or statecraft. I look forward to an America which will steadily raise the standards of artistic achievement and which will steadily enlarge cultural opportunities for all of our citizens. And I look forward to an America which commands respect throughout the world not only for its strength but for its civilization as well.[41]

A month later Kennedy was dead, killed by an assassin's bullet. In 1965 his successor, President Lyndon Johnson, signed legislation establishing the National Endowments for Humanities and for the Arts as independent agencies of the federal government.

The years 1963, 1965. It was in the context of the various conflagrations and cultural shifts of the sixties—the Russian takeover of Eastern Europe and erection of the Berlin Wall; the civil rights movement; the women's movement; the escalation of the war in Vietnam and student resistance to the draft; the House Un-American Activities Committee investigating citizens, including a number of artists, poets, and performers—that the National Endowments for the Arts and Humanities came into being. Perhaps it was inevitable that the optimism about the arts proclaimed by John Kennedy—and framed, it should be acknowledged, by familiar and comfortable American voices (Frost, MacLeish)—would give way to dissent.

Kennedy had exalted the solitary individual, the loner, the modern equivalent of Milton's "one just man" standing up against corrupt or unthinkingly conformist society. But what would happen if the loner's resistance became widely persuasive? If the counterculture became the culture? If conscience and conscientious objection—or, alternatively, if self-absorption, experiment, mind alteration, and conscious excess—carried the day?

The artist as suffering loner, a figure derived from Romanticism and brilliantly expounded in Edmund Wilson's *The Wound and the Bow* (1941), derived his—"his"—pathos from his exceptionalism, the ugly-duckling syndrome. Whether he was a rebel (with or without a cause), a ninety-pound weakling, or a "brain" (the dismissive appellation for the geeks, nerds, and wonks of yesteryear), the artist stood proudly alone, *contra mundum.* The misfit, the outsider, the loner: these were recognizable American types. Out of the frontier mythology the New Frontier could champion its artists.

The phrase "rugged individual" has been an American truism since the middle of the nineteenth century, and was memorably employed by Republican candidate Herbert Hoover in the 1928 presidential campaign to differentiate the United States from the collectivism of Europe.[42] A half-century later, in the (once again) prosperous 1980s, Roger Rosenblatt noted that "everyone always says that rugged individualism is the back-bone, and the jawbone, of America," characterizing the term as "more aggressive than mere individuality, less narcissistic than the 'me' decade."[43]

As Raymond Williams has noticed, the word "individual" has had an interesting intellectual itinerary, moving from the early meaning of "indivisible" (almost the opposite of our current usage) through the later senses of a singular personage as con-trasted with a group, a collective effort, or a set of supervening social institutions like the family, society, or the state.[44] As for the word "rugged," from the same root as "rough," "shaggy," "hirsute," and "ragged," it may come uncomfortably close to the image of the long-haired artist or intellectual. (The word "rug," slang for wig or hairpiece, is a related term.)

Etymology has never trumped cliché in American political discourse, however, and it is unlikely that either Hoover or any of the term's more recent users was thinking of hairiness as a principal characteristic of this indigenous and idealized species, the rugged individual. And yet "long-haired" has its own lineage, as the *OED* makes clear in this unusually acerbic entry: "Having long hair; *spec.* applied, at various times (*a*) to Merovingians; (*b*) (freq. derog.) to aesthetes and intellectuals; (*c*) to cats with long fur; (*d*) to classical (as opposed to popular) musicians; (*e*) to beatniks and hippies. Sometimes without reference to the actual length of the hair: with or of intellectual or aesthetic pretensions."[45] In any case, the idea of the artist as individual, floating free of propaganda and heedless of ideology, was, it soon became evident, itself a myth of the West.

The belated revelation that the Central Intelligence Agency had for many years underwritten cultural conferences and fes-tivals, and funded respected journals like *Encounter* (edited by respected figures like the poet Stephen Spender and the scholar Frank Kermode), *Transition, Partisan Review, Sewanee Review, Ke-nyon Review, Poetry,* the *Journal of the History of Ideas,* and *Daedalus* (the journal of the American Academy of Arts and Sciences), made it clear that art and politics were, in the minds of many in the government, inextricably intertwined. The Congress for Cultural Freedom, run by émigré operative Michael Josselson, was begun as a result of a postwar conference for western intellectuals and artists held in Berlin in 1950, and continued in operation, supporting art exhibitions, musicians, and other cultural events, until its sponsorship by the CIA was revealed in 1967.

The Congress, whose title may strike some ears as an Orwellian coinage, had as its objective the weaning of leftist European postwar intellectuals away from Marxism and Communism. In the Kennedy years A-list intellectuals like Robert Lowell, Hannah Arendt, Mary McCarthy, and Stephen Spender were guests at the White House, at Bellagio, at Gstaad, and in top-drawer hotels in New York, London, Paris, and Rome, as well as on private yachts. Money was funneled through a variety of foundations, and the Congress's leadership fretted over such questions as who would get the Nobel Prize for Literature.[46] (An organized campaign against the leftist Chilean poet and writer Pablo Neruda in 1964 had the unforeseen, and unwanted, effect of clearing the way for the prize to be offered to Jean-Paul Sartre, who famously refused it. The Peace Prize that year was awarded to Martin Luther King Jr.)

News of the CIA involvement in underwriting "cultural freedom" hit readers of the *New York Times* forcibly when they opened their morning newspapers in April 1966. A year later, in May 1967, under the headline, "Receiver of Funds from C.I.A. Quits: Head of Freedom Congress to Leave Group in Paris," correspondent Gloria Emerson reported Josselson's resignation, "after having assumed responsibility for his group's accepting funds from the Central Intelligence Agency from 1950 to the summer of 1966."[47]

It is not my intention here to offer a blow-by-blow account of cultural programming in the cold war. My concern is both more localized and more pointed. Once again, what I want to stress is that by the mid-1960s, when the National Endowments for the Arts and the Humanities were presented as new, optimistic examples of government patronage, there had already existed in the United States and in Britain a long history of government arts patronage, political entanglement, and covert funding for select artists, writers, performers, and cultural organizations.

## *Climate Control*

The Declaration of Purpose for the National Foundation on the Arts and Humanities Act offered a manifesto, of sorts, for government sponsorship of the arts. It pushed back at the intensive and singleminded Sputnik-era focus on science, stating that "an advanced civilization must not limit its efforts to science and technology alone, but must give full value and support to the other great branches of scholarly and cultural activity." And it emphasized, in a curiously predestinarian passive construction, that "the world leadership which has come to the United States cannot rest solely upon superior power, wealth, and technology, but must be solidly founded upon worldwide respect and admiration for the Nation's high qualities as a leader in the realm of ideas and of the spirit." The Declaration further underscored the importance of the arts and the humanities to "the fostering of mutual respect for the diverse beliefs and values of all persons and groups" and the "multicultural artistic heritage" of American democracy—an early sighting of the language of diversity several years before it would be dismissed as mere "political correctness," although, as we will shortly see, this formulation was quickly used and abused to *resist* cultural critique in the name of universal and unchanging values.

The Declaration offered a caution about the interaction between the humanities and the arts and the federal government, which would come back to haunt both Endowments: "the Government must be sensitive to the nature of public sponsorship. Public funding of the arts and humanities is subject to the conditions that traditionally govern the use of public money." But most strikingly, the Declaration of Purpose spoke, enthusiastically and unselfconsciously, about the making of artists and scholars: "While no government can call a great artist or scholar into existence, it is necessary and appropriate for the Federal Government to help create and sustain not only a climate encouraging freedom of thought, imagination, and inquiry but also the material conditions facilitating the release of this creative talent."[48] Notice that the Declaration does not insist that art—or scholarship—be "great" in order to be subsidized. Quite to the contrary, what it mandates is a "climate" and "material conditions" that permit for creative work, including, signally, both "freedom of thought" and practical ingredients from money to space and time. Greatness would be a happy outcome of this process, but the responsibilities of necessity and appropriateness fall upon the government, not the grant recipient. It is a nation's ethical obligation to foster the making of art, and the advancement of learning.

Or so said the Declaration. Twenty-plus years later the two national Endowments, one for the humanities and the other for the arts, were to encounter vociferous opinions from some members of Congress, and other government bureaucrats as well, about community standards of decency and what was insistently described as "redeeming literary, scholarly, cultural or artistic value." What the works of art were to be redeemed *from*, or *for*, and whether without redemptive value they were intrinsically worthless (or worse), was never made explicit.

Michael Brenson has usefully summarized the shift from cold war to culture war in his account of the shifting fortunes of the National Endowment for the Arts. "As the Cold War wound down," he observes,

"the Kennedy and NEA balance between an ennobling view of art, which in the eighties came to be identified with museum art, and a commitment to artistic free expression, identified with contemporary art, became increasingly unstable. After the Cold War ended in 1989, the willingness of Congress to tolerate NEA support for free expression, and with it for contemporary art values, disappeared.[49]

What disappeared with it, signally and symptomatically, was support for the individual artist.

As is evident from the words of Kennedy and from the Declaration, the individual was the keystone of sixties optimism, and the tie-in between the arts and American exceptionalism, the spirit of The American Century. But perhaps paradoxically— we'll investigate in a moment whether this is really a paradox— the rise of Reagan-era triumphalism over the defeated Soviet Union, while it led to an increased faith in individual entrepreneurship in business, also marked a decrease of faith in the ruggedly individual artist.

An attempt had been made as early as 1968 to eliminate NEA and NEH grants to individuals, as the price of retaining grants to institutions. Representative William Scherle of Iowa declared to the House that "one of the most questionable features" of the arts and humanities program was "the system of individual grants." What he described as a "Government giveaway"—grants of $5,000 apiece to sixty painters and sculptors in the previous year—was, in his view, untenable, and he drew the conclusion, as Michael Brenson notes, that "the 'individual grant' program should be ended."[50] Other congressmen joined in the drive. Representative Paul Albert Fino of New York, who would later that year be elected to the New York State Supreme Court, urged that grants be given only to groups, not to individuals. "Aid to individuals is liable to turn out to be nothing more than a subsidy for hippies, beatniks, junkies, and Vietniks."[51] In other words, for *long-hairs* in a variety of styles.

An amendment to curtail grants to individuals was proposed by Rep. William Steiger of Wisconsin, and was passed, but a few months later the Senate rejected the House amendment, and renewed funding for the endowments. Individual artists of extraordinary interest and merit benefited from Endowment support in the subsequent years,[52] and changed the nature of the art world. But twenty-seven years later, in 1995, Congress voted to eliminate all grants to individual artists, except writers.

There were many reasons for this curtailment of government patronage for the individual artist. Two works chosen by institutions—and actually supported by institutional, not individual grants—became flash points: Andres Serrano's *Piss Christ* (a photograph of a plastic crucifix in a container of urine) and Robert Mapplethorpe's *X Portfolio* (elegant photographs of nudes, and erotic, statuesque images from sadomasochistic gay culture). In most cases the lawmakers who inveighed against these works did not see them in the gallery or museum exhibitions for which they had been chosen. Instead they responded to descriptions, photographs of photographs, and "translations" of their content into the lowest possible common denominator. "I know it when I see it."

Likewise the nation and its lawmakers professed to be scandalized by the solo-performance awards given to four artists who became known as the NEA Four: Karen Finley, John Fleck, Holly Hughes, and Tim Miller. Finley famously smeared her naked body with chocolate onstage in a performance work called "We Keep Our Victims Ready," protesting violence against women. Fleck and Miller are gay men; Holly Hughes is a lesbian. All four performed political art with the body as the site of exhibition. The fellowships recommended for them were rejected in 1990 by NEA chairman John Frohnmayer, an appointee of President George H. W. Bush, citing federal laws against funding lewdness and obscenity. The artists sued, and obtained compensation in excess of their original grants (all these numbers, except presumably for the lawyers' fees, were very small). However, in 1998 the Supreme Court upheld the use of the congressional decency test for the awarding of federal funding.

As was the case with Mayor Giuliani's condemnation of Ofili's "Catholic-bashing," it is unlikely that many who were so publicly outraged actually saw these performances, rather than hearing them salaciously described. (Try describing the plot of *Macbeth* or *King Lear*, much less *Oedipus the King*, and seeing if they pass muster as uplifting moral fare.) Nor was the general public, or the Congress, likely to have much in the way of context for performance art. In any case the result was to galvanize support for the ending of grants to individuals. Congress and its moral arbiter Senator Jesse Helms had the last snigger here in 1995, defeating NEA chairman Jane Alexander's attempt to save the program that had benefited so many visual artists since the inception of the Endowment. Ironically, however, Brenson notes, none of these supposedly offensive grants were actually awarded to individuals: the Serrano and Mapplethorpe works were part of grants to institutions. None of the NEA four received grants from the visual artists' fellowship program, the program Congress set out to kill.

### From Cold War to Culture Wars: The Fall of the Endowment

The post-Vietnam period was rife with injured and indignant cries about the "politicization of the arts." The "culture wars" of the 1980s and 1990s—a term memorably christened by Pat Buchanan[53]—intensified the sense of conflict by tendentiously conflating the disparate notions of "culture": as social beliefs and formations; and as artistic creation. Buchanan's prime-time speech to the Republican National Convention in 1992 explicitly invoked the comparison with the cold-war era: "There is a religious war going on in our country for the soul of America. It is a cultural war as critical to the kind of nation we will one day be as was the Cold War itself."[54] Buchanan's rhetorical denunciation of the Clinton administration targeted social issues like women in combat, gay and lesbian rights, "abortion on demand," pornography and "radical feminism." Nowhere— except perhaps in his mention of pornography—did he touch on works of art. But this did not keep culture warriors from making war on the arts and culture.

During the contentious 1990 hearings on the renewal of the NEA, Representative Dana Rohrabacher proposed an amendment that would bar grants to projects that seek to "promote, distribute, disseminate or produce matter that has the purpose or effect of denigrating the beliefs, tenets, or objects of a particular religion [or] of denigrating a particular individual or group of individuals on the basis of race, sex, handicap or national origin." In support of the NEA, Rep. Pat Williams (D-Montana) memorably noted, for the record, that this amendment, as anodyne as it might at first seem, would outlaw funding for works like Jasper Johns's flag series, *The Merchant of Venice*, *A Chorus Line*, *The Birth of a Nation*, and *The Grapes of Wrath*.[55]

Of equal concern was the Crane Amendment, proposed by Rep. Philip Crane (R-Illinois), which aimed to abolish the Endowment so as to "privatize" art. Both were defeated, and the Endowment was renewed. But it was clearly under attack both from self-appointed guardians of "core values" and from conservative Christian groups. Claims that the NEA funded "morally reprehensible trash" (letter to NEA from Rep. Dick Armey, R-Texas, signed by 107 members of Congress) and "openly anti-Christian, anti-American, nihilistic" art (Patrick Buchanan, column in the *Washington Times*) became commonplace. What was clearly at stake, in addition to "artistic freedom" and the pluralistic concerns of a society increasingly multicultural, transracial, and sexually permissive, facing issues of homophobia and AIDS, was the question of the Endowment's own freedom. As Hugh Southern, the acting chairman of the NEA, noted in 1989, the Endowment was "expressly forbidden in its authorizing legislation from interfering with the artistic choices made by its grantees. . . . The National Endowment for the Arts supports the right of grantee organizations to select, on artistic criteria, their artist-recipients and present their work, even though sometimes the work may be deemed controversial and offensive to some individuals."[56]

Here we have come full circle with that keyword, "individual," and its relationship to arts policy in America. Which "individual" had the stronger claim? The individual artist, or the collective "individuals" who made up the population of ordinary Americans? Recall again the optimistic words of the Endowments' Declaration of Purpose: "While no government can call a great artist or scholar into existence, it is necessary and appropriate for the Federal Government to help create and sustain not only a climate encouraging freedom of thought, imagination, and inquiry but also the material conditions facilitating the release of this creative talent."[57] What were the limits of that "freedom of thought, imagination, and inquiry"? If creative talent were not to be "released," would that mean it needed to be restrained?

The Mapplethorpe, Serrano, and NEA Four controversies continually brought to the surface these underlying issues about the limits and scope of government patronage. For example, the Corcoran Gallery of Art in Washington, D.C., announced in June 1989 that it was canceling the Mapplethorpe exhibition because it did not want to have a negative effect upon Congress's deliberations on the question of NEA funding. This act of self-censorship, which resulted in the exhibit's being moved to the Washington Project for the Arts, led to vehement protests against the Corcoran by arts groups and political groups alike, and two months later the Gallery's director offered a public apology:

> The Corcoran Gallery of Art in attempting to defuse the NEA funding controversy by removing itself from the political spotlight, has instead found itself in the center of controversy. By withdrawing from the Mapplethorpe exhibition, we, the board of trustees and the director, have inadvertently offended many members of the arts community, which we deeply regret. Our course in the future will be to support art, artists, and freedom of artistic expression.[58]

The question, again, was: who decides on funding, and on the support of an artist's work, or an exhibition? By what authority, and with what, if any, restrictions? The same issue arose when the new NEA chair, John E. Frohnmayer, first withdrew and then reinstated a $10,000 grant to Artists Space, a New York gallery that sponsored an AIDS-related exhibition, "Witness Against Our Vanishing." The renewed funding stipulated that the funds could not be used for the exhibition catalogue.

When federal legislators set themselves up as guardians of "artistic excellence" and admonish granting agencies to "exclude those works which are without any redeeming literary, scholarly, cultural or artistic value,"[59] it becomes clear that there are limits to the remit of government patronage. The NEA director is a government appointee, and the senators and congressmen who sometimes grandstanded on these issues were, of course, elected officials. Jesse Helms's diatribe against artists "who will engage in whatever perversion it takes to win acclaim as an artist on the 'offending edge' and therefore entitled to taxpayer funding"[60] is symptomatic, if (typically) extreme. A decade and a half later columnist William Safire would still be inveighing, though more urbanely, against "edgy art." But for Helms in the late 1980s an artist had become, by association and definition, an offensive and offending individual. And his invocation of the legislators' monitory mantra, "taxpayer funding" for the arts, underscored the tension between freedom and accountability. The issue that I have placed at the forefront of this study, the ambivalent relationship between the two meanings of "patronize," could hardly have a better (or a worse) exemplum.

### Peer Pressure

The National Endowment would also have to wrestle with one of the foundational issues concerning arts patronage: the question of how awards were to be granted. By "peer review"? By a blue-ribbon panel of experts chosen by the government? By something like a public plebiscite? From the vantage point of *American Idol, Survivor,* and other audience-participation television shows, the question is even more problematic than it was at the time: Web sites, 888-numbers, and the ubiquity of cell phones make the leveling role of publicity and notoriety and the "judging" of talent by acclamation a realistic, if unhappy, possibility. But in the 1980s, "peer review" was itself seen as insufficiently imbued with the right stuff, the right values. Besides the question of the reliable unreliability of individual artists, their boundary testing, political activities, hair or skirt length, substance abuse, and general unsettling nonconformity—as well as the startling, sometimes confrontational and unfamiliar nature of their work—the congressional overseers of the National Endowment had also come to fret about this troublesome business of "peers." Who got to choose the artists that did the funding? And by what criteria? Cutting-edginess, or manifest "greatness"? Work for the many, or for the few?

The word "peer" is like the word "patronize" in that it demarcates two distinct kinds of relationship. A peer is an equal in gifts, ability, or achievement, and also a contemporary or age mate; once it also meant "a companion; a fellow; a mate; a rival." But a peer is also a person of high rank, whether the dignitary in question is a "life peer" (chosen for merit) or a "hereditary peer" (inheriting rank and privilege). It's not hard to map these categories, imaginatively, across the spectrum of arts-review panels, to distinguish among reviewers who are (1) artists contemporary with and equivalent to the applicants, (2) artists senior in stature and perhaps also in age or career stage with the applicants, and (3) nonartists, in fact, patrons of the arts, whether entitled by wealth and family (for instance, Nelson Rockefeller), or by government connections and political office (most NEA chairs), or by celebrity in a cultural field different from that of the applicant (for example, Charlton Heston).

As we have seen with the discussion of CEMA and the Arts Council in Britain, so also in the United States there have been major debates around the question of who is to be served by arts funding. But there was, inevitably, a tension between those who wanted to fund artists, and those who wanted to fund art—not to mention those who felt active animosity toward the entire enterprise. Many politicians opposed and decried government activities they regarded as elite, effete, and intimidating.

Nelson Rockefeller, by personal inclination and family heritage a collector and supporter of art, was sufficiently intrigued by the example of the Arts Council of Great Britain to propose to President Eisenhower a similar agency in the United States, to be called the National Council for the Arts. At the time—1954—Rockefeller was an undersecretary in the Department of Health, Education, and Welfare in the Eisenhower administration. The plan went nowhere. (Nancy Hanks, later a very successful chair of NEA, reported that the attempt was dismissed as "the President's toe dance bill.")[61] But it was revived at the state level by Rockefeller when he became governor of New York in 1960. The Arts Endowment, when it was finally passed in 1965, included a National Council on—not "for"—the Arts. Its first members, named by Lyndon Johnson, included Marian Anderson, Leonard Bernstein, Agnes de Mille, Richard Diebenkorn, Duke Ellington, Helen Hayes, Charlton Heston, Harper Lee, Gregory Peck, Sidney Poitier, Richard Rodgers, Rosalind Russell, David Smith, John Steinbeck, and Isaac Stern, an extraordinarily distinguished roster of artists, performers, composers, and choreographers.

These were art and performance headliners, stars to catch the eye and the imagination of a nation seeking to develop its own profile as a place of artistic richness and complexity. Times change, and new initiatives obviously attract, and recruit, big names. But even taking that into consideration, it is clear that the current members, chosen "by law" by the president and "selected for their widely recognized knowledge of the arts or their expertise or profound interest in the arts"[62] are not in the main part luminaries but rather representatives of a range of worthy activities, several of them educational, critical, or fiscal: museum director, opera singer, visual artist, author/critic/educator, theater administrator, art director/designer, artist/illustrator, symphony orchestra conductor, critic/author, music educator, and three members each identified as a "patron/trustee." In other words, instead of celebrities these are arts professionals.

The idea of peer review was, and is, that practitioners make better judges than government officials, consumers, or the general public. In one sense this seems unobjectionable—except, of course, that interested parties do often take objection to it, claiming that it fosters cronyism, nepotism, and narrowness of vision. At a symposium convened in November 1993 by "conservative artists, intellectuals, and scholars," as part of "the cultural counter-offensive reflected in the election returns of 1994" (the words are those of David Horowitz, a former liberal turned libertarian), many speakers inveighed against the NEA for a variety of sins, from its supposed nepotism ("an entrenched establishment") to its supposed mediocrity and lack of universal values. One speaker, Frederick Turner, the author of books on value and on beauty, put forward a critique of peer reviews, and an alternative suggestion for arts funding.

Turner was genially acerbic about the state of arts patronage in this country. "Good art needs good patrons," he observed, citing such models as "Enlightenment aristocrats, the Viennese 19th century upper-middle class, the Medieval church, Renaissance kings, and so on." But since none of those just mentioned were available, who should be the new patrons for new art at the NEA? Not fellow artists, Turner thought—they were too self-interested and too self-replicating, and in any case he regarded contemporary art and art theory as vacuous, empty of ideas. In his view peer panels and arts administrators had to go. In their place, Turner thought America should develop a new class of patrons:

> We should create arts panels, if we have them, out of leading citizens in business, law, medicine, sciences, religion, philanthropy, the arts, entertainment, the academies, sports, and so on, who will be, in a sense, patrons. . . . I would expect that in the first 10 or 15 years they would be doing this, they would be funding trite, nice, pretty art. And then, after a while, they would begin to learn. It's the duty of patrons to learn. We just have to go through that period. You can't just go on having contempt for the people; you have to have the people learn how to be good patrons. We just have to put up with a bit of trite art.[63]

Turner's suggestion underscores the difficulty of imagining and sustaining a "democratic" notion of patronage. During the presidency of Richard Nixon, Nebraska Senator Roman Hruska memorably defended the nomination of a candidate for the Supreme Court by standing up for the principle of mediocrity: "Even if he was mediocre," Hruska declared about the proposed candidate, "there are a lot of mediocre judges and people and lawyers. They are entitled to a little representation, aren't they, and a little chance? We can't have all Brandeises and Cardozos and Frankfurters and stuff like that there." This point of view, from 1970, superficially resembles the idea that the nation needs to endure a decade or more of "trite art" as it educates "leading citizens" in how to be arts patrons. But where Hruska endorses mediocrity as representative of a subset of American opinion, Turner envisages a process of learning, training, and (a risky word here) sophistication. This task of creating taste for the new, and developing criteria for evaluation and judgment beyond what is familiar and recognizable, is not always consonant with the structure of democratically appointed juries and panels.

What remains of the NEA today is a rich range of fields—arts education, dance, design, folk and traditional arts, literature, media arts (film, radio, television), museums, music, musical theater, opera, theater, and visual arts. But grants in these areas are available only to institutions and organizations, not to individuals, except in "Literature Fellowships, NEA Jazz Masters Fellowships, and NEA National Heritage Fellowships in the Folk & Traditional Arts."[64] Literature fellows are creative writers or translators, and, in any case, are likely to make few waves compared to the Finleys and Mapplethorpes of yesteryear. The once politically suspect field of theater, the first to be jettisoned by the New Deal right wing, now survives and flourishes, supporting dozens of productions of new plays and reinterpretations of classic ones. Collaboration thrives in these settings, as it does in funding for dance and opera companies. As for the visual artists, they have been, for the most part, handed over to local residency and touring exhibition programs for selection and support. Perhaps this is a good thing; whatever they do, Congress can, if it has a mind to, avert its eyes, and swear that no one there is responsible. Most of the organizations involved are city agencies, or art schools, or outreach programs for children, summer tourists, or the elderly, or—in several cases—art journals. Although the occasional university or college can be found among the grant recipients, these grants are usually for events or special (for instance, anniversary or tie-in) programs: the twenty-fifth anniversary of the Rutgers University Center for Innovative Print and Paper, or a subvention for a book on studio craft to be published by the University of North Carolina Press. Safety, it seems, is in the local—and in support for "art" rather than for artists. The Endowment seems to have moved away from the wish, however utopian, to call "a great artist" into being (in the language of the Declaration of Purpose), and toward a Hippocratic, if not fully hypocritical, oath: first, do no harm.

### *Going Public*

Government funding and corporate sponsorship both depend upon a notion of the public, whether it is through the idea of community standards and values, commercial viability, or image enhancement. But the public has also emerged as a kind of patron in its own right, through the phantasmic projection and dispersal of its tastes and interests, and also through the material courtship of its financial contributions. The public as patron can go by the name of "the public interest," or "the local community," depending upon the underlying politics of the moment, but it is also manifest in titles like that of the Public Broadcasting System (PBS) and National Public Radio (NPR), which are, of course, underwritten by both government and private grants.

Projects for "public art," including the installation—often over community or local objections—of monumental contemporary sculpture, have raised the issue of "who speaks for art."

The U.S. General Services Administration (GSA), working with the NEA, commissioned hundreds of pieces of art through the Art in Architecture program, and while many were welcomed by communities and individuals, others became flash points for controversy. Richard Serra's *Tilted Arc* (1981), a 12-foot-high, 120-foot-long steel curve installed in New York City's Federal Plaza, was perhaps the most celebrated of these unwelcome additions to the public scene. Opposed immediately by the office workers who had used the plaza for lunch breaks and exercise, the sculpture was fiercely defended in the courts by Serra, who claimed First Amendment rights and regarded the community criticism as censorship. Suggestions that the piece might be moved to a different location were resisted by the artist, who insisted that the work was site specific. Artists, curators, and art critics spoke out in favor of *Tilted Arc* at a public hearing in 1985, while office workers expressed the view that it interfered with public use of the space, and encouraged rats, graffiti, and terrorism. The case dragged on for eight years. Serra lost, appealed, and lost his appeal. The sculpture was dismantled during the night on March 15, 1989, and the pieces hauled off to a scrap yard. "Art is not democratic, it is not for the people," Serra remarked at the time. "I don't think it is the function of art to be pleasing."[65]

Even the grounds of this dispute were disputed. Serra objected to the idea that it was an artist versus workers controversy, insisting, instead, that it was "a fight to protect my work from destruction and to assert moral rights for artists"[66] against the government's claim that its ownership and property rights permitted it to dispose of the work in any way it chose. "The Government is savage," he said at the time. "It is eating its culture. I don't think this country has ever destroyed a major work of art before."[67] As for the government, represented by William J. Diamond, the regional administrator of the General Services Administration, who had been trying to remove the sculpture for years—its verdict was a victory for "the public," which could now "enjoy the plaza again." In Diamond's view, this was a "revolution in our thinking—that open space is an art form in itself that should be treated with the same respect that other art forms are."[68]

The *Tilted Arc* saga received a great deal of urban and global publicity, since it took place in New York City, one of the acknowledged capitals of the "art world," and a place where art, even—or especially—edgy art, might have been thought of as both welcome and at home. But controversies about site-specific sculpture commissioned by the GSA—including a number of works by quite established artists—erupted around the country. The Alexander Calder sculpture called *La Grande Vitesse*, commissioned by the NEA for the city of Grand Rapids, Michigan (the title of the work a play on the title of the city), had both supporters and detractors; one supporter, then-Congressman Gerald Ford of Michigan (later president of the United States) backed the sculpture, hailing it as "the flowering of an exalted mind" as well as "the largest Calder in the western hemisphere." Ford later confessed to his congressional colleagues that "I did not really understand, nor do I today, what Mr. Calder was trying to tell us."[69]

Proposals by Claes Oldenburg for either a massive ashtray or an equally outsized baseball mitt were, however, rejected by Michigan's capital city, Lansing. Minimalist works by Donald Judd (*Dropped Plane*, at Northern Kentucky State University) and Carl Andre (*Stone Field Sculpture*, Hartford, Connecticut) met with ambivalent receptions, as did work installed, supposedly for the pleasure of the public, in Wichita, Kansas; Jackson, Mississippi; Concord, California; and even Pittsburgh, Pennsylvania, where a half-million-dollar, ninety-foot steel sculpture in Gateway Center, designed by Mark di Suvero as the "signature piece" for the city, was reviled and rejected by the citizenry in the late 1980s.[70]

Should "the public," whoever they/we are, have more control over arts programming and arts financing? In *Art Lessons: Learning from the Rise and Fall of Public Arts Funding*, Alice Goldfarb Marquis suggested, a decade ago, that the government get out of the arts-funding business by following an exit strategy familiar from politics and warfare: declare victory and decamp, leaving the field to the locals. "The best that those who love the arts can do for them is to try to stop finding those deserving of aid," wrote Marquis, by "withdrawing from the absurd exercise of trying to discern excellence amid the vast panoply of arts that this country produces. Instead, public funders should concentrate on providing all the people with access to all sorts of arts: performances, exhibitions, readings." She urges the finding of new arts venues, allowing "artists to test their talent in the only arena that ultimately matters, before the public."[71]

So here is that elusive, all-purpose, and culturally appetitive "public" again. But as usual, access to it turns out to be not quite direct. "The way to implement such a system," Alice Marquis proposed, "is to subsidize the hiring of a professional arts manager—a public impresario, if you will—for every locality or neighborhood. This person, aided by appropriate staff, would be responsible for an inventory of all spaces where exhibitions or performances could take place," including high schools, churches, shopping malls, and prisons. "The arts manager would then book these spaces for anyone wanting to use them."[72] The public impresario would also, she imagined, advertise cultural offerings, set admission prices, distribute vouchers entitling individuals to admission, subscriptions, and so forth, all at less cost than the public agencies (NEA and others) are currently spending "on the minority of arts that they support."

That this utopian idea has not come to fruition is hardly surprising, given that it requires not only institutional defunding and a congressional rationale for doing so, but also the establishment of a *different* bureaucracy under the guise of freedom and equal access. Please note the ominous aside "aided by additional staff."

In any case, though, this kind of arts programming and sponsorship "from below"—like similar initiatives under way in the so-called public humanities—while manifestly desirable at many levels, is not a viable substitute for real patronage: the support of artists and of artwork-in-the-making, the support of experiment, initiative, failed attempts, collaborations, wild art, and avant-gardes, not to mention the kind of art-making (whether visual, filmic, theatrical, or acoustic) that involves very large outlays of money for materials, space, teams of collaborators, apprentices, fabricators, and so on. Despite Marquis's suggestion that the arts impresario system would produce a "level playing field" and an engaged set of new audiences, such a system is also reactive rather than active, consensus driven and consensual rather than challenging and confrontational. While there is a good deal to be said for openness, there are also good reasons for vertical and horizontal ("level," open, community) initiatives in the arts.

Such a system could be supplementary, but it could not, realistically, be foundational. And if the pursuit of some imagined standard of "excellence"—legible to legislators as well as to arts professionals and to artists—turns out, indeed, to be a blocking mechanism rather than an enabling strategy for funding the most interesting artwork of the future, that structural (and human) failure does not mean that all modes of comparative judgment are anathema. Artists are judged and juried constantly. There are acknowledged pecking orders among galleries and gallerists, invitational exhibits, one-person shows and retrospectives, international exhibitions, museum shows and collections, and a host of other evaluative mechanisms in addition to the market for buying and collecting art. Indeed, "art world" plus "art market" together represent a system already in place and in play, although both, as we have seen, have their flaws, blinders, clubbiness, and media influences. That there should be fashions in artwork should not come as a surprise, or a disincentive or devaluation, to anyone who acknowledges that there are also fashions in intellectual work, in economics, in public policy, in philanthropy, and in all other aspects of human culture.

### *The Second Time as Farce*

And things are, perhaps slightly, looking up. A Boston conference of the national organization called Grantmakers in the
Arts brought together donors, trustees, and staff of public and
private arts organizations to discuss the role of public investment in the arts. The creation of the Massachusetts Cultural
Facilities Fund, which brings together funding from the state
legislature, the National Endowment for the Humanities, the
Wallace Foundation, and other grantors, is an example of the
kind of cultural partnership that is increasingly needed nationwide. As Ann McQueen, cochair of the Grantmakers in the
Arts Conference, wrote in the *Boston Globe*, "Art and business.
Art and government. These pairings are not as awkward as they
are made out to be."[73]

After decades in which the individual artist was regarded with
suspicion, as a radical, a willful child, and/or a trendy poseur
who could not be trusted with money, the pendulum has begun
to swing back a little toward the possibility—and the urgency—
of funding artists directly, rather than supervising them like mi-
nors with trust funds.

A nonprofit organization called Artadia, founded by New
York investment banker and art collector Christopher Vroom,
offers arts grants of up to $15,000 for local artists (in Boston,
New York, Miami, Atlanta, San Francisco, and Berlin), and also
offers the crucial elements of facilitation and critical exposure,
making the artists and their work part of a nationwide network
of curators and artists. Boston-area partners include the LEF
Foundation, the NLT Foundation, and the Mills Gallery at the
Boston Center for the Arts. As an editorial in the *Boston Globe*
observed, "Using private funds protects the art and the artists
from political wrath and the unpredictability of government
funding."[74]

Inspired in part by a 2003 Urban Institute study, "Investing in
Creativity: A Study of the Support Structure for U.S. Artists," a
new charity called United States Artists (in-your-face acronym,

"USA") announced that it would offer grant support to fifty artists annually, with a generous stipend of $50,000 each, "no strings attached."[75] The sum, "pegged at about what an entry-level art professor would make,"[76] was intended to allow grant-ees to spend a year working full-time on their art. Explicitly describing its fellowships as venture capital, funded by the Ford, Rockefeller, Prudential, and Rasmuson Foundations, and with support from arts patrons like Agnes Gund, and Eli and Edythe Broad, United States Artists aims to reverse the trend toward funding arts institutions rather than individual artists. The Urban Institute study had noted the defunding of NEA grants to artists whose work engaged hot-button topics like politics, pornography, and sexuality.

The phrase "no strings attached," which appears early on in the *Times* article, identifies—by this very stress on antipatron-age—both the problem and the tensions around a solution. The vetting system itself, which involves nominations by 150 "anony-mous arts leaders" and reviews of the resulting three hundred nominees by panels of "artists, critics, scholars and others in the arts," is aimed both at funding deserving artists in many dis-ciplines and many career stages, and at providing, for potential funders, a way of evaluating art-makers. As Susan V. Berresford of the Ford Foundation commented, "I believe there are individuals who would like to give to artists directly but worry that they lack a system to help identify talent."[77] The first list of fifty included photographer Catherine Opie, artists Layla Ali and Michael Joo, graphic novelist Chris Ware, theater and performance artist Ping Chong, writer Amy Hempel, and musician Nick Cave.

It may not be much of a consolation to veterans of the so-called culture wars of the 1980s to discover that their battles were essentially replays of the past, but American history, like all history, has a way of uncannily repeating itself. When the U.S. Capitol building was under construction in the early 1800s, a resolution was brought in Congress to commission four paintings for the Rotunda, to be executed by the Connecticut painter John Trumbull. (Benjamin Haydon, Lord Melbourne's persistent interlocutor, would have perhaps been glad to note that the government was undertaking to support history painting, Haydon's own forte.) Some in Congress queried whether it was "just or proper for the Government of the United States to become a patron of the fine arts."[78] But there was general public approbation; the *Albany Daily Advertiser* expressed itself as gratified that "the patronage of the government extended to the encouragement of the arts which refine and adorn society,"[79] and the "moral effect" of the proposed historical topics was singled out in the legislature for praise.

Until, that is, the paintings were presented for exhibition, at which point the legislators became art critics, and critics of the most critical sort. A senator from Maine complained that what should have been a "sublime" scene, the *Resignation of George Washington,* was absurdly diminished: "What do you see in this picture? Why, a man looking like a little ensign, with a roll of paper in his hand, like an old newspaper, appearing as if he was saying, 'Here, take it. . . . I don't want to give it up.'" And a congressman from Virginia, John Randolph, who had initially supported the project, changed his mind when he saw the results. To see the paintings in place was to feel "ashamed of the state of the Arts in this country," he announced. In particular Randolph singled out the "picture of the Declaration of Independence," which in his view ought "to be called the *Shin-piece,* for surely never was there before such a collection of legs submitted to the eyes of man."[80]

Commentary on government in the arts had an eerily familiar ring. An Ohio congressman, proudly describing himself as a "backwoodsman," said that decorating the Capitol with public money was "in a great measure, money thrown away." Several congressmen spoke out against government commissions for paintings, one declaring that "if the fine arts cannot thrive in this country without getting up Government jobs, why I say, let them fall."[81] Tristram Burges, a congressman from Rhode Island, suggested—in a way that will again seem familiar to culture-war aficionados—that Congress itself should be the judge: painters should bring their works to be inspected by the House of Representatives, so that the "public"—that is, the House members—could pick from among them "such as are most worthy of selection." To which Henry A. Wise of Virginia retorted that artists would hardly consent to submit their work to "every pretender who knows not foreshortening from coloring"[82]—which is to say, the House members, again. And so on.

The uproar about Trumbull's paintings might seem minor, however, next to the controversy provoked by Horatio Greenough's notorious statue of a George Washington clad in a toga and naked to the waist. The architect Charles Bulfinch described Greenough's Washington as looking as if he were "entering or leaving a bath,"[83] and the statue's stiff and upraised right arm also came in for adverse commentary. Philip Hone, a wealthy New York merchant who was briefly the city's mayor, wrote in his diary that the Greenough statue "looked like a great Herculean warrior—like *Venus of the bath* . . . undressed with a huge napkin lying in his lap and covering his lower extremities, and he, preparing to perform his ablutions, is in the act of consigning his sword to the care of the attendant."[84] As Lillian Miller notes, the statue became itself "a touchstone for evaluating American taste," with many visitors to the country dismissing the criticisms as naïve and untutored. And certainly there were American fans as well as detractors. Gouverneur Kemble, who had been U.S. consul at Cadiz (and imported from there the art of casting cannon), thought it was "second only to the Moses of Michael Angelo." Or at least so he told Edward Everett, the governor of Massachusetts, who himself regarded Greenough's achievement as "one of the greatest works of sculpture in modern times."[85]

Such risible comments and controversies are themselves local color, important here only to underscore the fact that government patronage of the arts is always susceptible to second-guessing by both members of the government and members of the public. If the vitriol of late twentieth-century disputes seems to be missing from these eighteenth-century art spats, that may be because we are inclined to regard the witty or sneering exchanges of the past with an indulgent eye. But the savage spirit of mutual denigration and dismissal is not absent from some of these observations, and if we feel unthreatened by Washington's naked—and buff—marble torso, or indeed by the stockinged shins of the Continental Congress, we should nonetheless bear in mind that the patriotic reverence of the time sought and found "offense" in unfamiliar depictions. It was ever thus, and remains the case today.

# 3

## MINDING THE BUSINESS OF ART

SIR ANDREW: *I would I had bestowed that time in the tongues that*
*I have in fencing, dancing, and bear-baiting. O, had*
*I but followed the arts!*

—TWELFTH NIGHT

CONTROVERSIES OVER the National Endowments, jousting and posturing by members of Congress, and a few rather tame but nevertheless headline-making scatological scandals that are now the stuff of urban legend—Karen Finley smearing herself with chocolate; Chris Ofili adorning paintings with, or balancing them on, elephant dung; Andres Serrano and his vial of urine—all this has somewhat obscured the fact that most arts funding in the United States does not, unlike in Britain, come from the national or state government. In fact, compared to other modes of organized patronage, government is just a bit player. The real action is elsewhere—in business patronage, cultural philanthropy, and corporate funding of the arts; in corporate art and collecting; in corporate sponsorship as an art form in its own right; in funding for art in public places; and in the new "venture philanthropy," motivated by the twin incentives of profit and social conscience, together with other high-ticket, hands-on activities in the public arena.

Unsurprisingly, these enterprises, too, are often riven by tensions between the two kinds of "patronizing": support for the arts, and well-meaning condescension, however generously intended. When patrons and artists mix, the combination is heady, volatile, and unpredictable. Among the issues that would emerge from this set of high-minded but pragmatic encounters were the concept of the sponsor as patron, the question of the blue-chip or celebrity artist as a material asset, and the deep desire to retain the arts, conceptually, as above or apart from commerce at the same time that, in practical terms, they were seen as effective enhancements for both the corporate image and the executive suite. Could "corporate art" ever carry a positive connotation? Or is it, like "elevator music," intrinsically oxymoronic, always at war with itself? And what about the artists? Were they to be supported from the beginning of their careers, instructed, nurtured, and offered professional and commercial opportunities by galleries or theater, opera, and dance companies? Was art-making, and the performance of art, a profession, a vocation, or an avocation? How could investment in the arts be aligned with the education and training of new artists? Again the recurrent question: How best to patronize the arts?

## Business and the Arts

In 1966 *Esquire Magazine* established a series of annual Business in the Arts awards to recognize the contributions of individual businesses to arts organizations. A year later, in 1967, David Rockefeller founded the Business Committee for the Arts (BCA), a national task force of heads of corporations committed to increasing philanthropic support for the arts. By 1968 the two art-and-business initiatives—the Business in the Arts awards and the Business Committee for the Arts—had been combined, and BCA became the cosponsor of the *Esquire* prizes.

Many of the early *Esquire*/BCA award winners had local tie-ins: the Brooklyn department store Abraham and Strauss was lauded in 1968 for its crucial funding of the Brooklyn Academy of Music (BAM), transforming that institution from a "languishing" to a vibrant center for contemporary art and performance. In the same year, Philadelphia Gas Works underwrote a program called Dance Happens in Philadelphia that increased the size, as well as the repertoire, of the city's Civic Ballet Company. Other corporations (IBM, S. C. Johnson, Polaroid, and so on) sponsored touring museum shows, nationwide telecasts, and other cultural events.

"Projects involving the arts," declared David Rockefeller, "are not just a kind fluffy periphery of American life. They are an integral part of the solutions to the problems that face our country today," whether the problems were an excess of leisure time or the "crisis in our cities."[1] It was the role of the modern corporation, now a "social" as well as an "economic" institution and indeed a "full-fledged citizen" with civic responsibilities, to support the arts so that they could "illumine and reinforce our individuality" in what he regarded as "our increasingly mechanized and computerized world"—that is to say, the very world that the modern corporation had brought into being, and upon which it depended for its profits.

This early wave of corporate participation in funding the arts, then, assessed the value of cultural activities for their intrinsic merits and public importance: the Rockefeller family's long-time connection with the arts thus encompassed public, civic, and private modes of philanthropy. Abby Aldrich Rockefeller helped to create the Museum of Modern Art; her son David succeeded her on the board of directors, and later became chairman of the board. Nelson Rockefeller, committed to politics and public life, had proposed a National Council for the Arts as early as 1954, although, as we have seen, the authorizing legislation for the National Endowments for the Arts and the Humanities was not passed until more than a decade afterward. David Rockefeller's development of a high-profile network of business patronage thus came at the same time as the government's entry—or reentry—into arts funding and support.

It is worth emphasizing at the outset that the dollar value of business and corporate arts support was then many times greater than that of the government, as it remains today. If we hear more about controversies involving the NEA than about who gets, and does not get, corporate funding, that is largely on account of the "mingling" and "meddling" of legislators and public officials, whether or not they are arts professionals or connoisseurs. The specter of "taxpayer's money" also plays an important role in public debates about government funding for the arts, even though that funding is dwarfed by the money pouring in from corporate sources.

Concerns about the aesthetic consequences of corporate involvement in the arts were dispelled early on. For instance, in the late sixties Leo Schoenhofen, the chairman of the Container Corporation of America—which made products he cheerfully acknowledged as "prosaic" but benefiting in the marketplace from "good design"—told a group of New York City businessmen gathered at Lincoln Center that the world need not fear the dehumanizing results of "amassing a distinguished corporate collection of paintings and sculpture":

> There is no doubt that some have viewed with alarm; have worried about the corruption of the artist in the executive suite; have wondered what will be the dire results of the fact that an increasing percentage of private gallery sales are to the corporation, rather than to the individual or the museum. I would remind those who think such dark thoughts, that except for a relatively brief period of world history—the most recent period, in fact—the dominant center of power was always the major stimulus to art, serving as a sponsor and patron. It seems logical that the role of art patron should be assumed by this new major force in society, the corporate management team. There is nothing either new or sinister in the fact that they are using fine art for their own ends. That has almost always been true of art patrons. Industry must begin truly to believe in the arts, believe in them enough to use them selfishly, to put them to work for business rather than serving merely as corporate decoration.[2]

The U.K. equivalent to the Business Committee on the Arts is the Association for Business Sponsorship of the Arts (ABSA), founded in 1976. Like BCA, ABSA gave highly visible awards to corporate sponsors, roping in members of the royal family to present them. Following the precept of Margaret Thatcher, who

had a low opinion of government-sponsored arts initiatives—
"You cannot achieve a renaissance by simply substituting state
patronage for private patronage," she declared in May 1980, in
a speech reported under the indicative headlines "Arts Cash
Still Low Priority" and "State Cannot Be Part of Arts Revival"[3]—
ABSA became even more active as a corporate recruitment
and lobbying group in the 1990s, as the attempt to woo private
funding increased.

Meantime, in the United States, the BCA continued to insist
that it was not only money, but also "marketing skills" and orga-
nizational expertise that the business community had to offer:
"in brief," wrote its president after the first decade of awards,
"ingenuity and closeness of company participation counted for
as much as financial support." Well, perhaps. In any case, BCA
confidently asserted that "business support of cultural activities has become the fastest growing area of corporate philanthropy."[4] Membership in the Business Committee for the Arts
was originally, and remains today, by invitation only, making it,
as one analyst observes, "an exclusive club for the higher ech-
elons of business."[5] Equally significant, there are no representatives of arts organizations on the board. This is a pro-business
organization that wants to patronize the arts—arguably, in all
senses of the word.

"I know many executives who, like myself, paint in their spare
time," wrote Robert O. Anderson, chairman of the Atlantic
Richfield Company and (then) chairman of the Business Committee for the Arts, in 1971, "and I know many more who are
sophisticated art collectors. Thousands of businessmen are amateur musicians or actors and an even greater number regularly
attend performances of music, ballet, opera or theater." Having
established, as he considered, the baseline of executive interest
in the arts, Anderson went on to underscore the difference between amateur attraction and professional expertise:

The corporation executive often has a dual role to play
in relation to the arts and unless it is understood, it can

evoke considerable resentment. The corporate executive
as art lover or theatergoer is one person; when he directs
his company's philanthropic program, he becomes another. He may warmly admire the works of a painter or
a sculptor or the performances of a ballet company. But
he expects that in all matters that lie outside artistic performance, relations will be reasonably business-like and
predictable. He expects the ballet company's administra-
tive practices and bookkeeping to be efficient, even when
its performances are inspired. He expects artists to keep
appointments and he expects arts organizations that receive financial support from his company to report how
the grant was used.[6]

This symptomatic passage neatly combines the rhetoric of calm
top-down instruction with a consistent undercurrent of gently articulated chastisement. The "considerable resentment"
evoked at the beginning of the paragraph (and ascribed, indi-
rectly, to the arts beneficiaries of corporate largesse) appears
in full flower by the end in another place altogether, when
the expectations of the hypothetical corporate executive are,
it would seem, doomed to disappointment by the haphazard
practices of the arts. The litany of "he expects . . . he expects . . .
he expects" predicts the answer "no." The two persons of the
corporate executive are related but distinct: the CEO as lover
of the arts can permit himself to feel emotions like wonder, joy,
or pathos, but the CEO as philanthropic director has his eye
sternly on the clock and on the bottom line.

Nonetheless, we are subsequently assured, "Hard-driving corporate executives and dedicated artists are not as dissimilar in
values or motives as a *prima facie* comparison of life styles would
appear to indicate. Despite the pressures of conformity that
exist in any large organization, business or arts, the successful
executive is usually the one who questions orthodoxies." At the
close of the essay the genial latent paternalism of this view of corporate patronage becomes artlessly if no less genially manifest,

with the reminder that "businessmen are parents," and that "many executives have had their attention turned to the aesthetics of our environment and the obstacles to improvements in the quality of life by the insistence of their children that these must not be ignored any longer."[7] Thus spoke the business community, or some of it, in the rebellious 1960s, when "the insistence of their children" began to claim, however briefly in the history of the nation between Eisenhower and Reagan, a different set of cultural values. Nothing in this account seems as dated, or as poignant, as this concluding acknowledgment of intergenerational strife.

Thirty years after the inception of the BCA, in the late nineties, certain patterns about business support to the arts had become clear.[8] The importance of an active arts community in the vicinity of the company sponsor was reinforced, as over 90 percent of business resources given to the arts were at the local level. The favored targets for patronage were performing arts and arts education programs, following a pattern that mirrored the preferred government spending areas—theater groups, orchestras, dance companies, "live arts performances," and K-12 education rather than, say, the funding of individual artists. The initiative came from the top. If the chief executive was interested in the arts, the company was far more likely to contribute.

At this point the emphasis was not yet on what would come to be called "venture philanthropy"; the 1998 BCA survey determined that the majority of business supporters of the arts in the previous year emphasized "giving to do good" over "strategic philanthropy."[9] Interestingly, "giving to do good" was described as "traditional philanthropy," marking an explicit shift in the making. The semantic difference between "strategic" and "venture" is itself a turn-of-the-century shift: venture philanthropy, also called "high-engagement philanthropy," "the new philanthropy," or "social philanthropy," endeavors to combine fiscal and social profit motives to do good while doing well. We will come to venture philanthropy later on, but it is worth emphasizing here the more "traditional" philanthropic assessment of the value of arts funding—indeed, of "The Value of the Arts," as expressed by the BCA on its Web site:

- The arts are essential to the quality of life in a community.
- The arts are a critical component in K-12 education.
- The arts are good for business.
- The arts affirm and celebrate who we are.[10]

It is perhaps understandable, given what is included—and excluded—in these tenets, that no museum directors, curators, arts administrators, or college professors are given a seat at the table.

The idea of the corporation as a public citizen and a moral actor voiced so eloquently by David Rockefeller is still paid some lip service today, but the intrinsic definition of a corporation has undergone a tremendous change. Corporations are now frankly run for investors, in order to maximize profits. Their cultural role is still considerable—perhaps even more considerable than in the sixties—but the goal is manifestly to edge out the competition, and/or to gain fame, good will, and prestige, and therefore to augment the bottom line. Thus the BCA has recently inaugurated a competition for what it calls "The BCA Ten" of the year—the "best companies supporting the arts in America." Arts professionals *are* represented on the nomination review committee, but the focus for winners remains on the benefits of marketing and publicity. Victory earns a corporate sponsor "use of THE BCA TEN in marketing, customer and client relations"; "an invitation to the THE BCA TEN gala"; "national and local media coverage"; a "feature story in *BCAnews*"—and a "limited edition print" specially created by an American artist.[11] "Any company selected for THE BCA TEN has a real competitive advantage," said J. Barry Griswell, Chair, President and CEO of the Principal Financial Group, and a Vice Chairman of BCA, "because employees and customers favor businesses that support the arts."[12] This contest, also described as for business "role models" who invest in the arts, is cosponsored by *Forbes* magazine.

Patronizing the arts in the "traditional" philanthropic model can yield great publicity and marketing benefits for the corporation as a whole. There are also significant personal and social gains for individual corporate sponsors. Although arts professionals were not invited to be members of the Business Committee for the Arts, corporate business executives, their wives (and sometimes husbands), and children, have been welcomed onto the boards of trustees of art museums in both the United States and Britain. Museum trustees bring to their work on the board a serious commitment to the arts, but many come to this privilege not through professional training or experience, but through the opportunities afforded by affluence—and, in the cases of spouses and children, by leisure. The museum board, long a space for social visibility and clout, was an attractive and attainable goal for the new rich as well as the custodians of inherited wealth. Money made in real estate, the stock market, and other booming enterprises came to match, and in some cases to dwarf, the funding offered by the traditional family philanthropy of the nineteenth century.

Furthermore, as Chin-tao Wu notes, museum trusteeship is a two-way street, giving collectors on the board advance notice about which artists' work will be "acquired or exhibited" by the museum, a move that is sure to enhance the value of all work by those artists. Wu cites Flora Biddle, then chairman of the board of the Whitney Museum, on the question of conflict of interest: "The board is full of collectors who are buying contemporary art. The problem the Whitney has generally is that as soon as we have a show or buy a piece, the artist's dealer raises his prices by 30 percent. What do we do about that?"[13]

### Absolut Power

Conflict of interest also leads to a besetting problem—or, from another perspective, a beguiling opportunity—for corporate donors. Sponsorship packages can often be explicit "tie-ins," like the 2006 show at the Metropolitan Museum of Art called

Anglomania: Tradition and Transgression in British Fashion, which was sponsored by—or to use the more usual high-culture euphemism, "made possible by"—Burberry, and trumpeted on the British clothier's Web site. For other companies, though, the opposite becomes possible, allowing the deflecting of public attention from actual corporate activities to high-visibility cultural involvements. Companies like ExxonMobil and Philip Morris have developed reputations for civic and cultural generosity as a result of their underwriting of exhibitions, public television, and similar events. Since tobacco companies are restricted in the amount of direct advertising they can do for their products, they have tended to try to improve their public image by sponsoring charitable and cultural activities. Performing arts companies like the American Ballet Theatre, the Houston Grand Opera, the San Francisco Ballet, and the Wolf Trap Foundation for the Performing Arts have all accepted tobacco-company sponsorship, as have museums and visual-arts exhibitions across the United States (Brooklyn Museum of Art; Cincinnati Art Museum; Museum of Contemporary Art, Los Angeles; and others).

It is not only exhibitions and performances that link the name of the sponsor with art patronage. By the last years of the twentieth century, it was clear that the "sponsor as patron" had become a crossover success story, beneficial at once to advertisers, artists, business, and the general art-loving public.[14] In this world of metaprojects that showcase their own histories (the institutional equivalent of the confessional memoir), coffee-table art books on arts sponsorship by corporations have been published in lavish editions underwritten by businesses and their foundations. As a result, large-format books about corporate art are now themselves art works, or, at least, objects of commercial and aesthetic cupidity and desire. Two striking examples issue from corporate sponsors whose real products are cigarettes and alcohol: *Art in Business: The Philip Morris Story*, published in 1979 "under the auspices of" the Business Committee on the Arts by Abrams, the fine arts publisher; and a handsome work entitled *Absolut Book: The Absolut Vodka Advertising Story.*

In 1985 Andy Warhol proposed painting an interpretation of the Absolut Vodka bottle to the president/CEO of Carillon Products, Michel Roux. The Absolut advertising campaign had been very successful, and Warhol, the editor, publisher, and owner of *Interview* magazine, had met Roux through *Interview*'s advertising director. Intrigued, Roux paid $65,000 for the painting, thus setting a ceiling for future commissioned work by artists in what would become a remarkable series of visual ads. Utlimately there would be hundreds of Absolut ads, commissions from many kinds of artists, painters, glassmakers, dancers, filmmakers, and so on, as well as myriad spoofs on the brand that turn the attention back to its status not as art but as alcohol.

The initial commission did not specify that the painting would be used as an advertisement; Roux already had, hanging in his office, a Warhol painting of another Carillon product, "a concoction of Armagnac and passionfruit called La Grande Passion."[15] Nonetheless, in short order artists like Keith Haring, Ed Ruscha, and Armand Arman were signed up to contribute to the Absolut art collection. By 1991 the campaign had expanded to the contemporary art of the American Southwest, with work by artists like David Alvarez, Lane Coulter, Robert Gallegos, and Rebecca Parsons, ranging from furniture and paintings to sculpture and folk art. Absolut Glasnost was a 1990 collection of works by twenty-six Soviet artists. Earth artist Stan Herd produced the image of an Absolut vodka bottle the size of twelve football fields and clearly visible from the air in a field in eastern Kansas. "Absolut Art of the Nineties," a glossy forty-page spread in the magazine *Art & Antiques*, displayed the work of thirty-six artists "who promise to be at the forefront of the emerging artistic trends" of the decade according to Absolut's own Web site. Meantime Absolut had also ventured into the world of fashion, with T-shirts, designer gloves by Donna Karan, and a solid gold dress, weighing sixteen pounds, created by Anthony Ferrara.

Perhaps inevitably, Michel Roux began to be described as a Medici figure—in fact, as "the Medici of Teaneck," New Jersey.[16] As Arthur Lubow commented in a *New Yorker* profile, "Instead of being merely a liquor salesman, he was now a patron of the arts."[17] The trade journal *Sales and Marketing Management* waxed similarly historical in announcing its annual Marketing Achievement Award for 1992: Absolut Vodka was, it declared, a product that "embraces the same commitment to quality, artistry, and charity that families like the De Medicis, the D'Estes, and the Guggenheims became known for during their respective reigns."[18]

### Smoke and Mirrors

Another high-profile corporate art patron in this period was Philip Morris, which fended off the bad publicity associated with its principal product line, cigarettes, and assiduously courted the good will of the art public, sponsoring and contributing to hundreds of exhibitions in museums, galleries, and other spaces for the visual arts. Renamed "Altria" in 2003—a corporate moniker that successfully cloaked the identity of the corporation's signature product and seemed in fact to imply its *altruism* ("devotion to the welfare of others, regard for others, as a principle of action; opposed to egoism or selfishness"[19])— the group set about to identify itself with arts funding. "The name change is entirely cosmetic in nature," said Martin Feldman, the tobacco-industry analyst at Merrill Lynch, and the chair and CEO described the change as "the right thing to do and the right time to do it."[20]

Philip Morris had supported dance companies and the visual arts since the seventies, in part because some of its former chief executives, like Joseph F. Cullman III and George Weissman, had cared strongly about the arts and culture. "Our program is not about our products; it's about reputation," Jennifer Goodale, Altria's vice president for contributions told the *New York Times*.[21] "Creativity and innovation are some of our greatest attributes. What better way to reflect that then to support the arts?" But in 2007, after years of support to performance groups and venues from the Brooklyn Academy of Music to the Dance Theater Workshop in Manhattan and the Urban Bush Women in Brooklyn, the Altria Group decided to discontinue its funding and to move its corporate operations out of the United States. "The goal of the breakup," wrote Andrew Martin in the *Times,* "is to give the foreign arm, Philip Morris International, more freedom to pursue emerging cigarette markets without being hindered by the regulatory and legal problems facing its business in the United States."[22]

Arts institutions in New York were devastated, wondering where, or whether, they would find other major patrons, seeking assistance from "companies, hedge funds, or real estate developers." But some onlookers expressed their satisfaction. Matthew L. Myers, president and chief executive of the Campaign for Tobacco Free Kids, told the *Times* reporter that Philip Morris had formerly sought the support of arts groups it sponsored in opposing a city bill to ban smoking in public places, and noted that he had himself declined to attend any cultural events sponsored by Altria.[23] And the *New York Times* editorial page saw both loss and gain in the change:

> The loss of Altria gives the art world a chance to shake its addiction to what has, in fact, always been tobacco money. Yes, that money was spent in the public interest, supporting institutions and programs and exhibitions that have greatly enriched us all culturally. But it's also worth wondering about the real costs of that funding—the fact that for so many institutions Philip Morris ceased to mean tobacco and came to mean mainly a reliable check.[24]

If there seems a little hindsight to this self-righteousness, or a little self-righteousness to this hindsight, the point is nonetheless well taken. Like René Magritte's famous painting, *The Treachery of Images*—the depiction of a pipe as if for a tobacco store advertisement, with the words *Ceci n'est pas une pipe* ("This is not a pipe") written in cursive script below—the corporate contributions to the art world were, and were not, representations from the real world of smoking and mirrors.[25] The invention of Altria helped Philip Morris's corporate image problem, offering a positive reflection upon its generosity. But the sponsored institutions that accepted Altria's "cosmetic" gift and subsequently found themselves without their major patron were now, perhaps, encountering another version of the treachery of images.

Cigarettes and alcohol were thus by the magical agency of marketing and sponsorship transformed from addictive commercial substances into the very stuff of art. That commercial products should be thus transmuted comes, of course, as no surprise, either in the history of cultural patronage or in the fetishism of the commodity. Without departing from the "traditional" model of cultural philanthropy and patronage, such corporations as Absolut, Philip Morris, and ExxonMobil sidestep negative publicity resulting from their business activities and court the glitzy visibility of the art world, making an art form of patronage itself. In effect, savvy advertisers seek—and perhaps receive—public "absolution" (remission of guilt or sin) by patronizing the arts.

### Art, Inc.

The crossover between "high" or "fine" art and commercialism is, of course, the oldest of stories, as well as the most persistent of complaints (and boasts). The phenomenon of the museum "blockbuster show" is likewise old news by now. A generalized ambivalence about this situation can be detected in much writing on the subject. A typical example here discusses Malcolm Rogers, the director of Boston's Museum of Fine Arts: "Since his appointment in 1994, Rogers has brought into the MFA Ralph Lauren's cars and Les Paul's guitars and Herb Ritts's photos of Madonna. He has sent Monets to Vegas. Moreover, he has brought in a management style that his most fervent critics say is far more suitable to the average corporate shark tank than an institution like the MFA." The word "unapologetic" appears twice in two pages: Rogers is "feisty and unapologetic"; his "embrace of the modern, and his equally unapologetic embrace of the commercial, has prompted questions elsewhere in the arts community as to whether, one day soon, behind the counter at the museum's luxurious gift shop, one might be able to purchase for oneself a piece of the museum's soul." Nice touch. And the word "corporate" is everywhere: "Large, splashy exhibits require large, splashy funding, often from large, splashy corporations. Corporate officers have started appearing more frequently among museum boards of trustees."[26]

The typical museum director "now was dealing with the wide corporate world, and with the kinds of patrons whom sports teams often refer to as 'casual fans,' people drawn to a specific exhibit and not to the museum itself."[27] There is more in this vein in almost any similar report or exposé (again, it's a fine line between congratulation and schadenfreude). We get the point. Who are these directors of "fine arts," anyway, with their corporate salaries and their corporate suits and their casual fans? This trend may be indicative of a larger ambivalence in corporate art patronage, namely between the older mode of cultural philanthropy and the newer strategic sponsorship that attempts to bring profit and social change into one package.

### Nothing Ventured, Nothing Gained

"Will Venture Philanthropy Revolutionize the Arts?" asked an article published in 2001 by a group called Americans for the Arts. Why, the authors asked, were venture philanthropists—that is, the recipients of "new wealth" in the boom years of the late 1990s—not supporting cultural organizations with the same zeal as they supported other causes? "Venture philanthropy" is modeled on "venture capital," the modus operandi of the for-profit sector. It marks a desire, on the part of these new-style philanthropists, to be "hands-on benefactors" who expect to be managing partners working with nonprofit organizations and to see what are described as "measurable results." Three reasons were set forward to account for the lag in cultural funding:

- "[V]enture philanthropists are simply not very interested in the arts," because they grew up at a time when arts education was not a priority in America, and they were so busy making money that they "have not had time to become socialized into a milieu of arts and culture (something that, according to conventional wisdom, is more likely to happen later in life)."
- "[I]nvestors in venture philanthropy funds have tended to be interested in making a 'social investment' in basic human needs," and in their view arts and culture projects do not qualify.
- Finally, there is "the difficulty of measuring outcomes in the arts," whether on the level of "increased artistic excellence or the actual effects of arts participation on people's lives."[28]

Despite these concerns, a few successful programs were cited, chief among them the National Arts Stabilization Fund, which had its inception in programs supported by major national foundations like Ford, Mellon, and Rockefeller in the 1970s, and which aimed to stabilize the financial situation for arts organizations like symphony orchestras, for which endowment funding had not been sufficiently effective. This model was also applied to local arts agencies, with the same "lessons" to be learned: the desirability of measurable results, accepting the philanthropist as a managing partner—long resisted by local arts agencies, which value their independence—and, signally, something called a "clear exit strategy to the donor."[29]

Venture philanthropy thus attempted to develop business models for the arts and culture. In the meantime, however, some businesses had already become heavily engaged in the arts, through the strategy of corporate collecting. Corporate art collections offered tangible pleasures, both to the collector and to the observer. They allowed knowledgeable and interested participants to purchase and exhibit high-end art bought with company money.

## Corporate Art

You might think that "corporate art" would be either a contradiction in terms or a description of a collaborative process. But you would be wrong. Corporate art is now not only a reputable and recognized category, but an employment opportunity, a genre of collecting art that has its own curators, galleries, and gallerists, as well as—inevitably—its own bibliography of high-end art books. A corporation is an institutional "person," and just as individual persons developed taste and the habit of collecting, so, over time, have corporations. Here is one description of "the modern corporation as a patron of the arts," from the perspective of a sociologist:

> Acting as collectors, some companies purchase art because of its investment potential. Other companies display it proudly in highly visible areas such as entranceways, boardrooms, lobbies or sculpture gardens open to the public. Some companies choose several important paintings for display in their annual reports, or invite important clients to tour their collections. Either as collector or publicist, the corporation in buying and exhibiting art realizes opportunities to gain public recognition and prestige. Art collections serve corporations well as expressions to both their public and their rivals. The function corporations give to art establishes its meaning so that particular styles may be reinterpreted in terms of organizational requirements, and this includes using aspects of artistic style (content, color, size, form) to express status or match furniture.[30]

There's nothing surprising here, except perhaps the frank acknowledgment that expressing status or matching furniture is a recognizable aspect of artistic style. But the cascading list of

status words ("proudly," "important"—twice in one sentence—
"recognition," "prestige," and so on) makes it clear that corporate art collection is part of a business plan. Surely no artist
wants his or her work to be itself described as "corporate." Yet
this study identifies "blue-chip" artists who make corporate investment secure (Romare Bearden, James Dine, Jasper Johns,
Ellsworth Kelly, Sol LeWitt, Roy Lichtenstein, Robert Motherwell, Barnett Newman, Louise Nevelson, Claes Oldenburg, Robert Rauschenberg, James Rosenquist, Frank Stella, David Smith,
and Andy Warhol), as well as the "ultimate status in corporate
collecting," the commissioning of a monumental lobby or plaza
sculpture by Alexander Calder, Mark DiSuvero, George Segal et
alia, or a mural by Lichtenstein, Stella, or Sam Francis.[31]

Inevitably any commentary on corporate art once again invokes the Medicis, as in this panegyric from a handsome, over-
sized book called *Art and Business: New Strategies for Corporate
Collecting*: "It has taken business over three centuries to evolve
a new form of patronage of the arts that brings entrepreneurship and enlightened connoisseurship into the kind of balance
achieved during the Italian Renaissance, when the Medici and
other Florentine merchant bankers patronized the contemporary artists and architects of the new humanism." *Art and Business*
takes a commendably global view, however, noting for example
that in Germany "many corporations have assumed the role of
contemporary art patron, in an atmosphere where it is still assumed that it is the obligation of the state to finance culture,"
in France "contemporary art centers, staffed by well-trained gov-
ernment-accredited curators [are] proliferating in towns and
cities all over the country," and that "Japanese speculators in the
art market" in the 1990s purchased work by "signature Western
artists" as tax-free shelters for skyrocketing capital gains.

A series of case studies explores topics like The New Breed
of Business Patron, Exhibitions and Their Influence, and Character and Quality in Art at the Office, as they are implemented
in corporate collections and commissioned works around the
world. At the book's conclusion, after some two hundred pages

of handsomely designed layouts and full-color photographs of artworks and buildings, the persistent reader will come upon the payoff: a small-print section called "Launching an Art Program: A Practical Guide," that yet *again* celebrates the Medici ("a hybrid dynasty of princes and businessmen") together with the "business patronage" of royal families and the increasingly restrictive and constrictive academies, and the "cultural leadership" now available for a joint enterprise between "the artist and the businessman." Both the neophyte and the "seasoned private collector" are urged to seek professional advice, and not to go it alone. "And don't let your emotions interfere with your business judgment when you are dealing with the arts."[32] Good advice, no matter what the underlying expectation.

Far from being blanded-out safe spaces for non-edgy art, corporate collections have sometimes been the places, and spaces, to challenge consumer verities. IBM started purchasing American art as early as 1939. The 1970s and 1980s saw a big upsurge in corporate art buying, according to Shirley Reiff Howarth, the editor of the International Directory of Corporate Art Collections. "That's when corporate collections began to dominate and even influence the art market, because they were buying large quantities of art. By the late 1980s, it had become such a popular phenomenon that the majority of the Fortune 100 and a large number of the Fortune 500 companies collected and displayed art in their workplaces." In 2005 Howarth listed for an interviewer some "myths" about corporate art collections, including the claim that businesses buy art for investment ("there are other, more secure ways to invest"), that "corporate art is dead," that is, "that corporations have stopped collecting" (a misconception fueled, she said, by sensationalism in the art press), and that "corporate art collections are all visual musak, art as wall paper" ("some corporate collections rival museum collections"). While she acknowledged that there was a wide range, nationally and internationally, her view—admittedly one from within the business of corporate art—was that "corporations are a force in the art world," despite their detractors.[33]

Howarth pointed to the mission statements of various corporations' art collections as indicative of the match between clientele and collecting style. Thus Microsoft focused on "presenting and interpreting international contemporary art of the highest quality by emerging and mid-career artists," mirroring the company's interest in young and nontraditional talent, while Progressive Insurance declared that its collection was "designed to surprise, to please, and even to provoke employees." Progressive quoted its curator, Toby Lewis: "What I don't want is the art that has 'the wallpaper effect.' This is a challenging collection."

Lewis, the ex-wife of Progressive's CEO Peter B. Lewis, has amassed a huge collection of over five thousand works, most now owned by the company. The head of the Cleveland Center for Contemporary Art, Jill Snyder, praised it as "arguably the best corporate collection of art in the U.S." When curator Lewis hung a controversial painting by Kerry James Marshall across from Progressive's employee cafeteria, the painting, called *Bang*, was met initially with resistance from workers who thought it stereotyped blacks; after a week during which the curator, the artist, and others met with interested employees, CEO Lewis spoke out about the transformative effect of art in everyday life: "People learn from this. I wish it would happen more often."[34] He recalled with special pleasure the company's 1974 purchase of Andy Warhol's portraits of Mao Zedong. There was widespread protest, but Lewis refused to take them down, and gradually the Warhols became classics; one was hung in Peter Lewis's office, another in Progressive's boardroom. No further protests were heard.

It is this same Peter B. Lewis, we should note, who in January 2006 pledged the sum of $101 million to Princeton University to support a major initiative "to enhance the role of the creative and performing arts in the life of the University and its community." The gift will establish a new Center for the Creative and Performing Arts, and a new interdisciplinary Society of Fellows in the Arts, to include writers, directors, actors, choreographers, musicians, painters, video and installation artists, and curators, and to provide studios and other accoutrements, with the expectation that the fellows will teach courses, perform, and participate in conferences and collaborative work. Lewis had already given Princeton substantial funds for a science library designed by Frank Gehry ($60 million), a center for Integrative Genomics ($35 million), and a gallery for contemporary art in the Princeton University Art Museum ($1 million). His own interests were not exclusively in the arts. But his gift for creative and performing art spoke directly to the question of patronage as a powerful steering mechanism for universities and their influence on culture. Princeton president Shirley Tilghman, a molecular biologist, said that the gift would be "transformative," bringing the creative and performing arts into prominence in a way they had not been "in the history of the university."[35]

This migration from the (for-profit) corporation to the (not-for-profit) university is, in terms of arts patronage, a distinction of degree rather than of kind. Universities are prime expansion areas for both individual and corporate patronage of the arts. The donors are often the same, the incentives considerable, the hands-on possibilities for participation readily available, and the combination of business expertise and loyalty to an alma mater—or a locally valued institution—attractive to all parties. For all these reasons the university has become a timely site for patrons of the arts, and especially for patrons who are interested in supporting and following the careers of emerging artists.

## *Celebrating Patronage*

As we have seen with the Absolut ad campaign, corporate patronage can celebrate art and turn sponsorship into a phenomenon of the art world. Patrons themselves can come to be celebrated, too, their names associated with paintings and performers, with museums, performing arts centers, and schools—their own generosity turned into the stuff of art.

In the winter of 1999–2000, an exhibition at the Phoenix Art Museum celebrated Taos Artists and Their Patrons: 1898–1950 by exhibiting paintings, drawings, and sculpture by artists like Georgia O'Keeffe, Walter Ufer, Robert Henri, and John Marin, together with a life-sized study for the 1937 San Antonio post-office mural by Howard Cook—part of the federally funded mural project. The idea was to explore the several types of patronage that were at work simultaneously in Taos—"private collectors, corporate collectors, promotion through national exhibitions and awards, and various levels of government commissions." Particularly on view were documents attesting to the patronage of three influential women—Mabel Dodge Luhan, Millicent Rogers, and Helene Wurlitzer—who brought modernist painters to the Taos art colony. As the museum dryly acknowledged, "some of these relationships were mutually beneficial, while others tested both artist and patron. Yet, these support systems enabled the creation of the art works presented in this exhibition."[36]

Patrons, it seems, are not only behind the scenes, but increasingly in front of them. The Phoenix Museum collection proudly showcased the influential individuals who acquired the art on display: "spectacular paintings originally acquired by private patrons such as John D. Rockefeller, Thomas Gilcrease, Carter Harrison, and William Klauer," as well as "works collected by the Santa Fe Railway for promotion of its expanding tourist business." Of course there was an opportunity for museum visitors to become patrons themselves, and to anticipate, in some far-off day, an exhibition of work supported by the new patrons of the twenty-first century.

Trolling for patrons has become a major business, as we've seen, and the connection with the corporate world makes the process easier, smoother, and "even more valuable," as the New York Philharmonic notes, since corporations often match charitable contributions. The Donor Patrons, Supporting Patrons, Sponsor Patrons, Sustaining Patrons, Benefactor Patrons, and those who achieve the fiscal empyrean of the President's Circle, the Chairman's Circle, the Philharmonic Circle, or the Leonard Bernstein Circle, can presumably hear the music of the spheres (*harmonia mundi*) while also helping to "sustain the future of the Orchestra and classical and contemporary music." The International Association for Jazz Education has only one category, Super Patron, but the Patrons of the Los Angeles Opera can scale the heights of Benefactor, Premier Benefactor, Grand Benefactor, Silver Benefactor, and then (perhaps running out of new terms) of Premier Silver Benefactor, Grand Silver Benefactor, and finally, Opera Council. Each level has a dollar amount and a list of perks, from receptions and dinners with the artists, to attendance at dress rehearsals, "behind the scenes at the costume shop," and patron salons. At the very highest levels, patrons also get access to founders' parking—a genuine perk in L.A.[37]

But how are new patrons to be educated and nurtured? The Museum of Contemporary Art Cleveland had a "social networking party" aimed at the summer associates from the city's most prominent law firms, and the Summer Art Circle in New York City did the same, inviting summer associates of top law firms, "a small army of patrons-to-be who they hoped might grow up to be the junior committee leaders, season subscribers, donors, board members and art buyers of the future."[38] New York firms like Sullivan & Cromwell paid $375 per person for their young associates to attend the cocktail party, where they encountered representatives from major art museums and dance companies, all eager to sign up new recruits with optimistic financial futures. An auction for the Boston Institute for Contemporary Art had the same goal, producing the next generation of donors. Patterned on the way universities cultivate young alumni, getting them into the habit of giving, these arts institutions invite new patrons to travel to art fairs with museum buyers and give them private tours behind the scenes. "People may not have the dollars in the beginning," said a trustee of the Boston Museum of Fine Arts, "but they need to be trained early on and exposed to what philanthropy is." And the rewards are palpable.

"They feel like they're insiders," reported the director of the Fund Raising School at the Center on Philanthropy at Indiana University[39]—an institution that describes itself as "the only school of its kind." At least for now. One of the school's goals, unapologetically set forth, is to "Replace apology for fundraising with pride in philanthropy."[40] Which would seem to be the goal of the arts institutions as well.

### For Love or Money

"Like all art institutions, Dia:Beacon couldn't exist without money, specifically rich people's money," wrote *New York Times* business correspondent Joe Nocera in an article plangently titled "The Patron Gets a Divorce." The figure of speech is striking, and apt. The word "love" surfaces often when the arts are in question, and the story Nocera has to tell, of the passion of donor Leonard Riggio ("a Brooklyn cabbie's son who built Barnes & Noble into the dominant bookseller in America")[41] for contemporary art is an object lesson about objects, patrons, and institutions.

Fund-raisers have long called the actual pitch to donors "going for the ask," a culmination of the courtship that is preceded by careful steps so as to set up a favorable response. Dating services now use the same phrase ("Julian still does a run-through before going for the ask, because it builds his confidence—and his success rate," says Match.com, advising first-daters on how to move forward online.)[42] But, as we have already seen, when love and money mix, as they do in the patronage relation, the results are hard to predict and control.

In Nocera's retelling, Riggio's love for the sculpture of Richard Serra, and for the works of artists like John Chamberlain, Dan Flavin, and Donald Judd, led to his generous support of Dia projects and especially of the vast art museum built by the Dia Foundation in the Hudson River Valley town of Beacon, New York. But marriage, unlike love, is an institution and a formal covenant. The patronage relationship was mediated by a curator, Michael Govan, and ruptured when Govan left Dia for the Los Angeles County Museum of Art (LACMA). Riggio characterized the sundering with Govan in terms that might have motivated the article's provocative title: "Looking back," he told Nocera, "I guess we had a separation of sorts." The article builds on this figure, insistently describing the patron-curator relationship in personal terms ("Govan is the one who brought Riggio on the board, who whispered in his ear about which pieces of art to buy for the new museum"). And yet the divorce metaphor seems at least equally to pertain to the relationship between the patron and the works of art he helped the museum to acquire. Nocera's article describes a man who wanted to be the sole benefactor of the new museum. ("Because Riggio was writing the checks, he felt that his opinion was the only one that mattered. He made little effort to create a collaborative board or even to invite much in the way of discussion. . . . 'I am the patron,' he would say, 'and I will make the decision.'") Govan, the curator, not only supported this tactic but seems to have regarded it as essential and normative, invoking the phantasmatic image of the modern Medici: "when you look at the big gestures in the history of art, it is a story of individuals, whether it's the Medicis or J. Paul Getty."[43]

Monogamy and exclusivity, while they may be goals for a marriage, are unlikely outcomes for this kind of love relationship, especially in the arts. Art objects are polygamous, seductive, fickle, teasing, and standoffish; there is no contract that will make them love you back. "I have a vacuum in my life as far as art is concerned," Leonard Riggio told Nocera. The curator was the go-between. The fantasy is not only one of Medici power, and Medici taste and influence, but also of immediacy, an unmediated connection between patron and artwork that is somehow not paradoxically mediated through experts on the hand, and money, on (or *in*) the other. Nocera's article captures the tension well in a shrewd stylistic turn between paragraphs: "sometimes, everybody lives happily ever after. And sometimes they don't," he writes in his "author" voice, predicting the end of the love story. The next paragraph directly summons the voice of the patron—speaking in the present tense, the tense of enduring devotion, untouched by times or circumstance: "'I love this piece,' Len Riggio said."[44]

## The Medici Moment

Collectors and venture philanthropists who suffer from (or, more likely, take pleasure in) Medici envy might spare a thought for the fact that the Medici not only became powerful patrons, and commissioned and purchased art; they also founded art schools, among the first and most influential of their kind in Renaissance Italy. Lorenzo de Medici employed the sculptor Bertoldo di Giovanni to supervise instruction and care for his collection of antique and modern works; his most famous pupil was Michelangelo, who lived in Florence with the Medicis from 1490 to 1492. A generation later, Lorenzo's son Cosimo proposed to the painter and biographer Giorgio Vasari that he found an academy, the celebrated Accademia del Disegno. The faculty of this highly successful venture included Bronzino, Ghirlandaio, and Pontormo, among the painters; as well as specialists in sculpture, engraving, and architecture.

Academies of art developed throughout Europe in the seventeenth and eighteenth centuries, from the French Académie Royale de Peinture et de Sculpture (1648) to the Royal Academy of Art (1768) founded by George III in England. Instruction in drawing and painting, sometimes by copying paintings, sculpture, and antique casts, sometimes with the use of live models, formed the basic curriculum, which, while rigorous, could also be tedious. In 1816 the French academy of painting and sculpture was combined with two others (music and architecture) to create the Académie des Beaux-Arts (Academy of Fine Arts), which, in rejecting the work of artists like Manet and Whistler, led to the brief state sponsorship of the Salon des Refusés, the Salon of the Rejected, in 1863, and again in 1874, 1875, and 1886. To be "refused" had become a sign of cultural distinction.

Today there are Salons des Refusés aplenty, though none of them state sponsored: the Slamdance film festival in Utah supplements the tonier Sundance; works rejected by the Whitney Biennial, by the Toronto International Film Festival, or, indeed, "art which has been refused from any juried show" are actively sought in some arts venues.[45] Refusedness has become a category of art, and one that points, with some bitter amusement, at the devaluation of what is now highly conventional high-culture art, by painters like Courbet and Pissarro, and indeed all the Impressionists. (It's useful to keep this history in mind as we revisit the culture wars of the 1980s, where the "refusal" came from a government agency—the NEA—rather than from a private or independent sponsor.)

The idea that great patrons should be benefactors to institutions of art instruction, as well as to museums and to private collections, is one that has caught the imaginations of some generous donors in the twentieth and twenty-first centuries. The Tisch School of the Arts at NYU is the fruit of one such instance. The Sam Fox School of Design and Visual Arts at Washington University in St. Louis is another. The University of the Arts in Philadelphia has been the beneficiary of a single interested donor's recent generosity, and such instances are, happily, increasingly common. Yet at the same time, there still remains, in the minds of some, the idea that art-making is somehow natural, not learned, or certainly not learned in a school or academy. The myths of independence and rugged nonconformity that have developed around some mid-twentieth-century artists (Pollock, Kerouac), and the sponsorship by insightful private patrons of others (Smithson), have made "art school" seem sometimes rather tame by comparison. Though perhaps films like *Art School Confidential* will change all that.

So here is our next paradox, one that bears a striking resemblance to those we have already considered (the paradox of "patronizing" as both endorsement and condescension; the paradox of "public taste" as both blockage and goal). Is art-making to be considered something extrinsic to education, or essential to it? Is talent (and "artistic genius") bestowed in some ineffable way upon gifted persons who, untutored and untainted, are spontaneously creative? Or is "minding the business of art" also a matter of bearing in mind the necessity of professional training, both for skill and for advancement?

Artists and performers increasingly seek out professional training and, indeed, professional degrees and certification. Just as the sponsorship and support of art has become increasingly interesting to business professionals, so, at the same time, the training of artists has become more professionalized at the institutional level. For this, too, is the "business of art." Along with other "professional schools," like medicine, law, and business, conservatory and vocational training for artists—dancers, actors, directors, set designers, painters, sculptors, and filmmakers—appeals to talented young students, some still in secondary school, as starting points for careers in the creative and performing arts. In some fields, like dance and music, an early start is essential. In others, dedicated professional training might come after a more traditional liberal arts experience. But increasingly such schools, representing a wide range of art practice, became the fast-track entry into professional dance or theater companies, orchestras, or (in the case of artists) major galleries. Like college (or high school) sports teams, these schools became training grounds for the big leagues, with agents, big contracts, and multiyear commitments all within the range of the possible, or, at least, of the dream.

## Fine Distinctions

The term "fine arts" has often been employed to distinguish the useless, or nonutilitarian arts from the useful ones (decorative, mechanical, industrial, folk art, craft). As so often in culture, uselessness tends to denote high value and leisure, whereas "use" is a word for the everyday. So the fine arts, like the French *beaux-arts* and *belles-lettres*, has had a certain cachet, as in the titles of museums like those in Boston, Houston, and St. Petersburg: "MFA," Museum of Fine Arts. But the term also carries a certain perfume of the past. Most twentieth- and twenty-first-century art movements are resistant to this kind of categorization, in part because it fits so uneasily with issues of world art, outsider art, media arts, pop art, industrial minimalism, and other cross-cultural and performative modes. I once had a conversation with a sculptor who dismissed ceramics as "craft," even though he himself did welding, molding, and woodworking for a living. The word "craft" remains a lightning rod in art circles, alienating some arts practitioners while it is celebrated as authentic and hands-on by others.

Here is a brief institutional anecdote: In 1997, when a long-standing Harvard department decided to change its name from "fine arts" to the more commonly used "history of art," some old Harvard hands were bewildered: why did they want to call it a department of "history," one wondered out loud. It took the department chair an extra session of persuasion, and some printouts of other departmental names and descriptions across the country, to convince these longtime denizens of zip code 02138 that virtually no one else today called such a department of art history "fine arts." As the chair told the official university news organ, "The name sends out a confusing message. Nationally and internationally we're perceived as a department of studio art."

Another colleague added that "fine arts" was based upon a hierarchy of painting, sculpture, and architecture, on the one hand, and the decorative arts on the other, and that the department preferred not to rank the arts in this, or any similar, fashion.[46] Indeed, the original name, dating from 1875 when Charles Eliot Norton took up his post as the program's first professor, was, as it turns out, "history of art." A 1956 *Report of the Committee on the Visual Arts at Harvard University* had in fact strongly recommended "that the Department of Fine Arts revert to its first name: History of Art," adding the following explanation of its reasoning: "Although the expression 'fine arts' has an honorable history, its connotations have too little connection with modern society. The older title is at once less pretentious, less esoteric, and less exclusive. Literature, music, and other arts have good reason to object to the preemption of 'fine arts' by the visual arts."[47]

It is worth noting that the professional association to which art historians belong, the College Art Association, also includes "all *practitioners and interpreters* of visual art and culture, including artists and scholars,"[48] and has done so from the very beginning—declining to separate out the makers of art from the scholars, cataloguers, critics, and historians. The CAA, founded in 1911, thus combines—and has apparently always combined—the two groups, artists and scholars, practitioners and interpreters, in a single unified organization.

In the meantime, while Harvard's department abjured it for every good reason, the abjected term "fine arts" has returned in triumph and taken on a second life. It now denotes, in some places at least, the complex of interdisciplinary study of art and art-making. "Fine arts" has, for example, been adopted by Boston College as an umbrella phrase encompassing academic programs in art history, studio art, and film studies. Alcorn State uses the phrase to cover musical performance, art, speech, and theater, as does Michigan Tech, and indeed it seems clear that "fine arts" in the twenty-first century has become a newly useful, "repurposed" term, covering all these art media and practices, with no particular emphasis on supposed "high art" culture: the musical options include band and jazz, and other standard fields under the fine-arts rubric are digital media, sculpture, ceramics, and theater. What ties these various activities together, besides a common emphasis on creativity and the mixing or crossing of media, is, of course, yet another institutional element, the degree. In this case, the degree of Bachelor of Fine Arts (BFA), as contrasted with the Bachelor of Arts (BA) or Bachelor of Science (BS or BSc).

The National Association of Schools of Art and Design lists 264 U.S. institutions which grant the BFA degree, in areas like acting, musical theater, ceramics, dance, drawing, fiber, film production, furniture design, graphic design, illustration, industrial design, metalworking, new media, painting, photography, printmaking, and sculpture. Graduate schools of the arts offer a master's degree, or MFA (Master of Fine Arts) program, and some of these programs, notably those at places like Columbia, Yale, and UCLA, have become the sites of serious art speculation for collectors who want to get in at the beginning of an upwardly mobile artist's career.

Successful artists may seem to come from nowhere into the public eye, but in fact most are trained in art schools or other graduate programs: a recent alumni listing from the Rhode Island School of Design (RISD) included sculptor/installation artist Janine Antoni (MFA '89), installation/public artist Jenny Holzer ("dubbed 'America's artist laureate,'" MFA '77), and installation artist Kara Walker (MFA '94). Antoni and Walker are both also winners of MacArthur "genius" grants. Professional training in the arts might not have pleased a nineteenth-century purist of amateurism like William Hazlitt, but these art schools and masters' programs are the equivalent of the studios, workshops, and ateliers of an earlier time.

### Art Ed

The *New York Times* ran a revealing series of articles on its Arts pages under the general heading of "Making Artists," about the training (and marketing) of young artists. The piece on graduate students in contemporary art, for example, began with an eye-catching anecdote about a Manhattan dealer who had traveled to Columbia and to Yale, in the company of a venture capitalist, in search of hot new artists to showcase, represent— and collect. The dealer was described as "known for exhibiting the art of graduate students," and the dean of Columbia's art school offered words of both encouragement and caution.

"It's a double-edged sword," Dean Bruce Ferguson is quoted as saying. "The potential for making a living is greater for these young artists, but so is the danger of being exposed or pre-exposed." Indeed much of the article worried aloud about this over- or pre-exposure, the influence of a hot art market and a hot art world full of "art stars," many of whom teach at least part-time in MFA programs—stars like Kara Walker, Janine Antoni, and Andrea Zittel at Columbia, or John Baldessari and Mary Kelly at UCLA. Cautionary tales about being picked and then dropped (or bought up and then sold off), as the advertising mogul and collector Charles Saatchi had done with the Young British Artists and their "Sensation" show in the 1990s, were much in the minds of the faculty. Collectors and art students both expressed concerns. One student told the reporter, "I don't want to be discovered and then canned in five years," and a Los Angeles collector said he had stopped going to open studios in search of new work, since it gave the artists "the wrong idea about what to expect. The chances of finding the next Warhol in a student show are zero."[49] Since the article containing this quotation, however, bore the headline "Warhols of Tomorrow Are Dealers' Quarry Today," the reader—and dealer, and collector—may be pardoned for continuing to feel some ambivalence and some lingering taste for what the director of Sotheby's contemporary art department, Tobias Meyer, called "a hunting sport."

Interestingly, the *Times* article and its featured and quoted experts avoided the word "patron" completely: one collector described his activity as "mentoring" young art students, and Michael Ovitz, the former Hollywood talent agent, is characterized as a "scout of student art," and explicitly denies being a "speculator."[50] Probably "patron" seems too high-end, too stuffy, and too, well, patronizing at this level. But the patron functions performed by these mentors, scouts, gallerists, and other snappers-up of unconsidered trifles are very real.

An article on acting in the same series bore an equally telltale headline, "So Many Acting B.A.'s, So Few Paying Gigs." The accompanying article included the information that "the number of undergraduate acting degrees has never been higher," and that the National Association of Schools of Theatre lists 146 members, not including behemoths like NYU's Tisch School of the Arts or Juilliard, the latter of which began as a school of music, but added dance in 1951, and drama in 1968. Both dance and drama programs offer a BFA degree, as well as an alternative certificate program. The college-level music degree is a bachelor of music. As for Tisch, it is said to have graduated more than three hundred actors in June 2005. This represents a huge shift in the way acting is taught, and also a considerable shift in undergraduate college priorities. As reporter Bruce Weber points out, "There was in fact no such thing as an undergraduate degree in acting until the mid-60's, and you could probably count the number of schools offering one on two hands for more than a decade after that."[51] The result, perhaps inevitably, has been the addition of how-to courses that attach to these how-to courses: courses in how to find an agent or succeed in an audition.

A closer look at the Tisch School, not only the largest but one of the most distinguished of the places where undergraduates can enroll to study acting, shows that it includes in its curriculum not only a roster of courses in theater studies and theater history, and electives in stage combat, masked drama, clowning, lighting, scenery, and costuming, but also a pragmatic upper-level course "designed to teach actors how to manage their careers and lives in order to live independently and economically as working artists." Some of the areas covered in the course are: "pictures, résumés, postcards, mailing and follow-up, interviews, auditions, agents, casting directors, managers, answering services, unions, information publications, regional theatre, and goal setting."[52] I hasten to say that this is not very different, mutatis mutandis, from the kind of information I have tried to impart to my own PhD students in English literature as they prepare themselves for what we unapologetically call the "job market." In the case of Tisch's actors, this is a credit-bearing lecture course, but it represents a very small, if crucial, part of the actor's preparation. All such comparisons are inexact, but we might consider the necessity for advanced laboratory-science students to learn about writing grant proposals—again, a nuts-and-bolts topic, but one that, properly mastered, will allow them to properly and gainfully practice their profession.

Not all acting programs are in New York, of course, although the proximity to Broadway and off-Broadway theater is undeniably a draw. But the University of Michigan, for example, offers dozens of courses in theater and drama at the undergraduate and graduate levels, and awards three undergraduate degrees: BFA in performance, BFA in design and production, and bachelor of theater arts. The theater program at Florida State University gives BFA degrees in acting and musical theater as well as a BA in theater. Carnegie Mellon University's College of Fine Arts gives degrees in art, architecture, design, drama, and music. An undergraduate in search of specialized training, and a degree, in theater, art, acting, and performance has a wide range of options nationwide.

Subsequent articles in the *Times* "Making Artists" series offered equally interesting glimpses of a world in transition, both within academia and within the arts. The piece on opera described the difficulties of performers with "big voices" and late-maturing talents in a field where light, flexible voices that can sing a wide range of roles and "hit all the notes" were more highly valued in music conservatories. Voice teachers in the conservatories often, the article claimed, go directly from their own conservatory training to teaching, and thus don't have significant stage experience or a sense of singing in a large house. And aspiring opera singers in the United States now move through a series of steps, "from a music degree and graduate school to a residency with a smaller house, to, ideally, a place in one of the top programs for young artists," like those sponsored by the Lindemann program at New York's Metropolitan Opera, the Center for American Artists at the Chicago

Lyric Opera, or the San Francisco Opera's Merola program. Perhaps inevitably, many established performers are advising young singers to "skip the apprentice programs and start performing," or to "skip the conservatory and get a liberal arts degree, learn languages and study voice on the side."[53] These performers suggested that there was no substitute for actual performance experience. At the same time, what was singled out both in this article and in the art-schools piece as the specter of "our 'American Idol' culture," was an ethos that encouraged young artists to seek and expect instant fame, rather than slow maturation.

Dancer Mark Morris gave Erika Kinetz his own opinion about conservatory training. "I mostly think it ruins people," he said. Morris, who had himself begun his career right out of high school (beginning with folk dance in Macedonia), believes the best training for dancers was to dance. As for college degrees in dance, they are, he thinks, not only extraneous, but also time-consuming, in a profession in which youth and stamina are key ingredients. Yet dance programs at college and universities have expanded over the last several years, spurred on, according to the program director of the National Dance Education Organization, by the equal-opportunity legislation of the 1970s— Title IX in 1972, and the Equal Education Opportunity Act in 1974. Both placed emphasis on funding physical education for women, which, in practice, led to programs in dance. "In the 1980's and 90's," Kinetz reports, "most of these programs migrated out of the gym and into fine-arts departments."[54]

But paying positions for dancers remain few, and difficult to get. The Tisch School offers both a BFA and an MFA in dance, with courses spanning dance composition, kinesthetics of anatomy, and music theory in the first year, and courses in dance history, music literature, acting, improvisation, and choreography to follow. The course of study includes some general education courses, but the emphasis is strongly on all aspects of dance, whether theory, history, or performance. Barnard College, located in New York City, the home for many professional dance companies, has a separate Department of Dance, offering BA (not BFA) degrees. Cornell's Department of Theatre, Film, and Dance also offers a BA, as does Brown's Department of Theatre, Speech, and Dance, and Washington University's Department of Performing Arts. It's not the BFA that is itself determinative, except that a fine arts degree is often favored for teachers of professional practice. In the meantime, many serious dancers get their real training in independent studios, not in any school.

And there's yet another plus to dedicated training and education in the arts, especially for those crossover BA programs. What careers do dance students at Brown follow in the years after college? As reported to the *Times* by Julie Strandberg, the university's director of dance: "Some become performers or scholars; others become doctors or lawyers who later serve on the boards of dance companies."[55] So there you have it: what goes around, comes around. University programs in dance can produce—patrons.

### *Limbering Up the Joints*

Some opportunistic partnerships for joint degree programs have been formed between liberal-arts universities and nearby music conservatories: for example, Columbia College has a five-year program with the Juilliard School of Music, and Harvard College has a similar program with the New England Conservatory. These programs are academically demanding—the colleges require that students complete a full load of regular coursework for the BA in addition to studio and performance work in music—and as a result only a small number of students have been able to complete the five-year master's degree in music. Oberlin College has long offered a five-year double-degree program with the Oberlin Conservatory, admitting some twenty to twenty-five students a year for the degrees of bachelor of arts and bachelor of music, and emphasizing that academic majors may be either "closely related" or "quite unrelated" to music (examples of each, given in the admissions materials, are "Voice and French or German" and "Piano and Government"). Bard College offers an integrated double-degree program with its Conservatory of Music, and again provides an example—a five-year sample plan of study for a student at the Conservatory who "has chosen to moderate into the Biology program (specializing in biochemistry)" as evidence that "it is possible to complete the double-degree program even with one of the most demanding majors in the College."[56] Northwestern's School of Music offers the possibility of double-degree programs with the university's liberal-arts college or with the School of Engineering and Applied Science. As is typical of these joint programs, admissions materials specify that "every requirement demanded by each degree must be fulfilled."[57] Students at Northwestern's music school may also apply to a five-year program with the School of Journalism that culminates in a bachelor's degree in music and a master's in journalism.

A variety of other joint- and double-degree programs in other arts are also available at universities and colleges nationwide. Such programs are "demanding," to use Bard's nicely personified term, and they are also often somewhat cumbersome. Because they require true double majors, and thus a very great commitment of time, relatively few students are able to take advantage of them. But programs like these are pointing in the right direction, and the next decade or so should allow for institutional streamlining. The key issue here is visibility and stature. The more the creative and performing arts are integrated into an academic curriculum, the more the general populace, from the top academic officers to the entering student body, will consider the arts as part of education, and not as a decorative add-on or enrichment.

### *Amateurs, Professionals, Patrons*

University and college training in the arts has clearly expanded over the past several decades, in concert with both a liberalized

notion of the liberal arts and the unstoppable preprofessional-
ism that affects other disciplines, from engineering to premed
to business. When I was in college in the 1960s, many of the
arts, including theater as well as painting and sculpture, were
considered "extracurricular" activities, as the slightly invidious
phrase went. You could engage in them, and indeed you could
focus on them, but you couldn't get academic credit, or a degree, for being an actor or a director or a cellist. At least at the
school I attended, Swarthmore College. Under this regime I
and my friends did prosper, after a fashion: we wrote, directed,
and acted in plays; we sang (or rather, they sang; no one would
ever urge me to do so) in choruses. Musicians played in bands
and orchestras; visual artists made work and displayed it. Encouraged by the opportunity to do so, I even cowrote and co-
directed a musical comedy with a friend, and had the pleasure
of seeing it performed. But those who were determined on
a professional career in these areas knew well, going in, that
they would have to make the connections (through summer
theater, auditions, and so forth) outside of the confines of the
college. As, indeed, many did.

Today Swarthmore has degree programs in music and dance
(history, theory, composition, practice) and in theater studies
and in studio art. The Department of Art, which now encom-
passes both art history and studio art, posts this information
for students: "Growing numbers of the Department's gradu-
ates go on to attend professional art schools, specializing in
areas as varied as painting, sculpture, graphics, and ceramics;
architecture and urban planning; photography, film, and television; and commercial and industrial design."[58] As we've seen,
similar expansions into the visual and performing arts have
transformed offerings at small colleges, and state and private
universities across the country.

Yet many successful practitioners still have doubts. The other
side of "patronizing," the side that suggests a certain degree
of genial condescension, is not infrequently directed by prac-
ticing artist-professionals at institutes that offer certain kinds

of professional training. We noted this above with regard to opera singing, and I have heard it voiced by successful Ivy League-educated actors and directors who went right from an undergraduate major in something else to the big time. The resistances here come both from those who went immediately into art practice—like Mark Morris—and those who used their college years to combine high-level (though still "amateur," or "extracurricular") work in the arts with conventional scholarship and education. For some in the latter group, especially those educated at elite schools in the 1950s and 1960s, these improvised spaces of creativity represent a halcyon time, and one they are often reluctant to see transformed into (mere) professional, or preprofessional, arts programs.

Here is John Lithgow's characteristically droll account of the relationship between his Harvard education and his acting career, offered in commencement remarks to the class of 2005:

> I actually had two Harvard educations. The first one concluded on the day I graduated. Shortly thereafter, I launched myself into the acting game where, for the next twenty years, I virtually kept my Harvard degree a secret. Somehow it never seemed to come in all that handy when I was auditioning for a soap opera or a potato chip commercial. My second Harvard education began when I was invited back into the fold, in 1989. In another example of Harvard recklessness, I was asked to run for the Board of Overseers, presumably to redress the fact that no one from the world of the Arts had been on the Board since the poet Robert Frost in the 1930s.[59]

Having been duly elected, Lithgow began shaking things up. He proposed an Overseers' Ad Hoc Committee on the Arts, a springtime festival of undergraduate arts activity called Arts First, and an annual Harvard Arts Medal, to be awarded each year, during Arts First, to an alumnus or alumna who had gone on to a career in the creative arts.

By definition none of the recipients of the Harvard Medal had majored in the creative arts, since there were no arts degrees offered. Medal winners like Pete Seeger, Bonnie Raitt, Yo-Yo Ma, and Peter Sellars had all majored in more academic subjects, even while pursuing their "extracurricular" interests in the arts. John Lithgow himself studied English history and literature. But these tales of emergence from nowhere to stardom are often slightly exaggerated. The brilliant Peter Sellars, who has made his name as a theater, opera, and television director, had early honed his skills at Phillips Andover Academy, where "his reputation for artistic precocity" caught the attention of Harvard's Office for the Arts. As a freshman at Harvard he successfully petitioned the committee on dramatics to allow him to direct a production on the Loeb mainstage, a privilege heretofore restricted to upperclassmen. Yo-Yo Ma studied at Juilliard in its precollege division, where his principal teacher was Leonard Rose. By the time he came to Harvard he was an accomplished cellist. Lithgow's mother had been an actress, and his father was a theater director and producer; he knew "the business" firsthand before he came to Harvard on a scholarship.

Ma's official biography says he "sought out a traditional liberal arts education to expand upon his conservatory training."[60] But he'd had, or begun, his conservatory training long before he got to Harvard. In 1970, two years before he entered Harvard, he performed at a fund-raising event for the Kennedy Center, under the sponsorship of Leonard Bernstein. Likewise, John Lithgow, however he might have concealed his Crimson ties when auditioning for a soap opera or a commercial, had some family experience in show business to add to what he learned in college. Peter Sellars did not go to professional graduate school, but after graduation he "studied in Japan, China, and India before becoming the artistic director of the Boston Shakespeare Company at age twenty-four."[61] In his hometown of Pittsburgh, Sellars had apprenticed himself, at age twelve, to a puppeteer, and in college he directed dozens of productions in a variety of unusual venues—a swimming pool, a set of underground tunnels—as well as a professional production at the American Repertory Theatre in his senior year, at the express invitation of the ART's new head, Robert Brustein. These were, in short, unusual individuals, with unusual gifts, and, as it turned out, unusual opportunities. Despite the fact that several received MacArthur "genius" awards, we do not need to set them aside in the category of "genius" in order to see that they were, collectively and individually, both original in what they did, and focused in how they did it.

Sellars's audacious initiative, and its lasting effects upon both the university and his own career, recalls an earlier moment of similar creativity at the same, admittedly privileged, institution, one that produced a powerful patronage initiative based upon the heady blending of artistic, social, and academic communities. The moment I have in mind is the founding, in 1928, of an organization called the Harvard Society for Contemporary Art by three well-connected undergraduates, Lincoln Kirstein, Edward Warburg, and John Walker, with the backing of upscale patrons from art scholar Paul Sachs to collector John Quinn to Warburg's banker-father, Felix. (Providence art collector and Harvard alumnus John Nicholas Brown, who was the chair of the Committee on the Visual Arts at Harvard University in 1954–56, and a major author of the committee's visionary report, was another early supporter.) The three undergraduates rented space above the Harvard Coop and set about borrowing major works of modernism, with the idea of shaking up the art scene in staid, moneyed Boston and beyond.

The charter of the new Society declared that "this venture, at present in the nature of an experiment, will not only fill an important gap in the cultural life of Harvard University and Radcliffe College, but it will provide the only place in greater Boston where the friends of modern art can see changing exhibitions of the various forms of artistic endeavor." It was, in fact, the first organization of its kind in the country. With works like Brancusi's *Golden Bird* and the Dymaxion house of a young artist named Richard B. Fuller (later R. Buckminster Fuller), the Harvard Society for Contemporary Art immediately caught the attention, positive and negative, of cultural society and the press. Prestigious New York galleries—Valentine, John Becker, Downtown, Reinhardt, and others—were happy to lend work, and regarded the Society as "an avenue to their future collectors."[62]

Edward Warburg went on to become a force in the Museum of Modern Art, and Kirstein, especially, in the world of ballet. In 1933 Kirstein wrote with excitement to another friend, A. Everett Austin Jr., the pioneering director of the Wadsworth Atheneum, about his fascination with, and faith in, the works of Georges Balanchine:

> My pen burns in my hand as I write: words will not flow into the ink fast enough. We have a real chance to have an American ballet company within 3 yrs. Time. When I say ballet—I mean a trained company of young dancers—not Russians—but Americans with Russian stars to start with—a company superior to the dregs of the old Diaghilev Company. . . .
>
> It will not be easy. It will be hard to get good young dancers willing to stand or fall by the *company*. No first dancers. No *stars*. A perfect *esprit de corps*. . . . He is an honest man, a serious artist, and I'd stake my life on his talent.
>
> We have the future in our hands. For Christ's sweet sake let us honor it.[63]

From the perspective of the twenty-first century this seems like—and indeed it is—a completely different world. After World War II, as we have seen, arts patronage began to change, to become both more expensive and more public. As Nicholas Fox Weber notes,

> Since the Second World War, art exhibitions, ballet performances, and opera premieres have become part of a national, multi-million-dollar industry. The costs have increased dramatically, and the government and giant

corporations have taken much of the responsibility. Even extremely wealthy patrons like Paul Mellon or J. Paul Getty have made their decisions in carefully structured collaboration with universities or federal agencies. If Lincoln Kirstein had previously engineered ballet performances in the Warburgs' backyard, now he could arrange them in a large public theater with the support of New York City and countless other donors."[64]

However far away this moment seems, with its privilege, its insider connections with the art world, society, and academia, it is nonetheless suggestive. If elite institutions like Harvard have had their moments of incubating patronage, so in the modern and postmodern world have many other universities and colleges, private and public. More to the point, the opening-up of the art world beyond these—or any—bastions of privilege seems in itself both a necessity and an opportunity. In a changed world it is not, or not only, wealthy individuals or the government that will need to exercise wise judgment and, at the same time, take prudent—and occasionally imprudent—risks. But the model for such big-picture risk-taking today, as we will see in the next chapter, is in the sciences, not the arts.

# 4

---

## ARTS OR SCIENCES

PROSPERO: *I have bedimmed*
*The noontide sun, called forth the mutinous winds,*
*And 'twixt the green sea and the azured vault*
*Set roaring war; . . .*
*graves at my command*
*Have waked their sleepers, ope'd and let 'em forth*
*By my so potent art.*

—THE TEMPEST

THE PHRASE "ARTS AND SCIENCES" has become a university catch-all, describing, or circumscribing, the wide range of curricular offerings that lead to an academic degree. Within modern universities and colleges, and indeed in general cultural usage, the "arts" are usually grouped with the "humanities," and for what seems to be a perfectly good reason. Humanities scholars study the *history* of literature, film, art, architecture, and music, and for most departments in modern universities, that "history" continues to the present day. But historical, formal, textual, and political analysis of the arts, while essential to a university and to the study of culture, is quite different structurally, from *art-making*. Grouping the arts with the humanities, though thematically plausible, is in fact a category mistake, and that mistake has had consequences deleterious to the seriousness with which the arts are taken within and beyond the walls of the university.

To find a better analogy for the activities of art-making, we should look to the sciences. The word "science" comes from the Latin word for "knowledge" (*scientia*), and was not distinguished from *art* in English until the late seventeenth century. Classical education was based on the trivium (grammar, rhetoric, and logic) and the quadrivium (arithmetic, geometry, music, and astronomy), also known as the "seven sciences" and the "free" or "liberal arts." So the disciplines that we now think of as absolutely opposed, in fact, coincided. These arts were sciences; or these sciences were arts.

The arts are far more analogous to the sciences than to the humanities. Let us count the ways. Artists, like scientists, work in localized spaces where the tools and materials of their work are kept and tended. (Artists call them studios; scientists call them laboratories.) Artists often, and increasingly, work in collaboration with one another on projects (this is increasingly the case with the more sophisticated technology now available to art-makers), and, indeed, their technological needs are often very expensive. Artists try things out, often in a variety of media. They repeat processes, they test materials, they prize their tools. They work long hours at a stretch. Like laboratory scientists, they often must work in their studios because the size, style, or situated nature of their work precludes their taking it home.

Art is often regarded as "subjective," and science as "objective"; art as personal, science as disinterested; art as expressive, science as socially beneficial. The degree to which these categories are themselves the result of historically bound thinking rather than of timeless truth has been fruitfully explored, in the twenty-first century, by historians of art and historians of science. As Caroline Jones and Peter Galison suggest, "much of [the] focus on art and science as discrete *products*" ignores "the commonalities in the *practices* that produce them. Both are regimes of knowledge, embedded in, but also constitutive of, the broader cultures they inhabit."[1] From the perceptual work of Gestalt psychologists in the fifties and sixties like Rudolf Arnheim and Anton Ehrenzweig who explored similarities in modes of creativity to the "image studies" of scholars like James Elkins and Barbara Maria Stafford, the analogies and interrelationships between art and science as ways of seeing and ways of knowing have been intrinsic to pioneering work in both realms.[2] Yet these parallels have sometimes been obscured by an emphasis on outcomes rather than on processes. And this in turn is directly connected to what Thomas Kuhn has described as "the inextricable connections between our notions of science and of progress."

"For many centuries, both in antiquity and again in early modern Europe," Kuhn reminds the reader of *The Structure of Scientific Revolutions*,

> [P]ainting was regarded as *the* cumulative discipline. During those years the artist's goal was assumed to be representation. Critics and historians, like Pliny and Vasari, then recorded with veneration the series of inventions from foreshortening to chiaroscuro that had made possible successively more perfect representations of nature. But those are also the years, particularly during the Renaissance, when little cleavage was felt between the sciences and the arts. Leonardo was only one of many men who passed freely back and forth between fields that only later became categorically distinct. Furthermore, even when that steady exchange had ceased, the term "art" continued to apply as much to technology and the crafts, which were also seen as progressive, as to painting and sculpture. Only when the latter unequivocally renounced representation as their goal and began to learn again from primitive models did the cleavage we now take for granted assume anything like its present depth.[3]

That many of the practices we now call "art" began as a kind of science (photography, film, gesso and fresco, the mixing of paints, the strength of materials for sculpture and architecture), and that many of the practices we now call "science" were pioneered by individuals famous in their time as artists (Alberti, Leonardo, the architects of the flying buttress or the geodesic dome) is a reminder that these boundaries are permeable and flexible. Alliances between sculpture and engineering, between robotics and animation, between film and scientific inquiry are not only possible but ongoing. A reconsideration of the relation between art-making and science will help not only in assessing the nature of the questions engaged by each of these practices and their practitioners, but also in understanding the importance of arts patronage in restoring an occluded, and under-recognized, commonality of interests and concerns.

## The Penthouse and the Basement

For a contemporary public used to assessing the competing merits of art and science, it's worth bearing in mind that the great ideological push during the cold war for advancement in science and technology was partnered with a desire to balance America's national interests by increased funding in the arts. In other words, the two impulses were considered not only compatible but mutually offsetting.

Thus the Declaration of Findings and Purposes of the 1965 National Foundation on the Arts and Humanities Act asserted that "an advanced civilization must not limit itself to science and technology alone but must give full value and support to the other great branches of scholarly and cultural activity in order to achieve a better understanding of the past, a better analysis of the present, and a better view of the future."[4]

This rather elegant rhetorical sequence, moving as it does from *understanding* to *analysis* to *view*, combines the usual sense of the humanities as the repository of past achievements (aka "greatness") with the equally familiar sense of the computational social sciences, and the life and physical sciences, as the guarantors of progress. The point is brought home forcefully in the next item of the document, cautioning against runaway scientific aspirations unless they are tempered by reflection: "Democracy demands wisdom and vision in its citizens. It must therefore foster and support a form of education, and access to the arts and the humanities, designed to make people of all backgrounds and wherever located masters of their technology and not its unthinking servants."[5] Only the year before, in

1964, Americans had flocked to the movies to watch *Dr. Strangelove: Or How I Learned to Stop Worrying and Love the Bomb.*

The relationship between the arts and the sciences was very much in the mind of the early proponents of the National Endowments for Art and for Humanities. As we've seen, John F. Kennedy's vision of the role of the arts and culture was part of the cold war push-back against "propaganda" and the arms race. American freedom meant also American cultural growth and expansion, in contrast with what was perceived as a repressive Soviet policy about the arts. The ideology of freedom was that free expression was, somehow, un-ideological, and that good art, the best art, transcended politics. At the same time, expressive individualism in the arts, like that of the Abstract Expressionists (dubbed by Nelson Rockefeller practitioners of "free enterprise painting") became an iconic sign of American freedom. As Alfred Barr of MOMA claimed, "the modern artist's nonconformity and love of freedom cannot be tolerated within a monolithic tyranny and modern art is useless for the dictator's propaganda."[6]

At the Rose Garden signing of the National Foundation on the Arts and Humanities Act in September 1965, President Lyndon Johnson had made the inequity explicit: "We in America have not always been kind to the artists and scholars who are the creators and the keepers of our vision. Somehow, the scientists always seem to get the penthouse, while the arts and the humanities get the basement."[7] Actually, the penthouse and the basement were often not even in the same building, or the same ballpark, since the budgetary allotments for the two kinds of enterprise were so vastly different. In 1968, for example, the United States appropriated $16 billion for the sciences, and $7.8 million for the arts endowment.[8] But in this period, nonetheless, the rhetoric in support of the Endowments (both the NEA and NEH) stressed the importance of balancing the equation. Roger Stevens, the first chair of the NEA, drew an explicit analogy between art and science: "People think science is exact, but it isn't. It is failure after failure. And so with the arts. The arts should be approached more tolerantly by the public and the critics. The artist should be allowed to fail, and he won't do any great work unless he stops being afraid to fail. In this country there is too much of a premium on success."[9]

"Support for individual artists is much like basic research in the sciences,"[10] claimed NEA proponents, arguing that in both cases the general public might not appreciate the value of pioneering work, work that is, by definition, stretching the boundaries of what is comfortably understood. Artist James Melchert, former director of the NEA's Visual Arts Program, used a similar analogy: "[A]rt can be thought of as esthetic investigation. Where would science be without research? The same question can be said about art."[11]

"Einstein's space is no closer to reality than Van Gogh's sky," Arthur Koestler claimed.

> The glory of science is not in a truth more absolute than the truth of Bach or Tolstoy, but in the act of creation itself. The scientist's discoveries impose his own order on chaos, as the composer or painter imposes his; an order that always refers to limited aspects of reality, and is based on the observer's frame of reference, which differs from period to period as a Rembrandt nude differs from a nude by Manet.[12]

So on the one hand art was very unlike science, according to these claims, and on the other hand it was very similar. It dealt with the realm of the spirit rather than with the material world, but it pushed the boundaries of knowledge, functioning by trial and error, experiment, and inquiry. In both ways art seemed meritorious, worthy of government patronage, and of patronage meted out by knowledgeable artists themselves. And it turned out that artists themselves were very interested in science. "In the sixties and seventies," observes Michael Brenson, "a number of influential artists, including Athena Tacha, Mel Bochner, Michael Heizer, Helen and Newton Harrison, Barry LeVa, Sol LeWitt, Dorothy Rockburne, Tony Smith, and Robert

Smithson, made art influenced by science."[13] LeWitt was one of several artists influenced by the locomotion studies of Eadweard Muybridge, as well as by the apparently infinite possibilities offered by the geometric cube. Smithson, who died in a plane crash in 1973 at the age of thirty-five, wrote that he had "moved into science because it seems to be the only thing left that's religious."[14] "Then came chaos theory, black holes, and multiple infinities. . . . By the midnineties, many artists were making work inspired by the eye-opening photographs sent back to Earth by the Hubble Space Telescope."[15] Equally to the point, technology had become fundamental to the processes of art, as well as to its materials, topics, and themes.

All too soon, though, these two claims for art would be inverted and reversed, as the intellectual and cultural climate changed, and as the perceived exigencies of the cold war gave way to a different social and economic vision under Reaganism. No longer airy spirits leading us to our better selves, artists in the 1980s and 1990s became described as materialist adventurers, "avant-garbage." And experimental risk-taking, the need to fail in order to succeed, which was at the heart of the original plan, became over the years, at least in the eyes of some lawmakers and government bureaucrats, a sign that the artists were out of step with the country, its tastes and values. Art was now expected to conform to norms and guidelines, not to put every single one of them in question. Peer-review panels were regarded, not as experts, but as cronies and elitist insiders. Precisely what had marked the goals of the National Endowment for the Arts at the beginning became what allowed it to be put in question. Art was now like science in the wrong way: expensive, technological, arcane. And it was *unlike* science in the wrong way, since it did not solve problems. Indeed, it produced them.

### Experiment and Theory

We might consider as a kind of shorthand index of this contrast the differential weight that is given in art and in science to the word "experimental." Since the Greeks, and with increasing energy since the seventeenth century, a definition of a certain kind of science—work done in a laboratory—has been described as experimental: that is, based upon experiment, on empirical evidence. Experimental physicists build their own devices for measurement. Experimental medicine tests the frontier of new drugs, devices, and procedures.

But what does "experimental" mean in the world, and the canons, of art? Something in the public mind much closer to risky, risqué, weird, and unsound. "Experimental theater" means nonmainstream theater. Companies known as "experimental" include the Bread and Puppet Theater, the Living Theatre, Mabou Mines, the Wooster Group, and the Playhouse of the Ridiculous, while a number of groundbreaking directors have instantiated "theater" movements of their own (Artaud's Theatre of Cruelty, Jerzy Grotowski's Poor Theatre). Harvard's American Repertory Theatre has a small black-box theater known as the Ex, a place for noncommercial productions. In the early 1990s the National Endowment for the Arts canceled grants to five artists in the "experimental art" category, including performance artists Karen Finley, Tim Miller, and Holly Hughes, as well as to Franklin Furnace, an experimental arts center in New York City.[16] The artists—who had been found culpable on grounds of "decency" because of their experimental art—later won compensation from the NEA in an out-of-court settlement resulting from their legal suit.[17] A *New York Times* article on the New York Video Festival described "the wild and woolly frontier of video art" as situated between "Pop culture and experimental art, reality television and virtual reality, trippy psychedelia and austere digital abstraction."[18] (And this was a *positive* review.)

Experimental science. Experimental art. Like the once famous distinction between a "public man" (a statesman) and a "public woman" (a whore), these modes of experimentation are very differently valued. Yet both are about testing the bounds of what is known, and what can be done, within the bounds of practice.

Not only is "experimental" a word that resonates differently in the context of art and of science—so also is "theoretical," a term readily claimed by scientists (theoretical physics, theoretical chemistry). Although "theory" began as a word related to looking, sight, and spectacle—etymologically it shares a Greek root with "theater"—it has evolved into a term for a systematic statement of principles or laws. Theoretical scientists became, during the period of the Second World War and the cold war, particularly high-status investigators. But when humanists, and especially literary scholars and philosophers, began to talk about theory, they were often lampooned or lambasted, either as poachers or as pretenders.

In a 1982 book entitled *Beautiful Theories: The Spectacle of Discourse in Contemporary Criticism,* Elizabeth Bruss argues cogently for the usefulness of the term "theory" as precisely that which crosses over between the arts and the sciences: "Theory pursues knowledge past usefulness, past even power, since one can achieve rudimentary control without really caring to know how or why. It is here, in its extremity, that the theoretical and the artistic enterprises overlap, which may explain why our terms of praise—*elegant, symmetrical, powerful, interesting, bold*—are so often the same."[19] Bruss's visionary book directly addresses—without either defensiveness or bravado—the correspondences between scientific theory and literary theory, by unpacking the differences between theoretical and observational (or "descriptive") language. Theoretical approaches put familiar characterizations in question, opening the way for a radical rethinking.

"Literature is a *mathesis,* an order, a system, a structured field of knowledge," declares Roland Barthes in *Roland Barthes.*[20] A "mathesis" is a mental discipline, especially one connected to mathematical science. Since Foucault, the term has also been used, in the way Barthes is presumably using it, to denote the science, or practice, of establishing a systematic order of things.[21]

A third useful term for artists, to partner with "experimental" and "theoretical," was "conceptual," although that word is now showing signs of trend fatigue. Conceptual art, inspired in part by Duchamp's readymades in the 1910s and 1920s, had its early heyday in the sixties and seventies, and is well described in artist Sol LeWitt's "Paragraphs on Conceptual Art":

> In conceptual art the idea or concept is the most important aspect of the work. When an artist uses a conceptual form of art, it means that all of the planning and decisions are made beforehand and the execution is a perfunctory affair. The idea becomes a machine that makes the art. This kind of art . . . is usually free from the dependence on the skill of the artist as a craftsman. It is the objective of the artist who is concerned with conceptual art to make his work mentally interesting to the spectator, and therefore usually he would want it to become emotionally dry.

LeWitt contrasted such art with what he called "perceptual" art: "Art that is meant for the sensation of the eye primarily would be called perceptual rather than conceptual. This would include most optical, kinetic, light and color art."[22]

Conceptual art is often unrepeatable, known only through documentation (photographs, written texts and objects, rather than the "work" itself, which is not a "work" but a concept and an action). Yves Klein's 1960 *Leap into the Void*, in which he jumps out a window and attempts to fly; Huebler's *one authentic secret* (1970) asking museum visitors to write down their secrets, which he made into a book—or his series of photographs of New York's Central Park, each taken after he heard a birdcall.[23] I should add here that this kind of conceptual work, while "wild" in one sense, is also both carefully documented and thoroughly discussed and analyzed within the art world.[24] Conceptual art in its early years seemed to involve questioning or subverting the gallery and museum systems, although commerce and commodification seem to have won out, at least in some postconceptual cases, as the art world adjusted to accommodate this new way of "making" in which, sometimes, nothing was actually "made."

Hypothetical figurative concepts in science may appear to have a more "productive" purpose, since they seek to explain physical phenomena and thus to be foundationally useful rather than resolutely useless. But the acts of conceptual imagination and, especially, counterintuitive imagination are in both kinds of cases profoundly and productively destabilizing, opening the way—and the eyes and mind—to a new way of "seeing."[25]

In recent years there has been considerable interest from the side of science in reestablishing the connection between experimental art and science. Books with titles like *African Fractals: Modern Computing and Indigenous Design* (by a computer scientist and ethnomathematician, Ron Eglash) and *The Art of Genes* (by a geneticist, Enrico Coen) have drawn attention to these affinities. The astronomer John D. Barrow contended in *The Artful Universe* that "the arts and the sciences flow from a single source; they are informed by the same reality; and their insights are linked in ways that make them look less and less like alternatives."[26] And another set of terms linking the two kinds of practice have come increasingly into play: terms like "elegant" and "beautiful."

### *A Beautiful Proof*

That numbers and proofs can be "beautiful" and "elegant" is a staple of mathematics. An "elegant proof" is economical, surprising, original, and generalizable. An ugly or clumsy proof is cumbersome, laborious, and conventional. The title of Sylvia Nasar's popular biography of mathematician John Nash, *A Beautiful Mind*, makes the point, as does her chapter title on his early work, "A Beautiful Theorem." And the annals of mathematical— and philosophical—writing are full of elegant (and beautiful) testimonials to the beauty of mathematics.

> Mathematics, rightly viewed, possesses not only truth, but supreme beauty—a beauty cold and austere, like that of sculpture, without appeal to any part of our weaker nature, without the gorgeous trappings of painting or music, yet sublimely pure, and capable of a stern perfection such

as only the greatest art can show. (Bertrand Russell, "The Study of Mathematics")[27]

Mathematics, as much as music or any other art, is one of the means by which we rise to a complete self-consciousness. The significance of mathematics resides precisely in the fact that it is an art; by informing us of the nature of our own minds it informs us of much that depends on our minds. (J.W.N. Sullivan, *Aspects of Science*)[28]

The mathematician's patterns, like the painter's or the poet's, must be *beautiful*; the ideas, like the colours or the words must fit together in a harmonious way. Beauty is the first test: there is no permanent place in the world for ugly mathematics. (G. H. Hardy, *A Mathematician's Apology*)[29]

So here is one of the quintessential values of creative art—including visual art, music, and poetry—standing in pride of place among mathematicians. And "beauty" thus conceived has a similarly high status in some other scientific discourses. For example, commenting on Schroedinger's discovery of his wave theory through a "beautiful generalization of De Broglie's ideas," physicist Paul Dirac observed, "I think there is a moral to this story, namely that it is more important to have beauty in one's equations than to have them fit experiment."[30] At the same time, however, it's worth noting that Dirac saw some differences, as well as some similarities, between the practices of art-making and science. In a conversation with Robert Oppenheimer he is said to have "gently reproached" him for his interest in poetry: "I hear," he said, "that you write poetry as well as working at physics. How on earth can you do two such things at once? In science one tries to tell people, in such a way as to be understood by everyone, something that no one ever knew before. But in the case of poetry it's the exact opposite!"[31] Poets might well take issue with this formulation, which suggests that poetry tells people what they all know in terms that no one can understand. But Dirac's perfectly turned chiasmus is itself an example of the power and pleasure of rhetoric, demonstrating that he himself is, at least in this instance, of the poet's party without knowing it.

## Art and Progress

Fundamental to the analogy, or dis-analogy, between art and science is the contestatory idea of "progress." The sciences, even—or perhaps especially—the theoretical sciences, are at least in some sense always concerned with problem solving, although the academic distinction between "pure" and "applied" science, math, and engineering may seem to partition off the theorists from the experimentalists and the pragmatists. Art, as we have seen, can be "useful" when it is connected to design, craft, architecture, or other practical values, but sometimes the "higher" the art the more useless it is conceived to be. In any case, the idea of artistic progress is somewhat out of fashion these days, having been successfully—and importantly—reframed in the context of social and economic factors, situatedness, class, gender, and so on. No longer are art historians very comfortable drawing a straight line that is "the history of (Western) art." Histories in the plural have replaced monumental history, in this as in virtually all other fields. So what can be said about the relationship between art and science under this new disposition?

I tend to resist the idea that art is "good for you," or "makes you a better person," or "improves society," or indeed does anything in this ethical-liberal realm. Art *is.* If it *does,* if it is performative, what it performs is *itself,* not some act of social adhesion. Nonetheless, I have often found myself saying, to colleagues who wonder what the place of the creative or "making" arts is in a university setting, that art is what the scientists—and political scientists and diplomats—are saving the world *for.* While this has a certain in-your-face patness about it, I actually think it is pretty true. And moreover I think many scientists would agree. Evidence of this often comes in the richness of scientific writing, in which analogies and patterns from the arts are instanced as a way of explaining, and expanding upon, scientific observations. These are activities along a continuum; they are neither opposites nor rivals. We need both, as we need all creative, imaginative, and boundary-breaking work, work that reframes questions, and that is constituted to lead to more questions, rather than to any final answer. Art and science challenge: they challenge complacency, truism, expectation, and law.

A half-century ago, E. H. Gombrich could write, with humane self-confidence, "the artist works like a scientist. His works exist not only for their own sake but also to demonstrate certain problem-solutions. He creates them for the admiration of all, but principally with an eye on his fellow artists and the connoisseurs who can appreciate the ingenuity of the solution put forward."[32] Gombrich cited in support of his view the opinion of the poet, essayist, and art historian Herbert Read, who drew directly on modern science for his assessment of progress in modern art: "for a painter to ignore the discoveries of a Cézanne or Picasso is equivalent to a scientist ignoring the discoveries of an Einstein or a Freud."[33]

But the question of art and progress had been addressed from a diametrically different viewpoint, as Gombrich himself acknowledged, by Romantic critics like Hazlitt who were adamant in their insistence that art was the product of individual genius, and thus could not be tied to any progress narrative. It was clear to Hazlitt that Shakespeare was a better writer than Pope, and Raphael a better painter than Sir Joshua Reynolds. Progress had nothing to do with it. Indeed, that was one way of distinguishing between science and art. As he wrote in an essay called "Why the Arts Are Not Progressive?":

The greatest poets, the ablest orators, the best painters, and the finest sculptors that the world ever saw, appeared soon after the birth of these arts, and lived in a state of society which was, in other respects, comparatively barbarous. Those arts, which depend on individual genius and incommunicable power, have always leaped at once from infancy to manhood, from the first rude dawn of invention to their meridian height and dazzling luster, and have in general declined ever after. This is the peculiar distinction and privilege of each, of science and of art; of the one, never to attain its utmost summit of perfection, and of the other, to arrive at it almost at once.[34]

Thus the sciences were in large part definable by the drive for perfection, or for solutions, whereas the arts were fitful, episodic, determined by the spirit of the age and the inventiveness of the individual artist-genius. In general, Hazlitt thought, despite the periodic appearance of greatness, the arts were in decline, while science marched forward. Hazlitt could not know, of course, that the next century would begin to define genius itself, not so much as an attribute of art, but rather as the special province and the gift of science.

### Genius Envy

Consider a symptomatic pair of titles: *Shakespeare in Love* and *Einstein in Love*. The first is the film hit of 1998, with a witty screenplay by Tom Stoppard; the second is Dennis Overbye's 2000 biography of the young Albert Einstein. Both portray card-carrying "geniuses" of the popular imagination in moments of off-stage intimacy. The Stoppard play imagines (cleverly, although entirely at variance with the facts) that Shakespeare's gift for writing brilliant plays was jump-started by falling in love with a beautiful, elusive, and ultimately unobtainable, female aristocrat. Before that he was a hack; afterward, a genius. Overbye's Einstein book takes a slightly different tack, tracing the early life of the handsome and self-sufficient Albert as he romances women and ideas. The timing of Einstein's two major creative feats, the equation $E = mc^2$ and the general theory of relativity, coincide with his first marriage (to Mileva Maric, a Serbian physics student) and then with his struggle to divorce

Mileva to marry his cousin Elsa. (Overbye notes that Einstein had inconveniently fallen in love with someone else, his cousin's daughter Ilse. He was willing to marry either, and left the choice to them.)

Neither of these accounts offers a portrait of the artist with feet of clay. Both are to a certain extent charmed by, and charming about, their famous subjects. But each offers a "human" genius. And signally in both cases the suffix "in love" is found finally to apply, not to the lady in the case, but to his art or science. To the theater, and to the universe.

The later Einstein became a cultural icon, personating "genius" in look and name. With his unruly shock of white hair, his ambling gait, warm ("absentminded") smile, and penchant for going sockless, he was himself an intellectual celebrity easy to "love," at least at a distance. The Einstein legend, already fully established in Einstein's lifetime, persisted long after his death. Walter Matthau played him as a warmhearted matchmaker in a fright wig, in a film called *IQ*; a photograph of Einstein with his tongue sticking out adorns a popular T-shirt; on many computers a shaggy-haired Einstein "office assistant" can be found ready to explain the mysteries of word processing. Roland Barthes put it most effectively in "The Brain of Einstein," discussing depictions of the famous $E = mc^2$ equation in popular culture: "*photographs* of Einstein show him standing next to a blackboard covered with mathematical signs of obvious complexity; *cartoons* of Einstein (the sign that he has become a legend) show him chalk still in hand, and having just written on an empty blackboard, as though without preparation, the magic formula of the world."[35]

"Genius" derives from the same root as "gene" and "genetic," and meant originally, in Latin, the tutelary god or spirit given to every person at birth. One's "genius" governed one's fortune and determined one's character, and ultimately conducted one out of the world. In some uses, and in some cultures, there were imagined to be two geniuses in every person, a "good genius" and an "evil genius," who competed for influence over the individual's character, conduct, and fortunes. The word soon came to mean a demon or spirit in general, as in the fairy-tale "genie" or "jinn." To this point, as will be clear, the "genius" is part of a system of what would be later called "psychology," since it was thought of as residing somehow both inside and outside the individual, and motivating behavior.

Through the Renaissance to well into the eighteenth century, the most familiar meaning of "genius" in English was something like "temperament" or "disposition": you might hear or read of someone having a "daring genius" or an "indolent genius," or, as in a phrase of John Evelyn's, a "rural genius, born as I was at Wotton, among the woods." A genius was an inclination for something. When applied not to persons, but to nations or eras, it became a distinctive opinion or sentiment: "the genius of the age," the genius of the Italians, or the Spanish, or the English. Thus a genius could be a tendency, or a prevailing characteristic, or a natural (that is, inborn) endowment. In other words, you could have a genius (for finance, say, or for elocution, or for adventure, or for mathematics). But you could not *be* a genius, unless you were a sprite or an allegorical personage: the Genius of Famine, say, to use an example from Shakespeare, or the "genius of the shore," to cite John Milton's funeral elegy "Lycidas," in which a drowned man is metamorphosed into a local deity.

Joseph Addison's essay "On Genius," published in *The Spectator* in 1711, laid out the terrain of genius in terms that are still operative today. According to Addison, there were two kinds of genius, natural and learned. The best of the best, the greatest of geniuses, were those who were the most original, who depended least on models, imitation, or example. Homer, Pindar, and Shakespeare were his examples of the first category; Aristotle, Virgil, Milton, and Francis Bacon, of the second. In very general terms this dichotomy—natural versus learned, genius versus talent, brilliant versus industrious—still attaches to the romance of "genius" today, despite Thomas Edison's oft-quoted adage that "Genius is one percent inspiration and ninety-nine percent perspiration." It's the inspiration that we dote on; we're willing to hear about sweat equity, but only after the results are in.

For a while in the history of English and Scottish letters, "genius" was the hottest of topics—far more central, among philosophers and "public intellectuals," than it is today. By the middle of the eighteenth century, dozens of works on this fascinating question were being published and debated.[36] Alexander Gerard, a Scottish theologian, natural philosopher, and literary critic, was among the first to stress the scientific as contrasted with the artistic or aesthetic possibilities of genius. Newton plays as big a part in his essay as do Homer and Shakespeare. The concept of modern genius owes, in fact, a great deal to the development of seventeenth-century science and to the founding, in England, of the Royal Society, whose new scientists, asserting their independence from Aristotle's notions of physics, became innovators and "inventors" in the strong sense of the term.

But the idea of the scientific genius took a backseat to that of the artistic genius. It is worth bearing in mind that for quite a long period of time genius was a term applied almost exclusively to the realm of arts and letters, and not to science or learning. "What is called genius," wrote Immanuel Kant in the *Critique of Judgment*, "is a talent for art, not for science," since "it is quite ridiculous for a man to speak and decide like a genius in things which require the most careful investigation by reason." Here is that split, again, between genius and judgment. "We can readily learn all that Newton has set forth in his immortal work on the Principles of Natural Philosophy, however great a head was required to discover it [writes Kant], but we cannot learn to write spirited poetry."

Romantic poets and critics like Coleridge and Shelley staked out genius as the territory of the poet. The test case, as so often, was Shakespeare. Was he a wild and untutored genius—Milton's image of "Sweetest Shakespeare, fancy's child, warble[ing] his native woodnotes wild"? In a public lecture called "Shakespeare's Judgment Equal to His Genius," Coleridge argued fiercely against this view: "Are the plays of Shakespere [*sic*] works of rude uncultivated genius, in which the splendour of the parts compensates, if aught can compensate, for the barbarous shape-lessness and irregularity of the whole? Or is the form equally admirable with the matter, and the judgment of the great poet not less deserving of our wonder than his genius?" The critic and essayist William Hazlitt likewise felt he had to grapple with Shakespeare's supposed imperfections—his irritating fondness for puns and wordplay; his unaccountable willingness to alter chronology and geography, changing the ages of characters and the locations of cities and countries to suit his dramatic pur-poses (the "seacoast of Bohemia")—without losing the sense of unique brilliance. Thus we get typical formulations like "His barbarisms were those of his age. His genius was his own." It was, in fact, "the universality of his genius" that somehow accounted for local flaws and faults in Shakespeare's plays. This notion of genius carried with it the idea of instinctual feeling, excess, ungovernability, and it was the standard praise-and-blame for Shakespeare over the centuries.

William James, writing in the pages of the *Atlantic Monthly*, expressed the view that "effective greatness" can only be nur-tured by congenial surroundings, and that "for a community to get vibrating through and through with intensely active life, many geniuses coming together and in rapid succes-sion are required."[37] It was one of James's students, Gertrude Stein, who would boldly claim the mantle of genius for the next generation of artists. As she writes in her autobiography, ventriloquized through the voice of her companion and secre-tary, Alice B. Toklas, "I have sat with wives who were not wives, of geniuses who were real geniuses. I have sat with real wives of geniuses who were not real geniuses. I have sat with wives of geniuses, of near geniuses, of would be geniuses. . . . [T]he geniuses came and talked to Gertrude Stein, and the wives sat with me."[38] The geniuses who paraded through the Paris home

Stein shared with Toklas in the Rue de Fleurus included painters and writers—Picasso, Matisse, Hemingway, Braque, and a host of others—but Stein blithely regarded herself as the chief among such "geniuses," a word she used early and often. "The three geniuses of whom I wish to speak are Gertrude Stein, Pablo Picasso, and Alfred Whitehead," declares the fictionalized Toklas in the *Autobiography*.

By the later nineteenth century, scientific analysis had been deployed to investigate the roots and nature of genius. Eugenicist Francis Galton's *Hereditary Genius* (1869) advanced the argument that "illustrious men" have "eminent kinsmen," and that genius, talent, and natural gifts are passed down through family lines.[39] In his 1904 *A Study of British Genius* Havelock Ellis produced a list of 1,300 distinguished names, based on the amount of space devoted to them in biographical dictionaries, especially the *Dictionary of National Biography*. What genius actually *was*, though, both Ellis and Galton debated within themselves. In later editions of his book Galton regretted the use of "genius" in the title, noting that he had only meant something like "ability": "There was not the slightest intention on my part," he wrote, "to use the word genius in any technical sense, but merely as expressing an ability that was exceptionally high, and at the same time inborn."[40]

Galton, importantly, downplayed the magical side of "genius," insisting that all he meant was "ability" or "natural talent." The other kind of genius he found unstable, dangerous, and indeed diseased: "If genius means a sense of inspiration, or of rushes of ideas from apparently supernatural sources, or of an inordinate and burning desire to accomplish any particular end, it is perilously near to the voices heard by the insane, to their delirious tendencies, or to their monomanias. It cannot in such cases be a healthy faculty, nor can it be desirable to perpetuate it by inheritance."[41]

With the invention of the notion of the "intelligence quotient," or IQ, came the idea that genius could be quantified. Not unexpectedly, this spelled the end for a certain kind of romantic vision of "the genius" as a different kind of being—akin to what the critic Walter Benjamin, writing of the unique work of art, called its "aura." It's not surprising, either, that the IQ was the invention of an American, Lewis Terman, a psychology professor at Stanford who first thought up this device for the scientific detection of brilliance at the beginning of the twentieth century. By dividing a test taker's "mental age," as revealed in French psychologist Alfred Binet's standardized test of human intelligence, by the individual's chronological age, Terman derived the number he dubbed an intelligence quotient, soon shortened and popularized into "IQ," a phrase that was easy to say, easy to put in headlines, and less scholarly sounding than the mathematical "quotient."

IQ was the DNA of its time. The magic initials seemed to spell certainty and destiny, predicting great things; the template here was social science rather than biology, but the possibility of telling the future, and, indeed, of rereading and rationalizing the past, offered tantalizing hints of power. In fact, once "genius" was a test result, it had lost much of its charisma and its mystery. This was the effect of social science, the quantification of the unquantifiable. The excitement about the idea of IQ was linked to "meritocracy"—instead of a hereditary aristocracy of the titled and the entitled, there would now be a new, more deserving upper class of eminent, and soon-to-be-eminent achievers. The next step, perhaps inevitably, was to find a means to identify the Nobel laureates, Pulitzer Prize winners, and Picassos that Terman's rigorous IQ testing had somehow failed to produce. To identify them, and then to enable them to pursue their gifts.

Since 1981 the John D. and Catherine T. MacArthur Foundation has given out what the press insists upon labeling "genius grants" to artists, performers, architects, scientists, and scholars of all persuasions. The twenty-three recipients for 2001, for example, included a physicist, a biographer, a public-interest lawyer, a professor of psychiatry, the executive director of a non-profit housing development, a theorist of art, a naturalist who has spent more than thirty years studying elephants in Kenya, and an astrobiologist and policy analyst whose expertise ranges from lunar geology to bioterrorism. Whether any of these gifted people would qualify as "geniuses" depends on one's definition, of course. The Foundation itself scrupulously avoids the term. Where "genius" actually enters the picture is more in the fantasies and the intentions of the founder, J. Roderick MacArthur, the son of John D., a financial wizard who parlayed an insurance firm into an empire that included Florida real estate, New York office buildings, and pulp-and-paper factories. "The idea behind this," Roderick MacArthur explained when the Foundation was established, "is that Albert Einstein could not have written a grant application saying he was going to discover the theory of relativity. He needed to be free." Recipients neither apply nor submit progress reports after they have received their grants. "There was no management association looking at Michelangelo and asking him to fill out semiyearly progress reports in triplicate," said MacArthur. "Our aim is to support individual genius and to free those people from the bureaucratic pettiness of academe."[42]

Leaving aside for a second the patronage battles and other stresses and strains that did hamper the Michelangelos and the Einsteins in the past—not to mention the vexatious question of whether the obstacles they encountered were perversely beneficial to their achievements—and acknowledging for the moment that academe, like any other business, has its share of bureaucratic pettiness, what is most striking here is the still-romantic expectation that geniuses "need to be free." Or perhaps, if we hark back instead to an older notion of "genius" as an attribute rather than a person, that freedom encourages people to develop their genius (or, as the Foundation prefers to call it, their "creative instincts"). As noted, the Fellows Program eschews the problematic G-word, but the criteria today continue to emphasize the C-word instead: in a passage of less than a hundred words the Foundation now cites the importance of "creativity" three times: the selection process is geared to identify individuals who demonstrate "exceptional creativity," potential for "subsequent creative work," and the ability "to exercise their own creative instincts for the benefit of human society." Some of the earlier animus against petty academe has vanished from the MacArthur's self-description, as the individual genius of the founder has given way to a more complex vision for the twenty-first century, but the current formulation reiterates the stress on independence from institutions: "The MacArthur Fellowship is a 'no strings attached' award in support of people, not projects."[43] If a certain vestige of the former hopeful romanticism lingers in the idea that there can be "no strings" attached to a significant financial award, both the caution and the hope are consistent with the Foundation's longtime goals, and the stress on usable outcomes ("for the benefit of human society") underscores the ultimate expectation of a connection between individuals ("their own creative instincts") and the social, cultural, or scientific communities in which they do their work.

In these genetically obsessed days, when "mind, brain, and behavior" has replaced "race, class, and gender" as the academics' mantra, and "cognitive" has become a term to conjure with in certain humanistic circles, it's not inconceivable that we might expect a return of the hardwired approach to "genius." From anthropometry to phrenology, from "eminence" to IQ, from romantic idealization to the designation of genius by committee, from "psychometry" and "historiometry" to DNA and cognitive mapping, the world has been on a scavenger hunt for the secret ingredients of genius. Not content with naming them (eccentricity, brilliance, originality, transgression, arrogance, obsession, pathos), we have made every attempt to categorize, derive, tabulate, and compare, as if genius were an identifiable objective, rather than the most sublimely subjective and elusive of qualities.

Who can forget the story of Einstein's brain, weighed, preserved, pickled, then for some time inexplicably lost, and finally the object of a scientific custody battle? Could investigators detect the anomaly that made for genius? As critic Roland Barthes put it, "Einstein's brain is a mythological object." Early photographs showed him cheerfully submitting to testing, his head wreathed with electrical wires, his brain waves mechanically recorded while he was instructed to think of relativity. "Paradoxically, the more the genius of the man was materialized under the guise of his brain, the more the product of his inventiveness came to acquire a magical dimension, and gave a new incarnation to the old esoteric image of a science entirely contained in a few letters." If magic was the old science, then science is the new magic.

"Among American scientists," writes James Gleick, "it became a kind of style violation, a faux pas suggesting greenhorn credulity, to use the word *genius* about a living colleague." But science writer Sylvia Nasar uses it consistently and unselfconsciously, on page after page, in her biography of mathematician John Nash. There are repeated references to "Nash the mathematical genius," to "the two geniuses" Nash and John von Neumann, to Norbert Wiener as "a genius who was at once adulated and isolated," and the "group of geniuses" in mathematics and theoretical physics who came to the United States from Europe after World War II. Not only is Nasar comfortable using the word, she is comfortable describing its attributes, signs, and symptoms. She writes that Nash's "arrogance was seen as evidence of his genius," that "[a] profound dislike for merely absorbing knowledge and a strong compulsion to learn by doing is one of the most reliable signs of genius," and that at MIT "Nash picked up the mannerisms of other eccentric geniuses," appropriating as his own Norbert Wiener's gesture of running his finger along the groove of the tiled walls of the corridor, D. J. Newman's condemnation of music after Beethoven, Norman Levinson's dislike of psychiatrists, Warren Ambrose's impatience with conventional social greetings. Eccentricity, in fact, seems one of the distinguishing marks of "genius." Indeed, a non-eccentric genius is something of a disappointment.

General Leslie Groves was delighted to find that his top scientist on the Manhattan Project, J. Robert Oppenheimer, had an expert command of Sanskrit.

The notion that there is such a thing as genius, and that the bona fide genius is to be found on the science side of the campus rather than the arts side, has an effect, both subtle and profound, upon questions of funding, prestige, and institutional support. The reputation of the modern university depends upon its exceptionalism as well as upon its consistency. The unquestioning assumption of Kant, Hazlitt, and Coleridge that genius was "a talent for art, not for science," and the heady optimism of Gertrude Stein, her salon receiving and disbursing artistic geniuses through every portal, has long been out of mode. But rather than choosing among or between these definitions and assumptions, it will be useful here to identify what they have in common: the unpredictable and inventive capacities of creative work, uncharted, unbounded, both intuitive and counterintuitive. Even if the discourse of "genius" has now migrated, as to a large extent it has, into the realms of popular culture (sports, celebrity, advertising), the place marked by that problematic term is of value: indeed it turns out to be one way of locating and reinforcing the kinship between art and science.

### The Studio and the Laboratory

The notion of "genius" was, as we have noted, often linked to the unique individual rather than the collaborative team. This romantic conception of the creative loner remains active in the popular image of the artist, and has tended to obscure another key similarity between art and science: the usefulness of collective work and of trial and error, correction, and repetition.

Works like Vermeer's *The Artist in His Studio* (ca. 1665), or Rembrandt's painting of the same name (1629) may give the impression that the artist worked alone, and in a relatively circumscribed and private space. But studio masters like Raphael,

Rembrandt, and Rubens in fact maintained large establishments of assistants and apprentices, many of whom, of course, went on to become celebrated and successful artists with studios, students, and assistants of their own.

Raphael, who died at the early age of thirty-seven, had at one time at least fifty artists working in his studio in Rome, and his celebrity was ensured, even beyond the popes and men of letters who were his patrons, by the wide circulation of engravings after his paintings by Marcantonio Raimondi, who functioned in effect as his publicist. Rubens, who was a diplomat and court painter as well as a skillful man of business, spent a good deal of his time consulting with patrons and clients, in person and by letter. He employed so many pupils and artists in his workshop that, by his own reckoning, he "refused over one hundred" applicants, including relatives and friends. His best-known collaborators included Frans Snyders, Jacob Jordaens, and Anthony van Dyck, but not all his assistants were named in his correspondence with patrons. Francis Kelly quotes a description of a painting from Rubens's studio as "Original by my Hand except a most beautiful landscape, done by the hand of a master skilful [*sic*] in that department."[44] Clearly the collaborative nature of the artwork was not something about which the master was either reticent or defensive; this was how art was made. The price of a work might depend upon how much Rubens was in a genuine "Rubens," but the studio itself was a place for collaboration, creativity—and commerce.

We might note that Rubens, too, had his engraver-publicist. In fact the circulation of designs from his workshop was so widespread that he took legal steps to keep other engravers from imitating them. Collaborations were usually between senior and junior artists, but not always; Rubens and Jan Brueghel the Elder teamed up to paint a series of mythological and religious canvases in the early seventeenth century, with Rubens painting the figures and Brueghel the landscapes and the flora and fauna. The best known of these is a series on the five senses.

The artists cosigned at least one of these works, *The Garden of Eden with the Fall of Man*.[45]

A studio was, thus, both a workshop and a school. It was also, de facto, a laboratory, in all early senses of that word: a place where people worked, experimented, and designed and created their own tools and materials, from canvases to pigments to optical devices. From the time of Dürer through to the invention of photography—and, indeed, from ancient times to the present—artists tested out various ways of representing perspective, dimension, light, and space, using (and depicting) devices like mirrors, the camera obscura, the camera lucida, the so-called Claude glass (or black mirror), named after the landscape painter Claude Lorraine, the pantograph, and the graphic telescope.[46]

The similarities between the studio and the laboratory as places for experimentation and creativity have been marked and noted from at least the time of Francis Bacon, for whom what he called the "vexations of art" were part of the natural and experimental "histories of man." Bacon's *New Organon* contains a catalogue of 130 "Particular Histories" he has it in mind to write, or to commission, beginning with the History of the Heavenly Bodies and moving on through seasons, elements, substances, and species on the way to two final, speculative books on "numbers" and "figures" in pure mathematics. (Bacon notes scrupulously that these last two imagined books would properly be called "observations" rather than "experiments.") The "Histories of Man" would begin with the body, anatomy, humors, excrements, motions—voluntary and involuntary—sleep and dreams, food, conception, life and death, symptoms and disease, and so on. Here, suggestively in order, are numbers 64 through 78:

64. History of Drugs.
65. History of Surgery.
66. Chemical History of Medicines.
67. History of Vision, and of things Visible.
68. History of Painting, Sculpture, Modelling, etc.
69. History of Hearing and Sound.

70. History of Music.
71. History of Smell and Smells.
72. History of Taste and Tastes.
73. History of Touch, and the objects of Touch.
74. History of Venus, as a species of Touch.
75. History of Bodily Pains, as species of Touch.
76. History of Pleasure and Pain in general.
77. History of the Affections; as Anger, Love, Shame, etc.
78. History of the Intellectual Faculties; Reflection, Imagination, Discourse, Memory, etc.[47]

As you can see, Bacon integrates the histories of art and art-making into his speculations about drugs, surgery, the senses, the affections, and the intellectual faculties in ways that seem strikingly "modern," or indeed postmodern. Art is not a realm apart; it is of a piece with science and with psychology.

Furthermore, after the histories of cooking, baking, sugar, the dairy, barbers, gold, hemp, and thread, he returns to list more of what we might today call the "making" arts, categorizing them, interestingly, by material as much as by craft or practice:

96. History of Weaving, and the arts thereto belonging.
97. History of Dyeing.
98. History of Leather-making, Tanning, and the arts thereto belonging.
99. History of Ticking and Feathers.
100. History of working in Iron.
101. History of Stone-cutting.
102. History of the making of Bricks and Tiles.
103. History of Pottery.
104. History of Cements, etc.
105. History of working in Wood.
106. History of working in Lead.
107. History of Glass and all vitreous substances, and of Glass-making.
108. History of Architecture generally.

109. History of Wagons, Chariots, Litters, etc.
110. History of Printing, of Books, of Writing, of Sealing; of Ink, Pen, Paper, Parchment, etc.

And so on to wax, basketmaking, matmaking, agriculture, jugglers and mountebanks, artificial materials (enamel, porcelain, and so on), salts, machines, and "Common Experiments which have not grown into an Art."[48]

How exhilarating it must have been to compile this list, a Borgesian encyclopedia before its time.[49] But beyond the fertility of imagination we should pause to admire the linkages and associations that construe these as logically sequent—if as yet imaginary—histories. What these days are called "crafts" are interlinked with the practices that came, in the interval between Bacon's time and our own, to be regarded as the "fine," or more refined arts. Equally noteworthy is the interrelationship between art and the body; not only the brain and "cognition" but the materials of digestion, excretion, alimentation, and so on. Painting and sculpture are near neighbors to touch, smell, and taste, as well as to pleasure and pain. The materials of printed books—ink, paper, parchment—are cognate to the materials used by brickmakers, stonecutters, tanners, and glassmakers. The tenor (books, writing, sealing) comes immediately after the vehicle (wagons, chariots, litters). Here is a Renaissance wonder cabinet of ideas and associations, in which what we think of as "science" and what we think of as "art" are inextricably intertwined.

Art historian Svetlana Alpers notes that "the relationship between the practice of art and the practice of science is particularly striking in the seventeenth century, when the studio . . . come[s] into its own." Even though there were often many people in an artist's studio—assistants, servants, students, and so forth—the iconography of the artist in the studio is conventionally solitary: not a place of collaboration so much as a place of contemplation and isolated genius. What Alpers calls "the link studio/laboratory" allows for the consideration of painting as an *investigation*, and also, importantly, for the idea that the studio itself is not merely a place for, but an *instrument of*, art.

It is worth noting that the word "laboratory," describing a place set apart for conducting practical investigations in natural science, is far older, in English, than the word "studio," denoting a space for an artist's production of work. ("Laboratory," interestingly related to the verb "elaborate" as well as to "labor," dates from the early years of the seventeenth century; "studio," from the Italian word for a "study," the workplace for a scholar, does not appear until the Romantic period; the first instance in *OED*, from the *Edinburgh Review*, is 1819.) Laboratories, initially associated with chemistry and chemical transformations, were part of the mise en scène of the alchemist, a figure signally poised, in the literary and scientific imaginary, on the borderline between art and science: in the opening stage direction of Ben Jonson's 1616 masque *Mercury Vindicated*, the location is described as "a laboratory or alchemist's workhouse."

The humanities began actively to reappropriate the term in the middle of the twentieth century, with "language laboratory" (or, more usually, "language lab"), a room set apart with tape recordings or other facilities for oral practice, a coinage of the 1960s. The "media lab" is now a fixture on many campuses, a place for digital arts and technologies. MIT's famous media lab, which includes such consortia as "Things That Think," "Digital Life," the "Communications Futures Program," the "Center for Bits and Atoms," and a couple of special-interest groups, or SIGs (everything has an acronym) with witty titles: "Counter Intelligence," focused on developing a "digitally connected, self-aware kitchen," and "Gray Matters," concerned with computation and communication in the lives of older persons. If this sounds like science, not art, read on, and you'll see shortly what happens when the life sciences meet the art world.

Universities across the country now use the term "media lab" (sometimes "digital media lab") to describe places for working on images, animation, sound and video, and digital projects. These labs actively combine technology, art, and science, in effect performing the merger of studio and laboratory that had been implicit in art- and science-making for the last several decades. At Brown University the Multimedia Labs are multi-computer facilities dedicated to the production and analysis of work in the arts and humanities, generating graphics, hypertext, video, animation, and sound.[50] Audio and acoustic labs serve various scientific and aesthetic/cultural purposes—UCLA's Department of Ethnomusicology, for example, has a Music Perception and Cognition and Musical Acoustics Laboratory that includes a library of "mathematical, signal processing, programming and statistical software." Also located at UCLA is a new Art/Sci Center, founded to pursue and promote research programs that "demonstrate the potential of media arts and science collaborations," with the goal of addressing ethical, environmental, and social issues within scientific innovations, and fostering artistic projects that "respond to cutting-edge inventions and research."[51] In these laboratory settings, and others like them, the close conjunctions between art and science, artists and scientists, are being recognized and reestablished.

### The Artist as Scientist

There was a time when scientists were artists, or artists were scientists. Leonardo da Vinci is one celebrated example, but there are many others. Piero della Francesca was an important Renaissance mathematician as well one of his age's most famous painters. Vasari's *Lives* mentions Piero's many mathematical treatises, of which at least three survive. Piero's *On Perspective* was the first treatise to deal with the mathematics of perspective, a topic of interest to Giotto in the thirteenth century, and to Brunelleschi in the fifteenth. The sculptor Lorenzo Ghiberti, famous for the bronze doors on the baptistery in Florence, published a compilation of medieval texts on the theory of vision and optics. In Germany Albrecht Dürer was known as a mathematician as well as an artist. He was the author of the first serious mathematics book published in German.

In all eras artists have also been technicians, developing and refining—sometimes revolutionizing—the tools and materials (from paints to cameras) with which they make their art. The Impressionists famously profited from scientific investigations into the behavior of light, and also, equally importantly, from the invention of something as fundamental as the collapsible metal tube, devised in 1841 to replace the traditional leather bladder pouch. This simple but revolutionary device enabled artists to purchase their paints, already ground and mixed, from color merchants like the Impressionists' friend and patron Père Tanguy.[52] Other mid-nineteenth-century innovations, like portable easels and stools, and lightweight sketching support to replace heavy wood and canvas panels, made outdoor sketching feasible and convenient.[53] Eadweard Muybridge (born Edward James Muggeridge) developed studies of animal and human locomotion that influenced not only his own photographic series but also the nascent film industry, through such motion-picture pioneers as E. J. Marey, the Lumière Brothers, and Thomas Edison. Muybridge's invention, the "zoopraxiscope," was able to simulate or recreate the illusion of movement by showing individual photographs in rapid succession, and his photographs of horses, ostriches, and nude athletes in motion have become modern icons. His eleven-volume work, *Animal Locomotion* (1887), was written at the University of Pennsylvania, where Muybridge's stay was facilitated by the support of the painter Thomas Eakins.

Harold Edgerton, an electrical engineer at MIT, invented in 1931 a technique for "ultra-high-speed and stop-action photography," allowing him to take pictures of objects in high speed as if they were stopped in time. Egerton's astonishing photograph of a drop of milk, entitled "Coronet," was featured in the Museum of Modern Art's first photography exhibit in 1937. Awarded the National Medal of Science by President Richard Nixon, Edgerton is also the inventor of the stroboscope, better known to today's club audiences as a "strobe."

Among twentieth-century sculptors, we might consider Richard Serra, whose works use materials like fiberglass, rubber, lead, and steel, and Robert Smithson, whose "earthworks," like the 1970 *Spiral Jetty* in the Great Salt Lake, reshaped the physical environment. For a work called *Double Negative*, completed in 1969, sculptor Michael Heizer blasted away 240,000 tons of rock in Nevada to produce a 1,500-foot-long, 50-foot-deep, 30-foot-wide chasm. The work thus pointed to negative space—space created by the displacement of earth and rock—and spoke to the question of how empty space could be seen as art. *Double Negative* is owned by the Museum of Contemporary Art, Los Angeles, and is "accessible for four-wheel drive vehicle." Heizer's present project, called *City*, is far larger even than *Double Negative*. Made of "mounds, pits, passageways, plazas and ramps," one and a quarter miles long and more than a quarter of a mile wide—a huge work of earth art that has taken him thirty-two years thus far to develop, and is not yet close to completion. In its substantiality and permanency, Heizer's *City* is appropriately contrasted by art critic Michael Kimmelman to the deliberately impermanent sculptural projects of Christo and Jeanne-Claude, who surrounded islands in Florida with pink woven polypropylene, wrapped the Reichstag for fourteen days, and whose saffron *Gates* were installed—and then de-installed—in New York's Central Park.[54] All such artworks take years to conceive, design, and execute, and cost millions of dollars.

Art-making is always in part concerned with the evolution of new materials, their limits and capacities. Thus fresco painting demanded a certain technology in order that the pigments would bond with the surface; developments in lithography, photography, acrylics, and digital technology all changed what was regarded as a "work of art." The scientific field known as "Strength of Materials," a staple of engineering, was crucial to changing concepts of sculpture.

Contemporary art-making, with its increasing reliance upon technology, digitization, and expensive machinery, has perhaps brought art and science closer than at any time since the Renaissance—even in the studio. Just to give one example, the C&C machine developed by Cybersculpture and Co. creates three-dimensional artworks from an artist's computer-aided design in 3-D, and has greatly changed the practice of sculpture and of conceptual art. Each of these machines costs over $100,000, and the objects they produce are physical artifacts, often of great size and technical perfection. (The C&C machine, an apparatus for making computer sculpture, was designed by a team of four: an artist and engineer, a writer and multimedia artist, an engineer and technical consultant, and a computer scientist.)[55] This is the kind of machine you might expect to find in a lab, rather than in an artist's studio. Certainly the price tag, while it might not raise eyebrows for a science dean, would strike a dean of humanities as astronomical. Digital arts have become commonplace in all artistic studio practice, and computer-generated artwork is now the rule rather than the exception in fields like architecture.

## The Scientist as Artist

Despite these correspondences, the connections between the sciences and the creative and performing arts have remained to a certain extent under the radar when it comes to institutional support. But this is beginning to change. And interestingly, the changes are often being effected from within departments of science, technology, or social science, rather than departments of art. Here are two examples, the first concerned with the neurophysiology of vision, the second with what is called bioart.

### SEEING OR BELIEVING

In a number of departments of psychology, an interest in brain science and "cognitive" approaches have succeeded, and superseded, the "psychology of art" investigations of earlier scholars like Rudolf Arnheim and Ernst Gombrich, for whom the "perceptual" and the holistic were central concerns. Issues like figure/ground and the famous "duck-rabbit" visual experiment underscored the way perceptions change as the mind seeks to organize and make "sense" of what we think we see. Max Wertheimer, who is credited with coining the term "gestalt," bought a toy stroboscope at the Frankfurt train station, and noted that he "saw" motion when in fact what was there was a rapid series of discrete sensory events. This phi phenomenon, as it was called, is also what makes "motion pictures" seem to move. But attention has now shifted from these perceptual issues to the question of how the brain participates in marking out the visual field.

"I am a neurophysiologist," explains Margaret Livingstone in the preface to *Vision and Art: The Biology of Seeing.* "I spend my time investigating why some nerve cells in our visual systems are sensitive to color whereas others are not. In the process I have become particularly interested in something that artists have been aware of for a very long time: that color and luminance (or lightness) carry different kinds of visual information."[56] Livingstone is one of several distinguished scholarly investigators currently at work on the relationship between art and science.

From the time of Zeuxis, and then of Alberti, questions of visual illusion and perspective have brought the science of seeing into the world of the artist. As we have already noted, ancient, medieval, and Renaissance painters were, of necessity and by predilection, inventors and scientific investigators. Dürer's woodcuts of a *Draftsman Drawing a Vase* (1525) and a *Draftsman Drawing a Reclining Nude* (ca. 1527) illustrate, as Livingstone points out, the same technique recommended by Leonardo da Vinci for making a two-dimensional drawing of a three-dimensional scene: "Position yourself two-thirds of an arm's length from a piece of glass and mark on the glass what you see beyond."[57]

Nobel Prize winner David Hubel underscores the nature of this work and its relevance to art-making: "In the future, visual neurobiology will enhance art in much the same way as a knowledge of bones and muscles has for centuries enhanced the ability of artists to portray the human body." Hubel makes the central point very clearly from the point of view of neurobiology: "[B]y understanding what goes on in our brains when we look at a work of art we can hope to deepen our appreciation of both the art and the science. That the two are so separated is an artificial product of the way our knowledge is subdivided in academic circles."[58]

## BioArt

One of the most recent and striking developments in the edgy world of art is the movement known as bioart or wetware, in which artists use the materials of life itself—cell lines, plants, animals, bacteria—as the medium in and through which they work. Here art and science—and sometimes artists and scientists—arc closely allied. Joe Davis, a sculptor often regarded as a key figure in American bioart, has worked alongside the biophysicist Alexander Rich at the Massachusetts Institute of Technology. In one of Davis's projects, he encoded a sixty-character fragment of a Greek text by Heraclitus into the white-eye gene of a fruit fly. In another, he encoded on the DNA of a strain of *E. Coli* the message "I am the riddle of life. Know me and you will know yourself."[59] Other bioartists who have achieved visibility in this field include Eduardo Kac, a "transgenic artist" who began in performance and visual poetry. Kac's transgenic artwork, *GPF Bunny*, included "the creation of a green fluorescent rabbit, the public dialogue created by the project, and the social integration of the rabbit." ("GPF" stands for "green fluorescent protein," isolated by scientists in the early 1990s and modified in the laboratory.) "Transgenic art," Kac explains, is "a mode of genetic inscription that is at once inside and outside of the operational realm of molecular biology, negotiating the terrain between science and culture."[60]

The Tissue Culture and Art Project at the University of Western Australia, with the participation of artist Oron Catts, is exploring what it calls a "new class of object/being—that of the

Semi-Living," that is, "parts of complex organisms which are sustained alive outside the body and coerced to grow in predetermined shapes." Among their projects have been *Victimless Leather—A Prototype of Stitchless Jacket Grown in a Technoscientific "Body," Pig Wings Project*, and *Biofeel*, an installation that featured what were called *Art(ificial) Wombs*. Exhibitions connected with these semiliving projects have been shown throughout the United States and in Europe as well as in Australia. Oron Catts, the cofounder and artistic director of SymbioticA, the first art and biology lab situated in a science department, was formerly a research fellow with the Tissue Engineering and Organ Fabrication Laboratory at the Massachusetts General Hospital (2000–2001). The *Pig Wings Project* was shown at the DeCordova Museum in Lincoln, Massachusetts, outside Boston, as part of the Boston CyberArts Festival, thus crossing over, in terms of its performative genre, from the laboratory to the museum/exhibition/display space.

"Bioart," noted Randy Kennedy in the *New York Times*, "represents a logical next step in contemporary art, which has eagerly embraced new approaches and nontraditional materials: video and computers beginning in the 1960's and 70's, digital technology and the Internet in the 90's."[61] But the bioconnection, especially in an era understandably spooked by bioterrorism, is both more direct and, potentially, more dangerous.

The group called the Critical Art Ensemble made headlines when artist Steven Kurtz was arrested on charges of mail and wire fraud in connection with a biological laboratory that grew and mailed bacterial cultures. The Critical Art Ensemble, a group of five artist-activists, proposed something called "fuzzy biological sabotage" (*fuzzy* here denoting legal ambiguity rather than cuddliness or G. W. Bush's "fuzzy math"). Some of the potential violations here have to do with the sharing of living samples, and with safety and ethics. Members have preferred to describe themselves not as artists—whom they see as catering to a luxury market in objects—but rather as "tactical media practitioners."[62] For example, Beatriz da Costa, who has worked with Critical Art Ensemble, uses robot technology in her art practice, and currently teaches at UC Irvine in the graduate program of Art, Computation, and Engineering (a nice combination), is described as an "Interdisciplinary Artist and Tactical Media Practitioner."

So some real action is happening to bring together arts practices and science practices. These enterprises, however small or big they are, require lablike spaces, and function interactively across the disciplines. But what is needed for the future is a far more extensive set of collaborative endeavors, with the appropriate level of funding, and other basic resources, whether of materials, personnel, or space.

In the nineteenth century the word "scientist" was created on the model of the preexisting word "artist."[63] Now it may be time to recreate the "artist" on the model of the scientist, with art laboratories, expensive and delicate equipment, and an atmosphere that encourages, recognizes, and rewards collaborative work. Patrons of science—and they are many, from government to business to foundations and individuals—are often, already, also patrons of the arts. The connections between and among both kinds of makers, and both kinds of patrons, can and should be strengthened, with mutual profit to each, and considerable benefit to the public, and the world. Art can be the science of tomorrow—as it was, indeed, the science of yesterday, and of thousands of years, from Zeuxis to Leonardo.

# 5

---

## THE UNIVERSITY AS PATRON

*My lord, you played once i' th' university, you say?*
—HAMLET

WHERE, then, should patronage of the arts reside today? The first answer is the easiest and most uncritical one—everywhere. Public, private, corporate, local, governmental—there seems no reason to discourage funding, or patronage, wherever it emerges, or wherever it happens, for residual, historical, or contingent reasons, to be located at present. But "everywhere" is also "nowhere." If the oft-cited Medici example, or the Victorian philanthropy model, or the captains of industry as founders of museums and libraries, or the federal and national agencies for the arts, or any other predominant support mechanism, have each had their moments of glory and their moments of blockage, what do the times now require, or invite, as a new way of configuring these goals?

What does it mean to educate the public to assess (and "consume") new and unfamiliar art in any of its generic forms? What is the place of the scholar in this volatile mix of dealer, artist, reviewer, gallery owner, museum board, collector, donor, and the elusive "public"? Art in universities is often what business calls a "loss-leader," that is, something put on sale at a non-profit-making price in order to attract buyers of other articles, or, in this case, other programs. A college or university can advertise its dance or theater or musical groups, or its art classes and art gallery, with handsome photos on the Web site and in the brochure, while at the same time reserving the major fund-raising efforts and major donors for science laboratories, international affairs, or engineering.

Even when a significant number of courses are offered in painting, sculpture, photography, filmmaking, creative writing, theater, and musical performance, many scholars and academic administrators remain uneasy with these elements of the curriculum. How can creative artists be judged by "tenurable" standards, they ask. Never mind that artists of all kinds regularly compete for grants, for entry into juried shows, for top-of-the-line galleries and publishing imprints, and for places—and prizes—in film festivals. And would an artist with tenure stop being a top-flight artist and become instead a pedagogue, a coach, a mentor? The same kind of catch-22 that affects the notion of patronage and patronizing also affects the reception of creative artists on the faculty. If they were really the best, doubters ask, why would they need to teach? (Here the market tells at least part of the tale: there are paying clients for the works of certain novelists and for certain painters, fewer clients for even the most highly regarded poets and conceptual artists, which is why universities and colleges can often snare very distinguished practitioners of both groups for faculty hires.)

Increasingly, however, artists are being tenured, and greater numbers of students are interested in making and performing art as well as studying the histories of the arts. Distinguished poets, novelists, and playwrights have long been tenured in English departments, but theater professionals who are directors and actors rather than writers are increasingly tenured at major institutions—as are dancers as well as dance historians, composers as well as musicologists. I am speaking here largely of liberal-arts institutions, not specifically of academies, art schools, conservatories, or other places dedicated to professional training in the arts.

It is also important to emphasize that more and more art-making these days, like more and more science-making, is a collaborative undertaking. I say "these days," but—as we have noted—the making of art, whether in craft, portraiture, landscape painting, architecture, sculpture, or, indeed, playwriting, was often (or "always already") collaborative, involving studio assistants, specialists, fabricators, coauthors, actors rewriting roles, and painters whose métier was the depiction of hands, animals, dead game, putti, or distant hills. The idea of the solitary artist, a useful but not exclusive or exhaustive category inherited from a previous century, has to a certain extent obscured the fundamental issues of experiment, collaboration, and investigation—formal, theoretical, material—that are far more typical of art practice at the present time.[1]

As the modern (or postmodern, or post-postmodern) university tries to reevaluate its role in a world at once more redundantly "global" and more culturally fragmented than at any time in recent history, wrestling at once with issues of basic education and of professional and preprofessional training, the arts may, surprisingly, be in a position to supply the missing piece that holds this edifice together. The stone that the builders rejected may become the cornerstone. What are the possible opportunities here for re-imagining the shape and scope of higher education? How might rethinking the place of the arts within the university, and concurrently the notion of "patronage," break down entrenched prejudices and resistances? The question, once again, is that of how best to "patronize" the arts.

### The Visual Intellectual

We are now in an era of what could be called the "visual intellectual." Students on college campuses and members of the general public flock to hear—and see—addresses by filmmakers, artists, and performers. When the Spanish cinema director Pedro Almodóvar came to Harvard University for an advertised "conversation" with students and movie buffs, the crowd was so enormous that the large lecture hall was jammed to overflowing. Restive attendees, many of whom had traveled long distances for this event, protested against police attempts to limit the seating because of the fire code. A crisis was averted by the decision to hold the event twice, allowing a second huge crowd to fill the hall as soon as the first crowd exited. Likewise, when artist Ed Ruscha spoke at the Carpenter Center for the Visual Arts, more than four hundred disappointed would-be audience members were turned away (and promptly fired off email notes suggesting that the organizers should have changed the venue). On a campus where there are many distinguished lectures in a variety of topics nightly, this was an unusually high response. A similar situation obtained a few weeks later, when the featured speaker was Maya Lin. Again literally hundreds of people were unable to get seats in the lecture hall, which accommodates just under three hundred.

Stars of visual art and culture regularly pack audiences for intellectual events. Where a decade or two ago it might have been Jacques Derrida who was the big draw ("a philosopher with a celebrity status equal to that of a rock star"),[2] and before that, say, a poet like T. S. Eliot, today it is more likely to be someone like Almodóvar, or Martin Scorsese, or Yvonne Rainer, or Christo and Jeanne-Claude, or Art Spiegelman. Derrida and Lacanian-Slovenian philosopher Slavoj Žižek have reappeared as film stars, featured in "adoring and adorable"[3] (or "complex and highly ambitious")[4] documentaries that present their philosophical work through visual as well as verbal encounters. Like cultural life in general, intellectual life has become infused with visuality, with looking as well as with listening. I think it is not—as the authors of the NEA study *Reading at Risk* contend—that we are less literary or literate as a society, so much as that cultural attention, and cultural primacy, have shifted to encompass installation, technology, the moving image, and performance. Phrases like "visual literacy," "aural literacy," "digital literacy," and "media literacy" are increasingly common.

The portmanteau word "starchitect," coined, it appears, in the early part of the twenty-first century to reflect the new attention on high-end real-estate projects with visual and cultural bling, is a fair indicator of the celebrity status now accorded to figures like Frank Gehry, Richard Meier, Michael Graves, Daniel Libeskind, and Enrique Norten. Sydney Pollack's film, *Sketches of Frank Gehry*, a conversation between filmmaker and architect, was described as a "seductive documentary" that resembles "a Gehry building itself, all brash, eye-catching, a tad vain, and attractively neurotic,"[5] while Gehry himself was characterized as "a lovable acclaimed architect,"[6] "an iconoclastic genius,"[7] "an artistic giant,"[8] and a "cheerful, energetic, self-deprecating man"[9] with "considerable charm and infectious enthusiasm."[10] Today the popular image of the architect is not the rough-and-ready loner of Ayn Rand's novel *The Fountainhead*, but instead a hypercivilized, elegant, cosmopolitan artist cum business magnate, whose most recognizable professional attribute is a pair of outsized eyeglasses. Le Corbusier's famous black spectacles, appropriately called "owlish," set the trend, and were copied by Philip Johnson in 1934. "Architect glasses" (available in your local Lenscrafters) now distinguish such trendsetters as Daniel Libeskind, Ken Smith, Rafael Viñoly, and Gordon Kipping.[11] In effect these eyeglasses have replaced the stereotypical artist's beret or the cloak and floppy hat of an earlier era. They are the half-ironic, half-knowing "visual" signature of a certain kind of "visual intellectual."

At the same time, theoretical developments in the humanities have also inflected contemporary art. Artists like Hans Haacke and Mark Dion regularly deal with issues and processes of art-making, politics, and art display in their work in ways that would be familiar to, and congruent with, current humanities scholarship.[12] Mark Tansey uses structuralism and poststructuralism actively in his work, commenting on thinkers from Hegel to Merleau-Ponty and Derrida. Some of his titles—*Derrida Queries De Man*, for example, or *Robbe-Grillet Cleansing Every Object in Sight*, or *Bridge Over the Cartesian Gap* (1990)—make it clear how much he is engaged with, and amused by, developments in contemporary literature, philosophy, and theory.[13] Tansey's *Close Reading*, from 1990, shows a young woman climbing a rock, and trying to decipher, close-up, the text of which the rock is formed. Another work of the same year, *Under Erasure*, is a waterfall cascading over a cliff made of text; the title refers to

Derrida's theoretical term *sous rature,* "under erasure," a concept borrowed from Heidegger: to write a word and cross it out, leaving both the word and the deletion, to indicate the imprecision, but the inevitable ghostly presence, of a term. In these cases the visual both critiques and also advances the theoretical turn. It is "theory," broadly conceived, that links these works. Theory, in this case, is an art practice.

As we have regularly noted, innovations by individuals in the arts have gone hand in hand with innovations in technology. In a digital age, the arts have more need than ever of connections, global and local, and also of expensive, delicate, and complicated tools and equipment. When the need for high-end equipment and money is combined with the need for more space and the acknowledgment of the importance of collaborative work, the result is a blueprint for something I will call—borrowing a formulation from developments in science—"Big Art."

## *Big Art*

What has come to be known since World War II as Big Science, the development of modes of scientific research that employ hundreds of scientists and vast amounts of funding, might serve as a model for a new national commitment to the creative and performing arts. The time may have come for Big Art (and indeed Big Humanities) to become more visible, better funded, and more imaginatively and collaboratively structured, housed, and managed in partnerships that engage government, business, private foundations, the university, and interested individuals.

The term "Big Science" gained currency with the increase in enormous (and enormously expensive) projects like the Superconducting Supercollider, controlled fusion, and Star Wars, to cite three of many examples from the mid to late twentieth century. Teams of high-energy physicists, astronomers, mathematicians, and engineers, each team numbering perhaps hundreds of players, work together on a single project. Collaborative efforts involving scientists from a variety of nations, each with their own scientific culture, changed the way research inquiry functioned. Whether in conjunction with industry and the military, or resolutely independent of them, large-scale science initiatives, funded by universities, think tanks, government, and commercial and private enterprises, tackled problems in new ways and began to think of funding in millions and even billions of dollars.[14]

Universities like MIT, Stanford, CalTech, and Berkeley, to name only a few, have readily invested in Big Science laboratories, faculties, and research programs. As Harvard's provost, Steven Hyman, explained in announcing an architectural competition to build a 500,000-square-foot research complex for science and technology, traditional disciplinary scientific practice "is being complemented by a new style of science that is interdisciplinary, involves larger groups of scientists, often involves large shared tools, and needs new kinds of space."[15]

A similar attention to open, collaborative spaces for art-making, with natural light, high ceilings, flexible flooring (for dance and other performance activities) and acoustical sophistication, state-of-the-art technology and technicians, and spaces for encounters and improvisation across art practices would go far in transforming the sense of the arts as central to the idea of a university.

Needless to say, scientists have patrons too, and from the same sources—government, business, and foundations.[16] These patrons underwrite research with certain ends in mind, and with a close eye on outcomes: drug trials, AIDS research, "abstinence only" policies, and so on. The university, eager for funding, is not always a disinterested host, and the sums involved are considerable, whether from NSF, NIH, NASA, or privately owned labs, clinics, pharmaceutical companies, or other interested parties.[17] The utility of science to do good in the world is an *interested instrumentality*, a function of the kinds of outcomes being sought as well as the open quest for knowledge. From the Manhattan Project to the present day, these ethical issues have been part of the process of patronized scientific research, always to be weighed by individuals and by host institutions. The fact that there are now entire journals and centers—as well as professorships—concerned with bioethics should be another indication that monitoring the desires of patrons and funding sources is part of the everyday life of anyone who receives external support for the creative and inventive work they do.

If Big Science is one kind of model for future patronage of the arts, another might be Big Sports. Here the affinities are quite different, but the energies of institutional investment are comparably high. Sports, like the arts, are ostensibly an "enrichment" (in the case of high-profile team sports, often in two senses) and not envisaged as at the center of university learning. But in terms of funding, recruitment, emoluments, space, and prestige, sports are integral to American university and college life.[18] Alumni boosters and booster-clubs—the "patrons" of these endeavors—get significant tax write-offs: up to 80 percent deductions on contributions to university sports programs.[19] For football, baseball, and basketball players, and indeed for athletes in a wide range of team and individual sports, many programs offer what is, in effect, preprofessional training and scholarship aid packages.

Upward of ten Division I-A universities pay football and basketball coaches a combined $3 million a year.[20] Nick Saban was hired by the University of Alabama to become the highest-paid college coach in history, with an eight-year contract worth some $32 million, prompting some to speculate on whether the next step was "paychecks for [college] athletes."[21] Compare this to the salaries of university presidents, just as a yardstick. The chancellor of the University of Texas system, for example, earns $693,677, less than a third of what the UT-Austin football coach is paid (the coach also has a much cooler Web site).

The presidents of Vanderbilt University and Boston University each make over a million dollars, but they are in the distinct minority, according to a survey from the *Chronicle of Higher Education*.[22]

From the athletes who are heavily recruited, to the general undergraduate population, often viewed as alumni-in-training, the emphasis at these universities has tipped toward sports as a lure.[23] College applicants are attracted by what has become known in the admissions trade as the Flutie Factor, named for quarterback Doug Flutie, whose prowess on the football field—and success in the media—led to a rise in applications to his alma mater, Boston College.[24]

On today's college and university campuses, museums, theaters, film, dance, music, and contemporary fiction and poetry all have their own "fans" and aficionados, and many have exhibition or performance venues, improvised or established. But they are no match for the lavish outlay and institutional attention afforded to competitive sports teams. Here too—as with science—the issue is not some imagined "parity." Nonetheless, there should be something appealing to alumni and donors, as well as to the public, in showcasing theater and dance, painting and sculpture, film and video, orchestras and chamber-music groups at the university and college level (could we call this the "flute factor"?). From presidents and chancellors to development officers, there is room for leadership on this question. Patrons are made, not born, and the priorities a university sets can be communicated to its members, whether they are current or former students, faculty, or longtime donors.

Large gifts from individuals, like the one that Peter B. Lewis provided for Princeton University, or those currently being sought by the Stanford Institute for Creativity and the Arts, are not the only way that universities and colleges can expand their arts programming or raise the profile—and the stakes—for the arts. Public and regional universities and colleges have also taken advantage of opportunities and adjacencies to begin new initiatives.

The University of Michigan, led first by Lee Bollinger and then by Mary Sue Coleman, has brought the Royal Shakespeare Company to Ann Arbor for three-week residencies. Members of the company interact with the university community, and the wider Detroit area, in Shakespeare performances, workshops, panel discussions, and master classes. The 2006 season featured three plays—*Julius Caesar, Antony and Cleopatra,* and *The Tempest*—in an exclusive U.S. engagement; only in Ann Arbor would the company be presenting these productions. Detroit is a strong art and music city, with an institute of art, a museum of new art, a symphony orchestra, and the roots of Motown, Detroit Techno, and jazz. But the importation of one of the world's great Shakespeare companies, for three weeks of the year, gave the university a chance to raise its profile as a patron of classic theater. When Bollinger moved to Columbia University, he worked to connect the university with local communities as well as with the New York art world, participating with NYU's president, John Sexton, in a symposium titled The Role of the Arts at a Research University, sponsored by NYU's Tisch School of the Arts, and copartnering with the University of Michigan to bring RSC's production of *Midnight's Children* to the Apollo Theater in Harlem.

Another traveling Shakespeare company, the Shenandoah Shakespeare Express (SSE), begun in Virginia in the late 1980s and supported by local and by NEH Funding, has visited schools and colleges across the country, in Canada, and in the United Kingdom. In 2000 SSE, renaming its educational entity the American Shakespeare Center, joined forces with Mary Baldwin College in Staunton, Virginia, to develop a master's program for Shakespeare in performance.

Money makes things easier, no question. But the issue here is also one of imagination and commitment. Urban universities and colleges have partnership and residency options with local museums, theaters, troupes, and individual artists. Small colleges, branch campuses of universities, and institutions dependent upon state legislatures for authorization, assessment, and funding, can find—as many already have—that the arts attract new supporters.

I have been suggesting that one important and significantly under-regarded place for the patronage of the arts is the college or university. In this account of what could be called "patronage and its discontents," we have considered the modern history of patronage in U.S. (and British) government, business, and corporate philanthropy, and then the assymetrical situation of arts funding vis-à-vis funding for the sciences, and the category mistake by which the arts have been linked with the histories of art rather than with the making activities that characterize the sciences. But perhaps this is the moment to set out, more schematically and emphatically, the reasons why arts patronage by the university would make sense, and how it might be accomplished.

The arts and culture are the foundation of what used to be called a liberal (that is, a free-minded) education. This should properly include not only the histories of the various arts, as represented by departments of English, or music, or the history of art, but also the question of practice, of art-making, whether the art in question is writing, or printmaking, or dance, or theatrical production. That makers of art should be housed in universities, at the undergraduate, graduate, research, and teaching levels, is as reasonable, natural, and logical as that the university should contain and nurture other makers: engineers, or chemists, or applied mathematicians. And like those other makers, artists, no matter what arts they practice, need space, materials, training, and assessment, as well as a tolerance of imagination, "genius," stubborn dedication, or eccentricity.

Universities are already accustomed to managing grants from government, industry, and private sources. As I have noted, this is one of the many homologies between art-making and the sciences, homologies that are often obscured by the romantic description of the arts as cultural enrichment, moral guides, or recreational activities to fill leisure time and what is now increasingly called "lifelong learning." With relatively little adjustment, federal and state funding for the arts, and funding offered by foundations and private individuals, could be channeled (still competitively) through the university, just as is the case with soft money in the sciences or computational social sciences. A glance at a single month's grants from the National Science Foundation makes it clear how much various research projects, from physics to genomes to statistics, are dependent upon small and large government grants. Even the smallest of these grants often compares quite favorably to the funds available to individual artists. Bigger, collaborative arts enterprises, like theatrical companies, dance companies, art museums, and so forth are often—but far from always—independent of university affiliations. But where such affiliations do exist, there may already be models for cooperation between the university and grantors.

For better or for worse, universities are full of experts. In a book called *Academic Instincts*, I had something to say about the uneasy and sometimes risible relationship between expertise as it is understood in the media (journalism, television, and so forth) and the academic scholar. Importantly, though, however we might choose to describe the practice of researchers, analysts, and critics, it is the expertise of such scholars that makes a university a university. And when proposals are vetted for funding, it is often to experts like these that they will, in the ordinary course of things, be sent. College and university professors, and administrators, and curators are used to assess proposals competitively, both for their historical context (is it innovative? does it come out of a tradition or a movement? what is at stake?) and for their boundary-breaking potential. So routing arts funding via either government or private foundation grants through institutions of higher learning is making use of the evaluative systems that are already in use: the same people, the same kinds of reports, and in many cases, presumably, the same outcomes.

Universities and colleges are pledged to a doctrine of "academic freedom" that, if actually put in practice, protects the innovations of artists and performers as much as it does scientists or political theorists. Under the heading of "Academic Freedom in Artistic Expression" the American Association of University Professors laid out its principles clearly:

> Faculty and students engaged in the creation and presentation of works of the visual and performing arts are engaged in pursuing the mission of the university as much as are those who write, teach, and study in other academic disciplines. Works of the visual and performing arts are important both in their own right and because they can enhance our experience and understanding of social institutions and the human condition. Artistic expression in the classroom, studio, and workshop therefore merits the same assurance of academic freedom that is accorded to other scholarly and teaching activities. Since faculty and student artistic presentations to the public are integral to their teaching, learning, and scholarship, these presentations no less merit protection.[25]

Colleges and universities should feel they have a stake in trying to attract young artists—and young people who might someday be artists—rather than losing them to conservatories, dance academies, or art schools. Just as technical schools for other, often scientific activities exist side by side with universities capacious enough to include those activities, so specialized training for artists should find a home within, and not just on the boundaries of institutions of higher learning. The benefits of this are manifest for both the institution and the artist, but there is also a corollary benefit to students (and faculty) who are not aspiring professionals in these fields, but who wish to have an opportunity to study, practice, and experiment in them.

Inevitably there will be crossovers: some who thought they wanted a life in art-making will choose something else, and others who had no idea this was their goal will develop a passion for one or another of the arts. Some arts, like dance and music, are like mathematics, in that giftedness in the field is often detected early. Segregating these populations fosters the idea that real artists avoid the university in favor of either specialized training or "real life" experience.

Finally, the university or college as patron of the arts—not only in undergraduate and graduate training, BFA and MFA degrees, and collaborative practices like performances and exhibitions, but also in the developing of art museums and cultural centers, performing and practice spaces, cinematheques and exhibition halls—can help to reverse the trend toward thinking of the arts as a recreational ("extracurricular") activity rather than a serious and arduous career. There is an irony in the fact that the other major extracurricular activity on most college campuses, competitive sports, is often extremely well funded, supplied with strongly courted recruits and highly compensated coaches, and with state-of-the-art facilities. How might the arts participate not only in the prestige of the sciences but also in the very different but comparable prestige of the athletic program, a culture with donors and patrons aplenty, even if they are often called boosters and fans?

Some schools, like Yale and Bard, have been successful in persuading alumni and other donors to support arts facilities and arts programs; a few, like Washington University and Stanford, are building major new structures to house these expanded programs. Many state and private universities, and perhaps especially many small colleges, have developed dance and theater programs with enviable facilities and strong student and alumni backing. But all the forces that have gone into making the story of arts patronage through the ages—wealthy individuals, passionately concerned mentors, national pride, rising arts consciousness among the middle class and across ethnic, social, and gender lines—find a natural and powerful home in the university, where freedom of expression, the toleration of difference, and the high value placed on originality and imagination have defined the very purpose and essence of the institution.

Let me be clear that it is not my intention to advocate for the university *instead of* private philanthropy, galleries and museums, or government programs—federal, state, or local—as the best or most suitable patron of the arts. There is plenty of work to go around, and plenty of space for patronage and collaboration. As I have said from the start, the testy and contested relations among artists, patrons, and the viewing public is part of the story of art, not so much a problem as a lively condition of existence. Nor, in suggesting that universities and colleges are among the most promising patrons of the arts for the present and future, am I proposing that this will "solve" the problem of arts patronage and its discontents. For one thing, we cherish our discontents and will relinquish them only with the greatest reluctance. A university is not a paradise devoid of influence from donors, political factions, and prejudicial or interested beliefs. Donors have been known to withdraw large gifts if they are not satisfied with either the progress, or the nature, of their implementation. But nonetheless the world sometimes sardonically known as "academia" has rules, practices, expectations, and standards that make it potentially hospitable to experimentation and even to transgression (aka, "pushing the envelope," or "thinking outside the box") in the service of intellectual, scientific, and artistic work. Artists have, in fact, been thinking outside the box—the white box of the museum gallery, the black box of the cinematheque—for a long time now.

If there is a problem to solve here, it is at least in part one of academic culture—the besetting ambivalence toward the arts as serious modes of practice that belong within the curriculum of a liberal arts education. The growth of "colleges of the arts" and of programs in performance and in creative writing, while they may seem to give lie to the idea of ambivalence, in fact, in my view, may sometimes underscore it, by setting the arts and creative work apart from the scholarly, critical, and investigative work of institutions of higher learning. Such schools—at the graduate level, as conservatories, as summer programs—do vital work. Again, this is not an either-or situation. But we should not segregate or outsource the arts on the grounds that they do not fit within university goals, schedules, priorities, or practices. The liberal arts and sciences can learn from artists and from art practice, even as they learn from scientists and scientific methods. Moreover, if business schools, law schools, and medical schools can learn from practitioners (and gladly welcome them as adjuncts, professors of the practice, or clinical professors), there is a real opportunity here for "arts and sciences" colleges to collaborate with artists and performers, and to consider adjusting their schedules and credit-granting structures to accommodate the ways the arts are practiced, exhibited, and evaluated. On an extremely practical level I would suggest, among other things, that efforts be made to underwrite free admission to all arts events on campus for registered students. A cultural education in contemporary arts is available through these experiences as well as in the classroom, and it is, incidentally, one of the best investments an institution can make. Today's patron attendee is potentially tomorrow's patron of the arts.

But, as we have had occasion to note, art-making, whether in studio or onstage, has often been considered *extracurricular*; both a high-culture avocation and a messy, hard-to-evaluate hands-on activity. To make the arts a meaningful part of the standard university and college curriculum would require new and expensive spaces and materials, faculty members dedicated to these fields, and—equally challenging—a rethinking of academic *work*. But of course this was once true also of training in the applied sciences, relegated to specialized institutions: polytechnics or institutes of technology, engineering schools. Today excellence in the sciences is the proudest boast of many liberal arts institutions, an excellence backed—as, again, we have seen—by substantial funding for professors, laboratories, space, and graduate students.

The making and performing arts are in themselves *polytechnics*, a word that literally means "many arts." Technical and vocational, mechanical (and increasingly digitized) as well as aesthetic, these art practices are at the same time insistently conceptual, theoretical, and, as is often said to their detriment, political—a word that seems out of place only if one believes that art is not part of society and culture, but somehow above (or perhaps beneath) such mundane considerations. Far from being extracurricular, the arts, touching at once on science, social science, and humanities, are properly at the center of any curriculum.

## The Paradox of the Artist

My argument began with the paradox of patronage. Let me end with a few words about the paradox of the artist. For just as the paradox I proposed about the ambivalent status of the patron can be explored within the double meaning of a key word, "patronize," where one of its senses is in productive tension with the other, the same can be seen to be the case with the paradox of the artist. Here the productive tension can be located within the double meaning of the word "work."

In *The Human Condition* Hannah Arendt distinguishes between labor and work as human activities, describing labor as "the activity which corresponds to the biological process of the human body," and work as "the activity which corresponds to the unnaturalness of human existence, which is not imbedded in, and whose mortality is not compensated by, the species' ever-recurring life cycle."[26] "Work" is the term by which she denotes the achievements of both science and art. But do these "unnatural" creative processes, science and art, produce useful effects? Or is art, in contradistinction to science, constitutively useless? What is the relationship between work and works?

Arendt argues that in the classical period the Greeks expressed contempt for artisans and art-making, including sculpture and architecture, because in these arts and crafts "men work with instruments and do something not for its own sake but in order to produce something else." The historic ambivalence about art is, she contends, directly linked to this (unanswerable) question of use and uselessness, work and works, fabrication and what Arendt calls "worldliness." And in modern life, "the ideal of usefulness permeating a society of craftsmen," she suggests, "is actually no longer a matter of utility but of meaning."[27]

The paradox of the artist is the paradox of human agency in the making of something that takes on a life of its own. Whether it is a film, a play, a photograph, a painting, an installation, a ballet, or a symphony, the artwork will grow and change over time, as it is interpreted, presented, and experienced. The patron supports the work; the collector acquires it; the institution houses or presents it. But the work always escapes. It escapes the control of the maker and the performer, too, since it will live to be re-seen, and re-made.

The artists I know do not tend to speak about the formal specificity of the objects they produce. Work (not "works") is what they make in their studios, or wherever their practice takes them. Work as a process, and work as a product or an object, provisional and subject to change. Art is a theory performed in practice. Art-practice is an inquiry, a celebration, a mourning, an intervention, a critique, an interested observation, an action, an act.

A full-page advertisement showcasing the new United States Artists fellows, each a recipient of a substantial $50,000 grant, put the matter squarely: "Art comes from Artists," it declared, in large block letters, red and black.[28] Below a montage of photographs of the winners, and in much smaller type, the organization reiterated the issue that had led to its foundation: "A recent survey shows that while 96% of Americans value art in their communities, strangely, only 27% value artists."[29] Elsewhere USA has called this a "strange paradox."[30] But, as we have seen, it is not so strange. The work is idealized, commodified, exhibited or performed, bought or sold, analyzed and archived. It survives, it tells a story, it attains a place—proper or improper—in the world. The artist is lionized, praised, vilified, psychologized, honored and dishonored, understood and misunderstood. The maker is not the same as the thing made.

We cannot know what will be "useful," or "useless," in the future, or, indeed, what may cross over from what we now call art to what we now call science, or vice versa. What we can know is that patronage of the arts is an investment in that future. Patronage itself is part of the process of art-making, the long trajectory from the inception of a project to its completion, and beyond—for there is a sense in which this process never really comes to an end, but rather renews itself, in new contexts, and for new audiences and observers. Whether as sponsor, supporter, collector, audience member, or critic, the patron collaborates with the artist. Indeed, patronage is itself a practice: not, or not only, a theory, a vocation, an avocation, or a way of living. I use the term "practice" in the strong sense in which the arts themselves are practices: experimental, investigative, repetitive, innovative, skilled. In this sense, the paradox of patronage need not be paradoxical: for institutions or for individuals, for universities, governments, foundations, or the public, a sustained, thoughtful, informed, and committed patronage is the best way to avoid merely patronizing the arts.

# NOTES

## Preface

1.  Sigmund Freud, "Group Psychology and the Analysis of the Ego." *The Standard Edition of the Complete Psychological Works of Sigmund Freud,* ed. and trans. James Strachey (London: The Hogarth Press and the Institute of Psycho-Analysis, 1955), 18:112.

2.  Potter Stewart, *Jacobellis v. Ohio,* 378 U.S. 184 (1964).

3.  Maria Rosario-Jackson et al., *Investing in Creativity: A Study of the Support Structure for U.S. Artists* (2003: Urban Institute), http://www.urban.org/url.cfm?ID=411311 (accessed November 13, 2007), and Kevin F. McCarthy et al., *Gifts of the Muse: Reframing the Debate about the Benefits of the Arts* (Santa Monica, CA: Rand, 2004).

## Chapter 1

1.  Kathryn Shattuck, "Look Carefully: The Donor Is in the Details." *New York Times,* November 6, 2005, section 2, p. 20. The phrase "who's who of Haarlem" is that of James H. Marrow, professor emeritus of art history at Princeton University.

2.  Francis Haskell, *Patrons and Painters: Art and Society in Baroque Italy* (New York: Harper and Row, 1963), 6.

3.  David H. Solkin, *Painting for Money: The Visual Arts and the Public Sphere in Eighteenth-century England* (New Haven and London: Yale University Press, 1992), 1–2.

4.  John Oakly, in *St. James's Chronicle,* April 25, 1761, 3. Quoted in Solkin, *Painting for Money,* 180.

5.  Joshua Reynolds, *Discourses on Art,* ed. Robert R. Wark (New Haven and London: 1975).

6.  In several poems Blake invokes the "outline," the art of the draftsman, as central to good art: "[They] never can Rafael it Fuseli it nor Blake it / If they can't see an outline pray how can they make it. . . . Madmen see outlines & therefore they draw them." ("All Pictures thats

Panted [*sic*] with Sense & with Thought," in David Erdman, ed., *The Poetry and Prose of William Blake* (New York: Doubleday, 1965), 502.

7.   Ibid., 507.

8.   Dianne Sachko Macleod, *Art and the Victorian Middle Class: Money and the Making of Cultural Identity* (Cambridge: Cambridge University Press, 1996), 12.

9.   Lady Eastlake in Sir Charles Eastlake, *Contributions to the Literature of the Fine Arts with a Memoir Compiled by Lady Eastlake*, 2nd edition (London 1870), 147.

10.   Dante Gabriel Rossetti to Ford Madox Brown, May 28, 1873. *Letters of Dante Gabriel Rossetti*, eds. Oswald Doughty and J. R. Wahl, 4 vols. (Oxford: Clarendon Press, 1965–67), 3:1175.

11.   Quoted in William D. Grampp. *Pricing the Priceless: Art, Artists, and Economics* (New York: Basic Books, 1989), 15.

12.   Their relationship is depicted in the 1987 film *Vincent and Theo*.

13.   For more on Picasso and the shaping of the modern art market, see Michael C. Fitzgerald's extensive study, *Making Modernism*.

14.   Langston Hughes, *I Wonder as I Wander: An Autobiographical Journey* (New York: Thunder's Mouth Press, 1956), 5.

15.   In 2007 the literary establishment was still reeling from this event. See article by Dana Goodyear, "The Moneyed Muse," *New Yorker*, February 19, 2007, http://www.newyorker.com/reporting/2007/02/19/070219fa_fact_goodyear (accessed November 8, 2007) and response by David Orr, "Annals of Poetry," *New York Times*, March 11, 2007, http://www.nytimes.com/2007/03/11/books/review/Orr.t.html (accessed November 8, 2007).

16.   Dorothy Spears, "The First Gallerists' Club," *New York Times*, June 18, 2006, section 2, 1, 33.

17.   Roberta Smith, "Chelsea Enters Its High Baroque Period," *New York Times*, November 28, 2004, section 2, 33.

18.   Michael Kelly, *New York Times*, July 12, 1992, 2:1; Jonathan Duffy, BBC News Online, October 31, 2003; *Art Review*, January 15, 2002, p. 19; Julian Nundy, *The Independent* (London), October 23, 1994, p. 12.

19.   Dylan Thomas, "A Visit to America," *Quite Early One Morning* (New York: New Directions, 1954), 232–33, 237.

20.   Charles Dickens, *Our Mutual Friend*, part 10, chapter 14 (New York: Modern Library, 1960), 405.

21.   S. N. Berhman, *Duveen* (Boston and Toronto: Little, Brown and Company, 1952), 169.

22.   Erika Kinetz, "How Much Is That Dancer in the Program?" *New York Times*, August 15, 2004, section 2, 1–8.

23.  Ibid.

24.  Ibid.

25.  Maura Egan, "The Next Cultural Establishment: Patron Sweethearts," *New York Times Magazine*, October 3, 2004, 85.

26.  Senator John F. Kennedy, letter to Miss Theodate Johnson, the publisher of *Musical America*, September 13, 1960. *Musical America*, October 1960, 11.

27.  At the request of President Kennedy, Frost altered the final line from its original form, "such as she *would* become," replacing it instead with "such as she *will* become."

28.  Ishmael Reed, quoted in David Strietfeld, "The Power and the Puzzle of the Poem: Reading between Maya Angelou's Inaugural Lines." *Washington Post*, January 21, 1993, D11.

29.  Derek Walcott, from "The Road Taken." In Joseph Brodsky, Seamus Heaney, and Derek Walcott , eds., *Homage to Robert Frost* (New York: Farrar, Strauss, and Giroux, 1996).

30.  Galway Kinnell, "For Robert Frost," in *The Voice That Is Great within Us: American Poetry of the Twentieth Century*, ed. Hayden Carruth (New York: Bantam Books, 1970), 600–601. Reprinted from Kennell, *Flower Herding on Mount Monadnock* (New York: Houghton Mifflin, 1964).

31.  There is a disturbingly "colonial" moment in this poem, too, a thoughtless patronizing glance at emerging postcolonial states around the world:

> We see how seriously the races swarm
> In their attempts at sovereignty and form.
> They are our wards we think to some extent
> For the time being and with their consent,
> To teach them how Democracy is meant.

32.  "Here Comes Poet Laureate," *New York Times*, February 1, 1986, 12.

33.  Erdrich, Dove, Reed, and the unnamed "prominent poet" all quoted in David Stretfeld, "The Power and the Puzzle of the Poem: Reading between Maya Angelou's Inaugural Lines." *Washington Post*, January 21, 1993, D11.

34.  "Bush Gives No Reason, but There'll Be No Rhymes." Associated Press, January 10, 2001.

35.  Andrew Marvell, "The Garden," *Pastoral and Lyric Poems 1681*, eds. David Omerod and Christopher Wortham (Nedlands, Australia: University of Western Australia Press, 2000), 183.

36.   Edmund Kemper Broadus, *The Laureateship: A Study of the Office of Poet Laureate in England with Some Account of the Poets* (1921; rpt. Freeport, New York: Books for Libraries Press, 1969), 226.

37.   Ibid.

38.   William Knight, *Life of William Wordsworth* (1889), 3:435. Broadus, 183.

39.   Knight, 3:436.

40.   Alfred Tennyson, quoted in Hallam Tennyson, *Alfred Lord Tennyson: A Memoir by His Son* (New York: Macmillan, 1897), 3:435. Broadus, *The Laureateship*, 187.

41.   Ibid., 14.

42.   Stephane Mallarmé, "Tennyson Viewed from Here," *Divagations*, trans. Barbara Johnson (Cambridge, MA: Harvard University Press, 2007), 86–7.

43.   Robert Pinsky, quoted in JoAnne Henderson, "Four Poets Laureate" (www.hazelst.com/writer/joAnne_henderson).

44.   Quoted in R. W. Apple Jr., "Robert Penn Warren Names Nation's First Poet Laureate," *New York Times*, February 27, 1986, 1.

45.   Quoted in David Remnick, "Warren Named Poet Laureate: New Temporary Post to Be Tied to Library's Consultantship," *Washington Post*, February 27, 1986, B1.

46.   Elizabeth Olson, "New Poet at the Top," *New York Times*, August 12, 2004, B2.

47.   Dinitia Smith, "Outspoken New Englander Is New Poet Laureate," *New York Times*, June 14, 2006.

48.   Verlyn Klinkenborg, "Donald Hall, Poet Laureate," *New York Times*, June 15, 2006, A22; "Beyond the McPoem," *Boston Globe*, June 15, 2006, A14.

49.   Motoko Rich, "Charles Simic, Surrealist with Dark View, Is Named Poet Laureate," *New York Times*, August 2, 2007, B1.

50.   David Orr, "Chaos Theory," review of Simic, *The Voice at 3:00 A.M.*, *New York Times Book Review*, April 6, 2003.

51.   Monica Hesse, "The Poet of the People," *Washington Post*, August 2, 2007, C1.

52.   William Safire, "A Gioia to Behold," *New York Times*, March 8, 2004, p. 19.

53.   Robert Bly, *Talking All Morning* (Ann Arbor: University of Michigan Press, 1980), 107–108.

54.   Quoted in Elisabeth Bumiller, "Threats and Responses," *New York Times*, January 30, 2003, A14.

55.   Katha Pollitt, "Poetry Makes Nothing Happen? Ask Laura Bush," *The Nation*, February 24, 2003.

56.   Ibid.

57.   Hillel Italic, "U.S. Poet Laureate Opposes War with Iraq," Associated Press, February 6, 2003, http://www.commondreams.org/headlines03/0206-07 (accessed January 7, 2008).


*Chapter 2*


1.   John Updike. Testimony, January 30, 1978, before the Subcommittee on Select Education of the House of Representatives Committee on Education and Labor, Boston, Massachusetts. Published in Updike, *Hugging the Shore* (New York: Knopf, 1983).

2.   Michael Straight, *Twigs for an Eagle's Nest* (Berkeley: Devon Press, 1980), 71.

3.   William Osborne, "The German Arts Funding Model." January 4, 2002, http://www.osborne-conant.org/funding_model.htm (accessed April 11, 2008).

4.   Andras Szanto, "Art/Architecture; the Dutch Give the Arts a Dash of (Cold) Water," *New York Times*, March 9, 2003.

5.   Graham Devlin and Sue Hoyle, *Committing to Culture: Arts Funding in France and Britain* (London: Franco-British Council, 2000), 24.

6.   *Comparing Cultural Policy: A Study of Japan and the United States,* eds. Joyce Zemans, Archie Kleingartner et al. (London: Altamira Press, 1999), 19–61.

7.   The Parisian Ministère has branched out into a range of more administratively localized, pluralistic structures, and the most recent (1993) data indicate that subnational organizations financially contribute significantly more than the centralized Ministère: of total public spending on culture, 40.9 percent was by communities, and 49.7 percent by the nation, of which only 19.8 percent was directly from the Ministry of Culture. "Projets et programmes." Ministère de la culture et du patrimoine historique classé. December 6, 2006, http://www.culture.gouv.sn/index.php3 (accessed April 11, 2008).

8.   "The National Arts Council Act." Staatskoerant van die Republiek van Suid-Afrika Act No. 56, 1997. As reprinted in the *Government Gazette,* vol. 389, no. 18426 (November 14, 1997).

See also the report of the NAC to the International Federation of Arts Councils and Culture Agencies. Available at: "Country Profile: South Africa." *International Federation of Arts Councils and Culture Agencies.* October 18, 2006, http://www.ifacca.org.

9.   John Joliffe, ed., *Neglected Genius: The Diaries of Benjamin Robert Haydon, 1808–1846* (London: Hutchinson, 1990), 158.

10.   For example, in Theodore Wiprud's "On the Money: New Music Funding in the United States," NewMusicBox, August 1, 2000, http://www.newmusicbox.org/article.nmbx?id-808 (accessed January 5, 2008).

11.   Harold Baldry, *The Case for the Arts* (London: Secker and Warburg, 1981), 3. Lord David Cecil, *Melbourne* (New York: Grossets, 1954), 245.

12.   Thus *OED* (II.5.b.) quotes the *ACLS Newsletter* for 1954 ("To abstain from the temptation to meddle into the inner affairs of other departments"), George Saintsbury's 1916 *The Peace of the Augustans* ("It is difficult to be certain whether he would have long meddled with the stage if he had not, as a political reward, got shares in theatrical patents," and *USA Weekend* February 28, 1993 "We had 12 years of hands-off Republican presidents who said government should not meddle in people's lives").

13.   Joliffe, *Neglected Genius*, 158.

14.   Ibid., 159.

15.   William Hazlitt. Quoted in David Bromwich, *Hazlitt: The Mind of a Critic* (New Haven: Yale University Press, 1983; 1999), 119. Bromwich notes that Hazlitt's "provocation in this instance came not from Haydon but from the *Catalogue Raisonné* of the British Institution (1816), and the aids-to-appreciation of Benjamin West's paintings that had been approved and in part dictated by West himself."

16.   Cited in Harold Baldry, *The Case for the Arts* (London: Secker and Warburg, 1981), 3.

17.   Cited in ibid., 13.

18.   Despite Lord De La Warr's official position, though, the energy for these developments came from the secretary of the Pilgrim Trust, Dr. Thomas Jones; Pilgrim had provided the initial grant of £25,000. Other key figures in these early years, beginning in the 1930s, were William Emrys Williams, the secretary of the British Institute of Adult Education, who organized touring exhibits of painting and sculpture called "Art for the People," and John Maynard Keynes, the Cambridge economist.

19.   Baldry, *The Case for the Arts*, 15.

20.   Mary Glasgow, "The Concept of the Arts Council," in Milo Keynes, ed., *Essays on John Maynard Keynes* (New York: Cambridge University Press, 1975), 260–61, 262.

21.   As Keynes's biographer Robert Skidelsky notes, Keynes the economist was wary of patronage as a "bottomless sink": the purpose of patronage was to enable non-profit-making activities to take

place—by way of capital endowment or loan, or guarantee against loss, not to provide permanent subsidies for loss-making enterprises. Keynes once said that if a patronage body were 100 percent successful it would end up by spending nothing, except on its own administration. "It would choose so well and back such uniformly certain winners that all loans would be repaid in full and none of its guarantees ever called." Robert Skidelsky, *John Maynard Keynes 1883–1946* (New York: Penguin, 2003), 725. Mary Glasgow, in Milo Keynes, ed., *Essays on John Maynard Keynes* (New York: Cambridge University Press, 1975), 267.

22.    Virginia Button, *The Turner Prize: Twenty Years* (London: Tate, 2003).

23.    James F. English, *The Economy of Prestige: Prizes, Awards, and the Circulation of Cultural Value* (Cambridge, MA: Harvard University Press, 2005), 229.

24.    Roberta Smith, "The Best of Sculptors, the Worst of Sculptors," *New York Times*, November 30, 1993, http://query.nytimes.com/gst/fullpage.html?res=9F0CE4DA1E3EF933A05752C1A965958260 (accessed November 8, 2007).

25.    John Adams, letter to Abigail Adams, May 12, 1780. In *The Book of Abigail and John: Selected Letters of the Adams Family 1762–1784*, eds. L. H. Butterfield, Marc Friedlander, and Mary-Jo Kline (Cambridge, MA: Harvard University Press, 1975), 260.

26.    Jerre Mangione, *The Dream and the Deal* (Boston: Little, Brown, 1972), 34.

27.    Alan Howard Levy, *Government and the Arts* (Lanham, MD: 1997), 64–68.

28.    Mangione, 217–18.

29.    John O'Connor and Lorraine Brown, eds. *Free, Adult, Uncensored: The Living History of the Federal Theatre Project* (Washington, D.C.: New Republic Books, 1978), 5–7. Levy, *Government and the Arts*, 71.

30.    Elmer Rice, *The Living Theatre* (New York: Harper and Brothers, 1959), 149.

31.    William F. McDonald, *Federal Relief Administration and the Arts* (Columbus: Ohio State University Press, 1969), 502.

32.    Quoted in "Federal Theatre Project," http://www.spartacus.schoolnet.co.uk/USARftwp.htm.

33.    George Biddle, *An American Artist's Story* (Boston: Little, Brown, 1939), 273.

34.    "Removing a Mural," *New York Times*, February 14, 1934, http://www.proquest.com.ezp1.harvard.edu/ (accessed November 8, 2007). For publicly accessible website (free abstract), see http://select

.nytimes.com/gst/abstract.html?res=F40E1FFF345F11738DDDAD099
4DA405B848FF1D3

35.   Francis V. O'Connor, *Federal Art Patronage 1933–1943* (College Park: University of Maryland, 1966), 20.

36.   Ibid., 13, 23.

37.   Ibid., 31–32.

38.   Holger Cahill, "Federal Art Project Manual," mimeographed. Works Project Administration, Washington, D.C., October 1935, cited in O'Connor, *Federal Art Patronage*, 28–29.

39.   Henry Morgenthau, Secretary of the Treasury, October 14, 1934, establishing the Section of Painting and Sculpture. Cited in O'Connor, *Federal Art Patronage*, 12.

40.   O'Connor, *Federal Art Patronage*, 28.

41.   John F. Kennedy, remarks at Amherst College, Amherst, MA, October 26, 1963.

42.   "We were challenged with a peace-time choice between the American system of rugged individualism and a European philosophy of diametrically opposed doctrines—doctrines of paternalism and state socialism." Herbert Hoover, campaign speech, New York, October 22, 1928, in *The New Day: Campaign Speeches of Herbert Hoover 1928*, 2nd ed. (Stanford: Stanford University Press, 1929), 154.

43.   Roger Rosenblatt, "The Rugged Individual Rides Again," *Time*, October 15, 1984, http://www.time.com/time/magazine/article/0,9171,923739,00.html (accessed November 10, 2007).

44.   Raymond Williams, *Keywords: A Vocabulary of Culture and Society*, 2nd ed. (New York: Oxford University Press, 1983), s.v. "individual."

45.   *Oxford English Dictionary*, 2nd ed., s.v. "long-haired," a.

46.   Frances Stonor Saunders, *The Cultural Cold War: The CIA and the World of Arts and Letters* (New York: The New Press, 1999), 1, 344–47, 349–51.

47.   Gloria Emerson, "Receiver of Funds from C.I.A. Quits," *New York Times*, May 14, 1967, 32.

48.   *Title 20*, Public Law 89–209, *U.S. Code* 10 (2000): 868.

49.   *Congressional Record*, February 27, 1968, 4321–22. Cited in Michael Brenson, *Visionaries and Outcasts: The NEA, Congress, and the Place of the Visual Artist in America* (New York: New York Press, 2001), 81.

50.   *Congressional Record*, February 27, 1968, 4321–22. Cited in Brenson, *Visionaries*, 81.

51.   *Congressional Record*, February 27, 1968, 4333–44. Cited in Brenson, *Visionaries*, 82.

52.   Brenson (pp. 85–86) cites the following: "Laurie Anderson, Siah Armajani, John Baldessari, Jonathan Borofsky, Chris Burden,

Ping Chong, Felix Gonzalez-Torres, Dan Graham, Hans Haacke, David Hamons, Newton Harrison, Gary Hill, Robert W. Irwin, Alfredo Jaar, Donald Judd, Allen Kaprow, Barbara Kruger, Sol LeWitt, Robert Mangold, Daniel J. Martinez, Gordon Matta-Clark, Robert Morris, Bruce Nauman, Maria Nordman, Dennis Oppenheim, Adrian Piper, Martin Puryear, Yvonne Rainer, Susan Rothenberg, Richard Serra, Joel Shapiro, Cindy Sherman, James Turrell, Bill Viola, and Ursula von Rydingsvard."

53.    James Davison Hunter's 1991 book, *Culture Wars: The Struggle to Define America* was the first to put the term in play in the 1990s. Buchanan, or his handlers, took the phrase and ran with it, all the way to the polls.

54.    Pat Buchanan, "The Election Is about Who We Are," speech to the Republican National Convention, Houston, TX, August 17, 1992, in *Vital Speeches of the Day* 58.23 (1992): 713–14.

55.    136 *Congressional Record* 28663. Cited in *National Endowment for the Arts et Al v. Finley et Al* 524 US 569. U.S. Supreme Court, October 1997.

56.    Cited in Margaret Quigley, "The Mapplethorpe Censorship Controversy: Chronology of Events," http://publiceye.org (the Web site of Political Research Associates).

57.    *Title 20*, Public Law 89–209, *U.S. Code* 10 (2000): 868.

58.    Christina Orr-Cahill, quoted in Elizabeth Kastor, "Corcoran Offers 'Regret' on Mapplethorpe: Statement Promises Support for Art, Artists and Artistic Freedom," *Washington Post*, September 19, 1989, http://www.proquest.com/ezp2.harvard.edu (accessed November 12, 2007). Article preview available via Google News.

59.    "Amendment No. 153 in disagreement," 101st Congress, 1st sess., *Congressional Record* 135, no. 134 (October 7, 1989): S12967.

60.    Senator Jesse Helms of North Carolina, Senate debate on reauthorization of the National Endowment for the Arts, 101st Congress, 1st sess., *Congressional Record* 135, no. 134 (October 7, 1989): S12986.

61.    Fannie Taylor and Anthony L. Barresi, *The Arts as a New Frontier: The National Endowment for the Arts* (New York: Plenum Publishing Group, 1984), 13.

62.    National Endowment for the Arts, web site, http://www.nea .org/about/index.html.

63.    Frederick Turner, "The Embattled Establishment," in *The National Endowments: A Critical Symposium*, ed. Laurence Jarvik, Herbet I. London, and James F. Cooper (Los Angeles: Second Thought Books, 1995), 75–81.

64.   National Endowment for the Arts, web site, http://www.nea
.org/about/index.html.

65.   Richard Serra, cited in "Culture Shock: Flashpoints: Visual Arts: Richard Serra's *Tilted Arc*." http://www.pbs.org/wgbh/
cultureshock.

66.   Richard Serra, "'Tilted Arc': A Precedent?" letter to *New York
Times*, April 30, 1989, section 2, 5.

67.   Richard Serra, quoted in David W. Dunlap, "Moving Day
Arrives for Disputed Sculpture," *New York Times*, March 11, 1989, section 1, 29.

68.   "Open Space Replaces 'Arc,'" *New York Times*, June 15, 1989,
http://query.nytimes.com/gst/fullpage.html?res=950DE3DB1F38F9
36A25755C0A96F948260 (accessed November 8, 2007).

69.   Alice Goldfarb Marquis, *Art Lessons: Learning from the Rise and
Fall of Public Arts Funding* (New York: BasicBooks, 1995), 192.

70.   Ibid., 191–99. Marquis's account draws extensively on an unpublished doctoral dissertation by Mary Eleanor McCombie, "Art and
Policy: The National Endowment for the Arts' Art in Public Places
Program" (University of Texas. Austin, 1992).

71.   Marquis, see note 69, 252–53.

72.   Ibid.

73.   Ann McQueen,"Investing in the Arts," *Boston Globe*, November 14, 2006, A19.

74.   "An Investment in Art," *Boston Globe*, November 13, 2006, A10.

75.   Stephanie Strom, "New Charity to Start Plan for $50,000 Artists' Grants," *New York Times*, September 5, 2006, B1.

76.   "Art for Our Sake," editorial, *Boston Globe*, September 25,
2006, A10.

77.   Quoted in Strom, "New Charity."

78.   *Debates and Proceedings in the Congress of the United States, 1789–
1824.* Cited in Lillian B. Miller, *Patrons and Patriotism: The Encouragement of the Fine Arts in the United States, 1790–1860* (Chicago: University
of Chicago Press, 1966), 46.

79.   *Albany Daily Advertiser*, February 3, 1817. Cited in Miller, *Patrons and Patriotism*, 46.

80.   Miller, *Patrons and Patriotism*, 46.

81.   McArthur of Ohio; William McCoy of Virginia. Cited in ibid.,
48, 50.

82.   Ibid., 53.

83.   Ellen Susan Bulfinch, ed., *The Life and Letters of Charles Bulfinch, Architect* (Boston and New York: Houghton Mifflin, 1896),
293.

84.   Allan Nevins, ed. *The Diary of Philip Hone* (New York: Dodd, Mead, 1927), 2:694.

85.   Miller, *Patrons and Patriotism*, 62–63.


## Chapter 3


1.   David Rockefeller, Foreword to Arnold Gingrich, *Business and the Arts: An Answer to Tomorrow* (Paul S. Eriksson: New York, 1969), xi–xii.

2.   Leo H. Schoenhofen, "Value of the Arts to a Corporation." In Gingrich, *Business and the Arts*, 53–54.

3.   Richard Evan, "Arts Cash Still Low Priority," *Financial Times*, May 28, 1980, and Tony Conyers, "State Cannot Be Part of Arts Revival," *Daily Telegraph*, May 28, 1980. Cited in Chin-Tao Wu, *Privatising Culture: Corporate Art Intervention since the 1980s* (London and New York: Verso, 2002), 54.

4.   Goldwin A. McLellan, president, Business Committee for the Arts, *"Business in the Arts" Awards: A Ten-Year History, 1966–1975* (New York: Business Committee for the Arts, Inc., 1975), np.

5.   Wu, *Privatising Culture*, 79.

6.   Robert O. Anderson, "The Businessman and the Artist." In Gideon Chagy, ed., *The State of the Arts and Corporate Support* (New York: Paul S. Eriksson, 1971), 5.

7.   Anderson, "The Businessman and the Artist," 6, 7.

8.   See Richard Evan, "Arts Cash Still Low Priority," *Financial Times*, May 28, 1980, and Tony Conyers, "State Cannot Be Part of Arts Revival," *Daily Telegraph*, May 28, 1980. Cited in Wu, *Privatising Culture*, 54.

9.   *1998 National Survey, Business Support of the Arts* (prepared for Business Committee for the Arts, Inc., by Roper Starch Worldwide, New York, November 1998), 29.

10.   http://www.bcainc.org/about.html (accessed May 13, 2006).

11.   "THE BCA TEN," Business Committee for the Arts, http://www.bcainc.org/thebcaten.html (accessed November 11, 2007).

12.   "Business Committee for the Arts Announces Search for Role Models—Nominations Now Being Accepted for THE BCA TEN: Best Companies Supporting the Arts in America," Business Committee for the Arts press release, April 25, 2005, http://www.emediawire.com/releases/2005/4/emw231513.htm (accessed November 11, 2007).

13.   Flora Biddle, quoted in Wu, 95.

14.   For a good study of this development, see Mark W. Rectanus, *Culture Incorporated: Museums, Artists, and Corporate Sponsorships* (Minneapolis: University of Minnesota Press, 2002).

15.    Richard W. Lewis, *Absolut Book: The Absolut Vodka Advertising Story* (Boston: Journey Editions, 1966), 65.

16.    Ibid., 67.

17.    Arhur Lubow, "This Vodka Has Legs," *New Yorker,* September 12, 1994, 68. Quoted in Rectanus, *Culture Incorporated,* 72.

18.    "Carillon Importers: The Art of 'Absolut' Marketing," *Sales and Marketing Management,* August 1992, 44.

19.    *Oxford English Dictionary,* 2nd ed., s.v. "altruism."

20.    "Company News; Philip Morris Changes Its Name to the Altria Group," *New York Times,* January 28, 2003, http://query.nytimes.com/gst/fullpage.html?res=9902E3D71339F93BA15752C0A9659C8B63 (accessed November 14, 2007).

21.    Andrew Martin, "As a Company Leaves Town, Arts Grants Follow," *New York Times,* October 8, 2007, http://www.nytimes.com/2007/10/08/business/media/08altria.html (accessed November 14, 2007).

22.    Ibid.

23.    Ibid.

24.    "End of an Era in Arts Funding," *New York Times,* October 9, 2007, http://www.nytimes.com/2007/10/09/opinion/09tue4.html (accessed November 14, 2007).

25.    The painting was the centerpiece of Michel Foucault's book on Magritte, *This Is Not a Pipe* (1973), transl. James Harkness (Berkeley: University of Chicago Press, 1983).

26.    Charles P. Pierce, "From Monet to Madonna," *Boston Globe Magazine,* February 5, 2006, 20–21.

27.    Ibid., 20–21.

28.    Jane Culbert and Thomas Wolf, "Will Venture Philanthropy Revolutionize the Arts?" *Monograph,* November 2001, 4–5.

29.    Ibid., 1–11.

30.    Rosanne Martorella, *Corporate Art* (New Brunswick, NJ: Rutgers University Press, 1990), 69.

31.    Ibid.

32.    Marjory Jacobson, *Art and Business: New Strategies for Corporate Collecting* (Thames and Hudson, 1993), 10, 14, 15, 17, 200.

33.    "Art in the Workplace . . . or Art in a Pinstripe Suit." Interview with Shirley Reiff Howarth, editor of the International Directory of Corporate Art Collections, May 22, 2005. The interviewer was Bruce Peterson.

34.    Thane Peterson, "A Corporate Art Collection That's Aimed at Outrage and Enjoyment," *Business Week Online,* December 21, 1999.

35.    Robin Pogrebin, "Princeton to Receive Record Gift for the Arts," *New York Times,* January 21, 2006, B6.

36. "Taos Artists and Their Patrons: 1898–1950," Phoenix Art Museum, http://www.phxart.org/pastexhibitions/taos.asp (accessed November 11, 2007).

37. "Patrons of the Philharmonic," New York Philharmonic, http://nyphil.org/support/patrons.cfm (accessed November 11, 2007). "Patrons of Los Angeles Opera," Los Angeles Opera, http://www .losangelesopera.com/support/patrons.htm (accessed November 11, 2007).

38. Erika Kinetz, "For Top Law Students, a Sidebar with the Arts," *New York Times*, July 23, 2006, 8, 9.

39. Geoff Egders, "Meet the Donors: They're Young, They're Connected, and They're Coveted by Boston's Museums," *Boston Globe*, August 14, 2005, http://www.boston.com/news/globe/living/articles/2005/08/14/meet_the_donors/ (accessed November 10, 2007).

40. "The Fund Raising School," Center on Philanthropy at Indiana University, http://www.philanthropy.iupui.edu/TheFundRaising School/ (accessed November 11, 2007).

41. Joe Nocera, "The Patron Gets a Divorce," *New York Times Magazine*, October 14, 2007, 68.

42. http://www.match.com.

43. Nocera, "The Patron Gets a Divorce," 104, 68, 72–73, 74.

44. Ibid., 68.

45. Newburyport [MA] Art Association, May 2002.

46. "Fine Arts Department to Be Renamed," *Harvard University Gazette*, October 23, 1997, http://www.hno.harvard.edu/gazette/1997/10.23/FineArtsDepartm.html (accessed November 10, 2007).

47. *Report of the Committee on the Visual Arts at Harvard University* (Cambridge: Harvard University, 1956), 10–11.

48. College Art Association, Mission Statement (2006).

49. Dean Valentine, quoted in Carol Vogel, "Warhols of Tomorrow are Dealers' Quarry Today," *New York Times*, April 15, 2006, A1, A17.

50. Ibid. The self-described mentor in the article is John Friedman, a venture capitalist.

51. Bruce Weber, "So Many Acting B.A.'s, So Few Paying Gigs," *New York Times*, December 7, 2005, http://www.nytimes.com/2005/12/07/arts/07maki.html (accessed November 10, 2007).

52. H28.0171, "Preparing for Profession," Tisch School of the Arts, Undergraduate Drama Course Descriptions, 2005–2006.

53. Anne Midgette, "The End of the Great Big American Voice," *New York Times*, November 13, 2005, http://www.nytimes.com/2005/11/13/arts/music/13midg.html (accessed November 10, 2007).

54. Erika Kinetz, "Practice, Practice, Practice. Go to College? Maybe," *New York Times*, December 21, 2005, http://www.nytimes.com/2005/12/21/arts/dance/21danc.html (accessed November 11, 2007).

55. Ibid.

56. "Double Degree Program—Curriculum," Bard College Conservatory of Music, http://www.bard.edu/conservatory/doublede gree/curriculum.shtml (accessed November 11, 2007).

57. "Programs of Study," Northwestern University School of Music, http://www.music.northwestern.edu/programs/ (accessed November 11, 2007).

58. "Art at Swarthmore College." Swarthmore College Web site and bulletin.

59. John Lithgow, "An Actor's Own Words," commencement address at Harvard University, Cambridge, MA, June 9, 2005 (text as prepared for delivery).

60. Yo-Yo Ma, biography. http://www.yo-yoma.com.

61. "Peter Sellars." 2001 Harvard Arts Medal, Office for the Arts at Harvard.

62. Nicholas Fox Weber, *Patron Saints: Five Rebels Who Opened America to a New Art 1928–1943* (New York: Alfred Knopf, 1992), 61.

63. Ibid., 179–80.

64. Ibid., 345.

### Chapter 4

1. Caroline A. Jones and Peter Galison, eds., *Picturing Science, Producing Art* (New York: Routledge, 1998), 2.

2. Rudolf Arnheim, *Art and Visual Perception* (Berkeley and Los Angeles: University of California Press, 1954); Anton Ehrenzweig, *The Hidden Order of Art: A Study in the Psychology of Artistic Imagination* (Berkeley and Los Angeles: University of California Press, 1967); James Elkins, "Art History and Images That Are Not Art," *Art Bulletin* 77, 4 (1995): 551–71, and *The Object Stares Back: On the Nature of Seeing* (New York: Simon and Schuster, 1996); Barbara Maria Stafford, *Artful Science* (Cambridge: MIT Press, 1994).

3. Thomas. S. Kuhn, *The Structure of Scientific Revolutions* (Chicago and London: Chicago University Press, 1962; 3rd ed., 1996), 161.

4. *Title 20*, Public Law 89–209, *U.S. Code* 10 (2000): 868.

5. Ibid.

6.    Alfred Barr, "Is Modern Art Communistic?" *New York Times Magazine*, December 14, 1952. Quoted in Frances Stonor Saunders, *The Cultural Cold War* (New York: The New Press, 1999), 268.

7.    Lyndon Johnson, September 29, 1965, on the occasion of the Rose Garden signing of the National Foundation on the Arts and Humanities Act cited in Fannie Taylor and Anthony L. Barresi, *The Arts as a New Frontier: The National Endowment for the Arts* (New York: Plenum Press, 1984), 49.

8.    Michael Brenson, *Visionaries and Outcasts: The NEA, Congress, and the Place of the Visual Artist in America* (New York: The New Press, 2001), 28.

9.    Center for the Study of Democratic Institutions, *The Arts in a Democratic Society*, by Gifford Phillips, including a discussion with Roger L. Stevens and others on the new program of federal aid for the arts (Santa Barbara: Center for the Study of Democratic Institutions 1966), 15.

10.    Quoted in Brenson, *Visionaries*, 29.

11.    National Council for the Arts notes, November 1980, 69. Published in the *Washington International Arts Letter*, March 1981, 2350. Quoted in Brenson, *Visionaries*, 29.

12.    Arthur Koestler, *The Act of Creation* (London: Hutchinson 1970), 253.

13.    Brenson, *Visionaries*, 98.

14.    Robert Smithson, quoted in Michael Kimmelman, "Sculpture from the Earth, but Never Limited by It," *New York Times*, June 24, 2005, http://www.nytimes.com/2005/06/24/arts/design/24kimm.html (accessed November 11, 2007).

15.    Brenson, *Visionaries*, 98.

16.    Eric Bogosian, "Un-American Activities," *New York Times*, February 10, 1992, A17. Kim Masters, "Panel Approves Rejected Artists; NEA Chairman to Rule Next," *Washington Post*, November 3, 1990, D1.

17.    Jacqueline Trescott, "NEA to Pay 4 Denied Arts Grants, but 'Decency' Rule Challenge Unresolved," *Washington Post*, June 5, 1993, D1.

18.    Stephen Holden, "Where Psychedelia and Digital Austerity Converge," *New York Times*, July 14, 2004, E5.

19.    Elizabeth W. Bruss, *Beautiful Theories: The Spectacle of Discourse in Contemporary Criticism* (Baltimore: The Johns Hopkins University Press, 1982), 49.

20.    Roland Barthes, *Roland Barthes*, trans. Richard Howard (Berkeley: University of California Press, 1994), 122.

21.   Michel Foucault, *The Order of Things: Archaeology of the Human Sciences* (New York: Vintage Books, 1994), 73.

22.   Sol LeWitt, "Paragraphs on Conceptual Art," *Artforum* 5, no. 10 (June 1967): 80.

23.   Other examples would include: Haacke's *Real Time Social System* (1971), photographs of New York City slum buildings coupled with financial details about the landlord who owned them. When the Guggenheim Museum rejected this work as inflammatory, and canceled a planned exhibition, Haacke retaliated by making another piece about the Guggenheim family's financial holdings. The work of Christo also fits into this category, from an early piece like *Iron Curtain* (1962), oil drums that created a traffic jam on a Paris street, to the more elegant—and elaborately funded—wrapping of the Reichstag, draping of coasts and islands, and construction of fabric "gates" in Central Park.

24.   As, for example, in the seventies journal *The Fox*. Douglas Huebler, for two decades the dean of the California Institute of the Arts (CalArts), was the teacher of Mike Kelley, and imprinted American conceptual art (and art students) with his imaginative and often playful combinations of photography and text.

25.   Likewise, books like *African Fractals: Modern Computing and Indigenous Design*, by a computer scientist and ethnomathematician, Ron Eglash (New Brunswick, NJ: Rutgers University Press, 1999), or *The Art of Genes: How Organisms Make Themselves*, by a geneticist, Enrico Coen (Oxford and New York: Oxford University Press, 1999), have drawn attention to the affinities between art and science.

26.   John D. Barrow, *The Artful Universe* (Oxford: Clarendon Press, 1995), 4.

27.   Bertrand Russell, "The Study of Mathematics," in *Mysticism and Logic and Other Essays* (London: Longmans, Green and Co., 1919), 60.

28.   J.W.N. Sullivan, "Mathematics as an Art," *Aspects of Science; second series* (New York: Alfred A. Knopf, 1926), 94.

29.   G. H. Hardy, *A Mathematician's Apology* (Cambridge: Cambridge University Press, 1940), 25.

30.   P.A.M. Dirac, "The Evolutioin of the Physicist's Picture of Nature," *Scientific American*, 208.5 (May 1963), 47.

31.   Robert Jungk, *Brighter than a Thousand Suns: A Personal History of the Atomic Scientists*, trans. James Cleugh (New York: Harcourt, Brace and Co., 1958), 21–22.

32.   E. H. Gombrich, "The Renaissance Concept of Artistic Progress," in *Norm and Form: Studies in the Art of the Renaissance* (London and New York: Phaidon, 1966; 2nd ed. 1977), 7.

33.   Herbert Read, *Contemporary British Art* (Harmondsworth, England: Penguin, 1951), 19.

34.   William Hazlitt, "Why the Arts Are Not Progressive?" in *The Complete Works of William Hazlitt*, ed. P. P. Howe (London: J.M. Dent and Sons, 1933), 18:6.

35.   Roland Barthes, "The Brain of Einstein,' in *Mythologies*, trans. Annette Lavers (New York: Hill and Wang, 1957, 1972), 69.

36.   William Sharpe's *A dissertation upon genius* (1755; rpt. Delmar, NY: Scholars' Facsimiles & Reprints, 1973), William Duff's *Essay on Original Genius, and Its Various Modes of Exertion in Philosophy and the Fine Arts* (London: Printed for Edward and Charles Dilly, 1767), James Beattie's *The Minstrel; or, The Progress of Genius* (London: E. & C. Dilly, 1771;1774) and Alexander Gerard's *An essay on genius* (London: Printed for W. Strahan; T. Cadell, 1774) were among the works that marked a major shift, from the earlier idea of genius as an aspect of personality ("a Man's Nature, Fancy, or Inclination") to the view of genius as superior or unique mental powers, as distinguished, for example, from the lesser attribute of talent. Genius was "the faculty of invention," the capacity to produce original works of art or new discoveries in science.

37.   William James, "Great Men, Great Thoughts, and the Environment," *Atlantic Monthly*, October 1880, 453.

38.   Gertrude Stein, *The Autobiography of Alice. B. Toklas 1933* (New York: Vintage, 1990), 87, 114.

39.   Francis Galton, *Hereditary Genius; An Inquiry Into Its Laws and Consequences* (London: Macmillan, 1869), 324.

40.   Francis Galton, preface to ibid., 2nd ed. (London: Macmillan and Co., 1892), viii.

41.   Ibid., x.

42.   Diane K. Shah with Richard Manning, "A Fund for Geniuses," *Newsweek*, August 13, 1979, 50.

43.   "Fellows Program Overview," John D. and Catherine T. MacArthur Foundation, http://www.macfound.org/site/c.lkLXJ8M QKrH/b.959463/k.9D7D/Fellows_Program.htm (accessed November 12, 2007).

44.   Francis Kelly, *The Studio and the Artist* (New York: St. Martins, 1974), 87.

45.   Alan Riding, "Partners? You Paint the Figures, and I'll Do the Rest," *New York Times*, December 23, 2006, B11.

46.   Kelly, *The Studio and the Artist*, 75.

47.   Francis Bacon, *The New Organon and Related Writings* (New York: Liberal Arts Press, 1960), 289.

48. Ibid., 290–91.

49. "The composition of vast books is a laborious and impoverishing extravagance. To go on for five hundred pages developing an idea whose perfect oral exposition is possible in a few minutes! A better course of procedure is to pretend that these books already exist, and then to offer a resume, a commentary. . . . More reasonable, more inept, more indolent, I have preferred to write notes upon imaginary books." Jorge Luis Borges, prologue to *The Garden of Forking Paths*, 1941, in Borges, *Ficciones*, ed. Anthony Kerrigan (New York: Grove Press, 1962), 15–16.

50. One of the two Multimedia Labs is located in the List Art Center on campus.

51. Even the spaces and their designs are innovative. The Broad Art Center, housing the departments of art, design, and media arts, and the Center for Digital Arts, will be constructed on the north side of the campus, and the new California NanoSystems Institute on the south side: streaming cameras and monitors will be in place, "always projecting the activities and events on the other side." Thus the interdisciplinary work of art and science will be pursued both within the arts building itself and in electronic conjunction with the NanoSystems Institute.

52. The collapsible paint tube was invented by John. G. Rand, an American artist in London who received patents for "Improvements in preserving paints and other fluids" and for "Improvements in making and closing metallic collapsible vessels." By 1842 "the tube was being sold exclusively by the firm of Winsor and Newton as "Rand's Patent Collapsible Tube," and by the 1850s the name Rand had been dropped, and the item was included in the firm's catalogue as the Winsor and Newton Collapsible Paint Tube. Alexander Katlan, "The American Artist's Tools and Materials for On-Site Oil Sketching," *Journal of the American Institute for Conservation*, 1999, vol. 38, no. 1, 21.

53. Katlan, "America Artist's Tools," cites a catalogue listing for a portable easel from Goupil and Co. in 1857, and notes that the Albert Bierstadt painting *Cho-looke, the Yosemite Fall* (1864) depicts both a portable easel and a portable stool.

54. Michael Kimmelman, "Art's Last, Lonely Cowboy," *New York Times Magazine*, Februry 6, 2005, 33.

55. From the Cybersculpture and Co. Web site:

We did not mention the Renaissance period by chance: the modern world was indeed thought out at that very time by artists and engineers together. CYBERSCULPTURE & Co wishes to keep up with this historical cross-fertilising tradition. The joint trials of an American enterprise, and of the cyber-sculptors Stewart DICK-SON and Christian LAVIGNE have thus led to a breakthrough in colour 3D printing. CYBERSCULPTURE & Co groups together a team of complementary talent (artists, computer engineers, software experts, gallery owners) and advisers at the highest level (from the industrial and academic world) to achieve the creation and production of the mini- or mega-artefacts of the 21st century, in architecture, cultural heritage, sculpture, industrial design.

56.   Margaret Livingstone, *Vision and Art: The Biology of Seeing* (New York: Abrams, 2002), 10.

57.   Leonardo da Vinci, quoted in ibid., 105.

58.   David Hubel, foreword to Livingstone, *Vision and Art*, 8.

59.   Randy Kennedy, "The Artists in the Hazmat Suits," *New York Times*, July 3, 2005, sect. 2, 1. Steve Nadis, "Science for Art's Sake," *Nature*, October 12, 2000, 668.

60.   Eduardo Kac, "GPF Bunny," http://www.ekac.org/gfpbunny .html. See also Eduardo Kac, "Transgenic Art," Leonardo Electronic Almanac, vol. 6, no. 11, December 1998. Republished in Gerfried Stocker and Christine Schopf, eds., *Ars Electronica '99: Life Science* (Vienna, New York: Spring, 1999), 389–96.

61.   Randy Kennedy, "The Artists in the Hazmat Suits," *New York Times*, July 3, 2005, http://www.nytimes.com/2005/07/03/arts/ design/03kenn.html (accessed November 11, 2007).

62.   Jon McKenzie and Rebecca Schneider, "Critical Art Ensemble: Tactical Media Practitioners," *The Drama Review* 44.4 (Winter 2000), 127.

63.   The primal scene of this invention, a series of meetings of the British Association for the Advancement of Science in the 1830s, was memorably recorded by William Whewell in the *Quarterly Review*, where "the want of any name by which we can designate the students of the knowledge of the material world collectively" was addressed by "an ingenious gentleman," in fact, the puckish Whewell himself. The third-person narration is worth citing at length, not least because it so well illustrates the combined talents of (literary) art and science:

There was no general term by which these gentlemen could describe themselves with reference to their pursuits. *Philosophers* was felt to be too wide and lofty a term, and was very properly forbidden them by Mr. [Samuel Taylor] Coleridge, both in his capacity of philosopher and metaphysician: *savans* was rather assuming, besides being French instead of English; some ingenious gentleman proposed, that by analogy with *artist,* they might form *scientist.*" (William Whewell, *Quarterly Review* 51 ([1834], 59f).

## Chapter 5

1. The budget for the National Science Foundation in 2006 included $4.33 billion for the research and related activities account, $796.69 million for the educational and human resources account, $190.88 million for the major research equipment account, and $246.81 million for salaries and expenses. In the same period the total budget for the National Endowment for the Arts in 2004, 2005, and 2006 was approximately $120 million, and the budget for the National Endowment for the Humanities was approximately $140 million. NEA: http://www.arts.gov/about/04Annual/2004AnnualReport.pdf; NEH: http://www.neh.gov/whoweare/2007budget.html; NSF: http://www.nsf.gov/about/congress/109/highlights/cu06_0112.jsp.

2. Anandhi Subramanian, "Interpreting Derrida," *Hindu Magazine,* October 24, 2004, http://www.hindu.com/mag/2004/10/24/stories/2004102400470400.htm (accessed November 14, 2007).

3. Elvis Mitchell, "Film Review: Peeling Apart Layers of Reality to Deconstruct a Philosopher," *New York Times,* October 23, 2002, http://query.nytimes.com/gst/fullpage.html?res=9E0CEFDA173CF930A15753C1A9649C8B63 (accessed November 14, 2007).

4. Elizabth Weitzman, *New York Daily News,* October 23, 2002.

5. Lisa Schwarzbaum, "Sketches of Frank Gehry," *Entertainment Weekly,* May 19, 2006, http://ezp1.harvard.edu/login?url=http://search.ebscohost.com/login.aspx?direct=true&db=f5h&AN=20910427&site=ehost-live&scope=site (accessed November 14, 2007).

6. Dennis Schwartz, "*Sketches of Frank Gehry,*" *Ozus' World Movie Reviews,* August 13, 2006, http://www.sover.net/~ozus/sketchesoffrankgehry.htm (accessed November 14, 2007).

7. Nathan Rabin, "*Sketches of Frank Gehry,*" *A.V. Club,* May 10, 2006, http://www.avclub.com/content/node/48302 (accessed November 14, 2007).

8. Todd McCarthy, "Sketches of Frank Gehry," *Variety,* September 21, 2005, http://www.variety.com/review/VE1117928278.html (accessed November 14, 2007).

9.    Glenn Whipp, "Building on an Architect's Constructions," *Los Angeles Daily News*, May 18, 2006, http://www.dailynews.com/film reviews/ci_3837728 (accessed November 14, 2007).

10.    Maitland McDonagh, "Sketches of Frank Gehry," *TV Guide's Movie Guide*, http://www.tvguide.com/movies/sketches-frank-gehry/review/280259 (accessed November 14, 2007).

11.    Ruth La Ferla, "Let Me Guess: You Must Be an Architect," *New York Times*, February 9, 2003, http://query.nytimes.com/gst/fullpage .html?res=9402E1D7153BF93AA35751C0A9659C8B63 (accessed November 14, 2007).

12.    In working with and altering print advertisements (for Tiffany, Mobil, and so forth), Haacke deals with materials also of consuming interest to scholars and critics in cultural studies, while Dion's work on collections, museums, and the cultural politics of display speaks directly to current issues in history and culture, museology, and the history of science. Haacke has collaborated with Pierre Bourdieu on a book (*Free Exchange*, trans. Randal Johnson and Hans Haacke (Stanford: Stanford University Press, 1995)) about art and politics, and his *Framing and Being Framed* (Halifax: Press of the Nova Scotia College of Art and Design and New York: New York University Press, 1975) intervened in some key debates about conceptual art.

13.    *Triumph of the New York School*, painted in 1984, depicts some twenty-three artists and critics—including Jackson Pollock, André Breton, Marcel Duchamp, Arshile Gorky, Clement Greenberg, Harold Rosenberg, David Smith, Barnett Newman, and Robert Motherwell—attired in military uniforms and signing a treaty commemorating the moment when New York replaced Paris as the capital of the art world. The defeated French wear World War I uniforms; the victorious Americans wear battle fatigues from World War II; an inset photograph in Arthur Danto's book compares the painting to its manifest model, Vélasquez's *The Surrender of Breda*. Arthur C. Danto, *Mark Tansey: Visions and Revisions* (New York: Abrams, 1992), 50–51.

14.    Please see note 1 above. As Peter Galison notes, Big Science, by the very nature of its size, "has become an economic, political, and sociological entity in its own right." Peter Galison, "The Many Faces of Big Science," introduction to Galison and Bruce Hevly, eds., *Big Science: The Growth of Large-Scale Research* (Stanford: Stanford University Press, 1992), 17.

15.    Lauren Marshall and B. D. Colen, "Allston Planning and Consultation Advance," *Harvard University Gazette*, September 15, 2005, http://www.news.harvard.edu/gazette/2005/09.15/01-allston.html (accessed November 14, 2007).

16. Please see note 1 above.

17. Periodic stories in newspapers and watchdog sites note the problem, under headings like "Authors of JAMA Study Did Not Report Financial Ties to Pharmaceutical Companies" (MedicalNews-Today.com) or "Drug Interactions: Financial Ties to Industry Cloud Major Depression Study" (David Armstrong, *Wall Street Journal*, July 11, 2006). A former editor of the *New England Journal of Medicine* told the *Wall Street Journal* that medical schools ought to have more stringent policies because "faculty members are just up to their ears in financial conflicts and academic medical centers are just not doing anything about it" (Jerome P. Kassirer, quoted by David Armstrong in "Medical Reviews Face Criticism over Lapses," *Wall Street Journal*, July 19, 2006).

18. See, for example, Murray Sperber, *Beer and Circus: How Big-Time College Sports Is Crippling Higher Education* (New York: Henry Holt, 2000). Andrew Zimbalist, *The Bottom Line: Observations and Arguments on the Sports Business* (Philadelphia: Temple University Press, 2006).

19. Selena Roberts, "Big-Time College Sports May Be Due for an Audit," *New York Times*, October 29, 2006, 4. When the University of Texas spends $150 million to expand its football stadium, or when programs like Auburn's make the news because a sociology professor offered "directed reading" courses to athletes, with A grades for "phantom courses" that enabled failing students to graduate (and evidence surfaces that grades were changed upward without another professor's knowledge), there is reason for concern. Pete Thamel, "An Audit Reveals More Academic Questions at Auburn," *New York Times*, December 10, 2006, http://www.nytimes.com/2006/12/10/sports/10auburn.html (accessed November 14, 2007). Pete Thamel, "Professor at Center of Academic Investigation by Auburn Is Suspended," *New York Times*, December 23, 2006, http://www.nytimes.com/2006/12/23/sports/ncaafootball/23auburn.html (accessed November 14, 2007). Pete Thamel, "Amid Questions, Brand Says N.C.A.A. Tax Status Is Merited," *New York Times*, October 31, 2006, http://www.nytimes.com/2006/10/31/sports/ncaafootball/31colleges.html (accessed November 14, 2007). In its response, the NCAA put the onus on presidents, chancellors, boards of trustees, and athletic directors, pointing out that Division I sports budgets were growing much faster than general university budgets—8 to 12 percent a year, compared with 3 to 4 percent for overall campus funding.

20. Urban Meyer at the University of Florida makes $2.1 million, Mack Brown at Texas, $2.6 million.

21. Shannon J. Owens, "Saban Windfall Raises Pay Questions." *Orlando Sentinel*, January 6, 2007.

22.   Selena Roberts, "Big-Time College Sports May Be Due for an Audit," *New York Times*, October 29, 2006, sect. 8, 1, 4. Michael Janofsky, "University President Salaries Soar into the Millions," *New York Times*, November 22, 2005. *Chronicle of Higher Education* figures are for 2003–2004, as cited in Janofsky. In 2003–2004 nine presidents of private universities earned more than $900,000 each, and fifty presidents of private universities earned at least $500,000, "a 19 percent increase over the previous year."

23.   A survey conducted by the National Collegiate Athletic Association in 2006 reported that almost a third of Division I football and men's basketball players said that participating in sports had "prevented them from choosing the major they really wanted" (Mike Knobler, "Athletes Choose Majors to Accommodate Sports," *Atlanta Journal-Constitution*, January 7, 2007, 1A). Laboratory sciences, for example, take up too many hours of the day. And increasingly top athletes are leaving college early, before they graduate, to take their chances in the professional draft. Nonetheless, despite these media concerns, and periodic news stories and editorials, there seems no likelihood of a downturn in the visibility, celebrity, or support for high-profile college sports.

24.   Boston College conducted its own survey of the Flutie factor, concluding that Flutie had increased applications to the college, "but not nearly as much as the public and the media believe or as academic planners at some institutions seem to hope in justifying the millions of dollars they invest in football." Bill McDonald, "Phenomenology: The 'Flutie factor' is now received wisdom. But is it true?" *Boston College Magazine*, Spring 2003, http://bcm.bc.edu/issues/spring_2003/ll_phenomenology.html (accessed November 14, 2007).

25.   American Association of University Professors, Committee A on Academic Freedom and Tenure, 1990.

26.   Arendt, *The Human Condition* (Chicago: University of Chicago Press, 1958), 4, 7.

27.   Ibid., 157, 323, 154.

28.   *New York Times*, November 18, 2007, p.10. The red type used in the headline was echoed in the organization's logo, and also in the (far more familiar) logo of the sponsor who paid for the ad, Target Stores.

29.   The USA website (http://www.unistedstatesartists.org) cites as the source of this figure "Urban Institute," *Investing in Creativity: A Study of the Support Structure for U.S. Artists* (2003), and Rand Research in the Arts, *Gifts of the Muse: Reframing the Debate about the Benefits of the Arts* (2004).

30.   "An American Paradox," http://www.unitedstatesartists.org.

# INDEX

World War I, 53
World War II, 53–55, 69
*Wound and the Bow, The* (Wilson), 72
WPA. *See* Works Progress Administration
   (U.S.)
Wright, Richard, 62
Wu, Chin-tao, 105
Wurlitzer, Helene, 118

*X Portfolio* (Mapplethorpe), 78–79

Yale University, 127, 191
Yeats, William Butler, 43–44
Young British Artists, 128

Zittel, Andrea, 128
Žižek, Slavoj, 181